'A lively and engaging study of a field of increasing popularity and importance. Klich and Scheer provide wide coverage of key issues and debates, supported by case studies of both emerging and iconic artists and companies.' – Steve Dixon, Professor of Digital Performance and Pro-Vice Chancellor, Brunel University, London, UK

'A welcome and important overview that effectively introduces concepts and terms of study for the area of multimedia performance. It will be of great use for undergraduate and postgraduate courses, and will likely become a standard text for the field.' – Thomas DeFrantz, Professor of Theater Arts, MIT, USA

Multimedia Performance provides an up to date account of the evolving relationship between technology and aesthetics in contemporary performance culture. Identifying key aspects of performance practice that are inspired by developments in audio visual media, the authors introduce the reader to the major artists, bodies of work and theoretical positions within the field.

Multimedia Performance is essential reading for students of theatre and performance working at all levels, as well as for scholars and practitioners interested in the live and mediated aspects of performance.

Rosemary Klich is Lecturer in Drama and Theatre Studies at the University of Kent, UK.

Edward Scheer is Associate Professor of Theatre and Performance Studies at the University of New South Wales, Australia and President of Performance Studies international (2007–2011).

Multimedia Performance

Rosemary Klich and Edward Scheer

First published 2012 by
PALGRAVE MACMILLAN

Palgrave Macmillan in the UK is an imprint of Macmillan Publishers Limited, registered in England, company number 785998, of Houndmills, Basingstoke, Hampshire RG21 6XS.

Palgrave Macmillan in the US is a division of St Martin's Press LLC, 175 Fifth Avenue, New York, NY 10010.

Palgrave Macmillan is the global academic imprint of the above companies and has companies and representatives throughout the world.

Palgrave® and Macmillan® are registered trademarks in the United States, the United Kingdom, Europe, and other countries.

ISBN 978–0–230–57467–0   hardback
ISBN 978–0–230–57468–7   paperback

This book is printed on paper suitable for recycling and made from fully managed and sustained forest sources. Logging, pulping, and manufacturing processes are expected to conform to the environmental regulations of the country of origin.

A catalogue record for this book is available from the British Library.

A catalog record for this book is available from the Library of Congress.

10   9   8   7   6   5   4   3   2   1
21 20 19 18 17 16 15 14 13 12

Printed and bound in Great Britain by
CPI Antony Rowe, Chippenham and Eastbourne

Contents

List of Figures

Acknowledgements

Rosemary Klich thanks the University of New South Wales and the University of Kent for providing the intellectual homes and funding that enabled this project, and her colleagues in Australia and the United Kingdom for their encouragement and support. A special thanks to her family, as always, but also to the many theatre companies whose commitment to innovation, often in challenging circumstances, produces insights and knowledge for us all.

Edward Scheer would like to thank his family for their forbearance and his colleagues and students at Warwick University and UNSW for the opportunity to discuss the key ideas in this book over a number of years. He also acknowledges the Australian Research Council for its financial support in enabling the completion of the project.

The authors and publishers wish to thank the following for permission to use copyright material:

A. T. Shaefer and Troika Rank for the image of '16 [R]evolutions' on p. 119;

Atsushi Nakamichi and Janet Cardiff/Galerie Barbara Weiss, Berlin and Luhring Augustine, New York for the image of 'The Forty Part Motet' on p. 146;

Bill Viola Studio LLC for the images from 'Five Angels for the Millennium' on pp. 137, 138, 139, 140, and 141;

Blast Theory and the Mixed Reality Lab, University of Nottingham, for the images from 'Desert Rain' on p. 149, and 'Can You See Me Now?' on pp. 173, 175 and 201;

The Builders Association for the images of 'Supervision' on pp. 57 and 59;

Byrn Hoffman Watermill Foundation for the image and libretto extract from 'Einstein on the Beach' on p. 43;

Chris Herzfeld and Australian Dance Theatre/Garry Stewart Louis-Philippe Demers for the images of 'Devolution' on pp. 199 and 200;

David Rokeby for the image of 'Silicon Remembers Carbon' on p. 158;

Emmanuel Valette and Dumb Type/Epidemic for the images of 'S/N' on p. 10, and '[OR]' on p. 52;

Eric Joris for the image of '"W' (Double U)' on p. 187;

Gina Czarnecki for the image from 'Nascent' on p. 108;

Greg Ferris for the images of 'Eavesdrop' on pp. 61, and 156;

Heidrun Lohr and Kate Champion/Force Majeure for the image of 'Same, same But Different' on p. 95;

Heidrun Lohr and David Williams/Version 1.0 for the image of 'Wages of Spin' on p. 79;

Hellen Sky/Company in Space for the image of 'Escape Velocity' on p. 109;

Klaus Obermaier and Ars Electronica Futurelab for the image of 'Le Sacre du Printemps' on p. 2;

Kurt Hentschläger/Epidemic for the image of 'Feed' on p. 183;

Miles Beckett for the image of 'Kate Modern' on p. 162;

The Museum of Modern Art, New York and Scala Florence for the image of 'Fresh Widow' on p. 25;

The Ohio State University and the Forsythe Company for the images of 'Synchronous Objects Project' on pp. 113;

Paul Kaiser/Openendedgroup.AD for the images of 'Ghostcatching' on p. 114, 'Hand-Drawn Spaces' on p. 115, and 'Loops' on p. 120;

Paula Court and The Wooster Group for the image of 'House/Lights' on p. 50;

The Estate of Peter Moore and VAGA, NYC for the image of 'TV Cello' on p. 33;

Rafael Lozanno-Hemmer and Antimodular Research for the images of 'Body Movies, Relational Architecture 6' on p. 168, and 'Under Scan, Relational Architecture 11' on p. 170;

Rom Anthoni and Chunkymove for the image of 'Glow' on p. 123;

Scala Florence and Heritage Images for the image of 'Muybridge's Horse' on p. 22;

Simon Kane for the image of 'Sarajevo Story' on p. 54;

Stelarc for the images of 'Exoskeleton' on p. 160, 'Prosthetic Head' on p. 163, and 'Movatar' on p. 197;

Stephanie Berger/Time Life Pictures/Getty Images, for the image of 'Biped' on p. 116;

Ulf Langenreich and Kurt Hentschläger/Granular Synthesis for the image of 'Modell 5' on p. 181;

Ulf Langenreich/Epidemic for the image of 'Hemisphere' on p. 183;

White Images and Scala Florence for the image of 'Filippo Tommaso Marinetti' on p. 24;

Every effort has been made to trace the copyright holders, but if any have been inadvertently overlooked, the authors and publishers will be pleased to make the necessary arrangements at the first opportunity.

Note on the Text Boxes

These boxes are used to focus on people – sometimes theorists or artists and groups – and ideas that the authors think require some highlighting or that would otherwise disrupt the flow of the discussion. As such they represent the written equivalent of the theatrical notion of the 'aside'.

Introduction: From Slide Shows to Powerpoint

Consider the following performance, simply entitled *Rites* and presented at the Festival Hall, London in July 2007. *Rites* was a 'live in 3-D' version of Stravinsky's *The Rite of Spring*, involving 3-D media art, dance, projection, and live dance. The London Philharmonic Orchestra performed the music, while at the side of the stage a lone dancer moved on a separate black-box platform. Her real-time image was projected via live feed onto an enormous screen above the orchestra, and when the audience donned the 3-D glasses handed to them in the interval, the screen came to life. Media artist Klaus Obermaier created a three-dimensional virtual effect which enabled the stunning and supple dancer, Julia Mach, to reach out and practically stroke the spectators' cheeks before pixellating into oblivion. The spectacular media elements worked functionally to illuminate the work as much as illustrate it, but it did so in ways which made the outlines of 'dance' and 'the virtual' seem to merge. The 'extension in space' of the dancer's body was not only corporeal but was enhanced via its 3-D mediation, and this mediation did not eradicate embodiment but extended it.

What genre of work is this? How do we account for this kind of development of the original composition of Stravinsky's orchestral project? What social and cultural processes explain this kind of aesthetic evolution? How does work like this challenge our habits of thought and perception? Where does this kind of work belong in the push and pull of our disciplinary envies and professional fealties? This book will chart some itineraries through these questions and attempt to answer some of them by focusing on how performance like this makes use of multimedia technologies and what this means for contemporary performance. In these chapters we are tracking the kind of performance work that highlights the ways in which representational, largely audio-visual, media can activate new aesthetic potentials and new spectatorial experiences.

Ontologies of performance

Through experimentation and innovation, contemporary performance is not only utilising new media technologies to create innovative aesthetic

Figure 1   *Le Sacre du Printemps,* a project by Klaus Obermaier and Ars Electronica Futurelab. Dancer: Julia Mach

forms, but it is also functioning as a training regime for the exploration of contemporary perspectives developing as a result of, or at least in conjunction with, audio-visual and information technologies. Multimedia performance, as a medium that incorporates both real and virtual, live and mediatised elements, is in a unique position to explore and investigate the effect of extensive mediatisation on human sensory perception and subjectivity. By celebrating the increasingly 'multimedial' nature of performance, and through both the overt and implicit representation of critical perspectives regarding the mediatisation of society, multimedia performance also presents an insight into, and a critique of, the impact of media technologies on contemporary culture.

As advances in technology and science alter our perception of the world, so then do our perceptions of the world inform our art-making. While the pervasiveness of digital media has been viewed by some as posing a threat to the cultural value of theatre and the ideas of the ontology of performance, increasingly critical opinion in performance studies has moved to endorse the new aesthetics of multimedia. Others argue that it is not simply theatre that is in crisis but the human itself as 'it attempts to understand its position in the space of technology' (Causey, 2002, p. 182). The discussions and analyses in these chapters attempt to track this crisis as it plays out in the forum of experimental performance, in which aesthetic forms such as theatre and performance art show the extent to which human sensory perceptions are affected and enhanced by media technologies in such a way that we will need to talk about the ontologies of performance rather than understanding performance as a singular essence.

New media and performance are continually reframing and colonising each other in inventive ways, and this book examines areas of practice that draw influence from both of these creative fields, that use digital technologies within the theatrical frame or in a performative mode, or that activate the participants or viewers in media spaces and virtual installation environments in performative ways. This book attempts to understand and explore these practices with questions such as: How do performers and artists respond to the technology-saturated consciousness of contemporary culture, and how do they employ media technologies to create live events relevant to and consistent with the aesthetic regimes of a mediatised society? How has the development of new audio-visual technologies changed how we perceive the basic non-technological elements of performance, the spectator, and the performer? What are the best ways of understanding the significance of these developments, what terms should be applied, and what are the key concepts needed to unpack multimedia performance?

The fundamental premise of this book is that any investigation of the contemporary moment of performance that does not examine the significance of the increasingly complex interaction between live forms and mediated experiences is bound to be anachronistic. However, artists and performers continue to explore the aesthetic potential of new technologies at a rate that makes any attempt to survey the field in the present tense essentially problematic. The approach taken here will be to examine particular examples of performance in terms of emergent patterns of practice and to discuss theoretical arguments which allow the significance of these patterns of practice to be understood.

Chapter 1 begins to respond to these topics by outlining some key terms that will be useful in the analysis of multimedia performance and by discussing recent relevant developments in the field of performance theory, especially discourses on post-dramatic theatre, virtual theatre, and new media performance in relation to the seismic shifts in culture towards a mediatised society. In Chapter 2 we outline the evolution of multimedia performance from two perspectives: one, the photographic genealogy from Muybridge and Marey and, two, the developments in experimental theatre and the notion of the 'total artwork' leading up to the 1960s. Both culminate in the emergence of time-based media art in the style of Paik and John Cage. In describing these differential genealogies, we focus on three key shifts: the move towards hybridisation, the transition from passive to active spectator, and the shift from object to action, from product to process. We argue that these developments are foundational to the aesthetics of multimedia performance.

Cage is also at the root of the Theatre of Images movement described in Chapter 3 and associated primarily with the early performance practices of Robert Wilson and Laurie Anderson. This chapter extends the discussion by describing a 'second wave' of the Theatre of Images founded on, and augmenting, the ideas and ideals of practitioners such as Wilson. The Wooster Group and The Builders Association are used as examples of this second generation. An overview of key Wooster Group works is provided alongside an exploration of their distinctive approach to performance composition, whereas the Builders Association are addressed through a thorough case study of their work, *Supervision*. This chapter also examines other case studies in this style, including the British multimedia theatre company, Lightwork's production, *Sarajevo Story*.

We argue that the legacy of the Theatre of Images extends into the arena of new media installation or, more specifically, that some forms of immersive new media installation remediate the Theatre of Images. The I-Cinema Centre for Interactive Cinema Research, based in Sydney and directed by renowned media artist Jeffrey Shaw, epitomises this extension of theatre into installation. Works such as *Eavesdrop*, the work presented in this chapter, remediate theatre on a 360-degree circular screen, and turn the participant into the key performer as they navigate through the cinematic image-scape. This raises the question about the limits of live performance, since the only live component here is the spectator and their remixing of the elements of the recorded performances.

Deconstructing liveness

In the following chapter we negotiate the difficulty of this question through a re-examination of Philip Auslander's seminal arguments in his *Liveness. Performance in a Mediatized Culture* (1999) concerning the debate between Live vs Mediated performance. These arguments are of central importance to the topic of multimedia performance since they represent the first steps in a deconstruction of the opposition between these two entities: the live and the mediated, or mediatised. The debate is conventionally understood as a clash between readings of the basic ontolog(y)ies of performance. On the one hand is Peggy Phelan's view that the determining condition of performance (its ontology) is that it occurs only once in time. Photographs, videos, or other documentations of the event are therefore necessarily second-order material and there can be no other kind of performance except that which occurs *live*. On the other hand, Auslander says that the difference between live and 'mediated' performances is a 'competitive opposition at the level of cultural economy' not at the level of intrinsic (or ontological) differences (Auslander, 1999, 16).

The discussion in this chapter explains these two positions in detail and suggests that the third term that best resolves the opposition, if not the debate, is 'multimedia performance'. In this chapter we define other key terms such as 'liveness', 'mediated', 'ontology', 'representation', 'intermediality' and the new term, 'remediation', which plays an important role throughout this study. The framework provided by the notion of intermediality moves away from the theoretical polarisation of the live and mediated and provides a lens through which to explore the patterns manifesting across media within the theatrical frame. Through a framework of intermediality we discuss the 'balance of media' within the frame of the performance work and examine how this works in a production, by Sydney-based company Version 1.0, which establishes intermediality in the *mise en scène* as a tool to underline thematic concerns. We also consider the ways in which the notions of intermediality and 'remediation', as defined by Jay David Bolter and Richard Grusin, overlap and manifest in contemporary performance. In this regard we turn to the performance art of the celebrated Marina Abramovic. As part of *Seven Easy Pieces*, performed at the Solomon R. Guggenheim Museum in New York in 2005, Abramovic re-enacted six major works of performance art by Joseph Beuys, Bruce Naumann, and others. This case study examines the status of the 'live' in the process of re-enactment and explores Abramovic's re-enactments as both a means of documentation and a form of 'remediation'.

There is a need to account for recent developments in multimedia not only in terms of performance history and theory or art history but also within a history of media theory generally. Accordingly, in Chapter 5 we trace the elaboration of media theory through the late twentieth century, addressing theorists such as McLuhan, Baudrillard and Virilio in terms of ideas concerning technological determinism and social informatics, simulation, and remediation. We contextualise discussions of digitalised, or 'virtualised', society in terms of a new media theory (Levy, Hayles) that describes a cultural paradigm of 'virtuality'. This paradigm is predicated on the dissolution of the separation of the corporeal and the virtual such that we see both these categories informing and performing the other. It is an important aspect of our reading of the contemporary cultural space of performance.

Another important contemporary site of the transformative use of media in performance is the area of dance. Chapter 6 takes as its point of departure an observation made by Auslander that the addition of screen projections to dance means that the dance is fused with the virtual and disappears because the audience watches the projection and not the dancing body. This argument about the telescoping of dance into virtuality is subjected to a critique based on the evidence of a plethora of live work in dance that makes imaginative use of virtual systems to re-imagine dance and to re-frame the body in dance rather than make it disappear entirely. In this regard we discuss a number of works, including work by Australian artists Company in Space and Chunky Move and the motion capture-based choreographic projects of the Openended Group, especially *Ghostcatching* with Bill T. Jones (1999) and *Biped* with Merce Cunningham (1999).

From the Motet to the Movatar: Mixed reality performances

Similarly, our discussion of immersion in Chapter 7 examines the ways in which video installation remediates theatrical experiences for the viewer. New media installation artists such as Bill Viola exploit the potential of the moving image to sensorially immerse the audience, not in an artificial world, but within the immediate 'here and now' of the presentation, as in performance. In this chapter we first explore the history and concepts of cognitive immersion vs sensory immersion before addressing the theorisation of immersion in new media via Bolter and Grusin's notion of remediation. We then use a number of case studies, including Viola's *Five Angels for the Millennium* and Janet Cardiff's sound installation *Forty 20 Part Motet*, (both 2001), to show how an emphasis on temporality and sensory immersion in multimedia work is creating new modes of reception, embodiment, and contemplation. The final case study in this chapter is *Desert Rain* (1999) from British performance company Blast Theory, which develops an experience in which participants are immersed in a composite reality constructed of both actual and virtual elements.

Blast Theory is a highly influential company and a significant force within the arena of multimedia performance. This company's work also features in Chapter 8 in a discussion on the use of interactivity in performance. As in *Desert Rain,* Blast Theory's interactive project *Can You See Me Now?* (2004) takes place in both real and virtual space and explores the ubiquitous presence of the virtual in urban spaces and everyday life as a result of media technologies such as mobile phones and GPS tools. The usefulness of these tools often consists in providing the occasion for interactions between people. Public art can function in the same way in works such as Rafael Lozano-Hemmer's public artworks, where the interactions between members of the public are a key aspect of the work's design. As a way of visualising the process of complex interactivity we consider Lozano-Hemmer's use of gigantic interactive projections of photographic portraits or video portraits in public spaces.

The final chapter represents the culmination of the experience of the subject in the age of digital media in the project of becoming 'posthuman'. We explore this notion primarily through the work of N. Katherine Hayles, who focuses on embodiment as cultural and informational (not natural or simply biological) and in which the body becomes a prosthesis to technology and information systems (not simply the origin or destiny). Hayles also argues that a human being is an embodied being that can seamlessly articulate with intelligent machines. This introduces the theme of cybernetics, which we also explore here in relation to Donna Haraway's eco-feminist arguments about the new gender and power relations being forged through cybernetic systems disrupting old hierarchies.

Two key sites emerge as essential topographies of the debate regarding the convergence of multimedia and performance in theatre practice: the posthuman and the virtual. It is in the form of these two modalities that the dimensions of materiality and information are specifically manifest in posthuman performance practice. This chapter mentions a number of 'posthuman' moments and events alongside more recognised case studies here, such as Granular Synthesis's *Modell 5* (1994), an immersive installation that presents images of the 'posthuman body', and Stelarc's cybernetic experiment, *Movatar* (2000). The importance of these case studies for this book is the way in which these works model a kind of cyborg performance in which bodies are in feedback loops with robots, or digital avatars, in such a way that the viewer cannot distinguish the behaviours of one or the other but only as a system. The implications of this for performance are perhaps obvious in that the human dramas of previous centuries are giving way to new modes of representation and performance in which, as Artaud imagined, 'man is only a reflection'. (Artaud, 1994, 116)

At the time of writing the Internet rules, media are digital, the image is ubiquitous, and the humble slide show has developed into the pervasive 'powerpoint'. Digital technologies have infiltrated nearly all aspects of human culture in the post-industrial Western world. As new media continue to have an impact on the conditioning of perception, media artists and performance makers continue to explore the creative potential of new media but in doing so question the ways in which media influence and alter experience and subjectivity. In such work, the technology and the artwork are inseparable ('the medium is the message') and as terms such as 'media art', 'computer art', 'networked performance', 'bio-art' and, of course, 'multimedia performance' suggest, the potential for the creative reciprocity of art and technology is expanding in a multiplicity of forms – which are the focus of the following chapters.

Chapter 1

Defining Medium?

Multimedia has been described as the defining medium of the twenty first century (Packer and Jordan, 2001, p. xiii) but the inferences of the term 'multimedia' have become increasingly vague as the term becomes more widely used. The word is often used to describe digital systems organised around online environments, virtual reality systems and computer games in the sense that these are systems that support the *interactive* use of text, audio, images, video, and graphics. While the notion of multimedia we develop in these pages is not directly related to the digital conception of the term, the insistence, in this model, on interactivity is worth noting. In addition, the idea that these different components of the system – text, image etc – must also converge in a single environment is also relevant to our discussion.

In the book *Multimedia: From Wagner to Virtual Reality*, Randall Packer and Ken Jordan suggest five characteristics intrinsic to computer-based multimedia: *integration*; *interactivity*; *hypermedia*; *immersion*; and *narrativity* (Packer and Jordan, 2001, p. xxx). This list, while not exhaustive, provides a useful point of departure from the discourse of digital culture and a starting point for developing a language in which to articulate the forms and processes inherent in multimedia performance. Taking these in turn, we discuss the emergent characteristics of multimedia performance in terms of the way different media and art forms are *integrated* or brought together in certain works.

Integration is therefore important in understanding multimedia performance as an intermedial and interdisciplinary formation in culture. This formation can be traced from the Futurist avant-garde at the beginning of the twentieth century through the Fluxists of the mid-century to recent developments in post-dramatic and postmodern staging. Of equal importance is the notion of *interactivity*, which Packer and Jordan describe in terms of the extent to which spectators or users can determine

8

the structure of the work through their own interactions with the work. This idea of a complex interactivity empowers the spectator or user not merely to experience the work in a more active way but to contribute to a re-iteration of the work in a modulated form.

The way that the different elements of a system speak and relate to each other is the subject of *hypermedia*. If the user follows the links and makes the connections, their experience of the work is more complete and there is a strong possibility for greater interaction with it. In performance culture we might speak of the way that the work is *remediated*, after Bolter and Grusin's 2000 study of the same name, across different media forms and environments. This refers to the way that a live performance can be recorded in the form of a video document and then remediated as a DVD, with the result that the same work can be experienced by the spectator as both a live event and a DVD and then even shared as a Youtube clip. The way in which the same work migrates across different media is the process of remediation, and it is one important means by which performance, not only multimedia performance, can occur in a range of media.

Our study also examines the function of *immersion* as the way multimedia creates a form of sensorial overload to exhaust the subjective experience of the object or event. Finally, whereas Packer and Jordan consider *narrativity* as a key aspect of multimedia in terms of the various forms of conceptual organisation (often non-linear narratives) used in the development of multimedia applications, we prefer the term *composition*. The idea of narrativity as a means of structuring and understanding a narrative may not be sufficiently broad to encompass those forms which do not make use of narrative conventions such as multimedia dance productions to name just one example. The broader language of *composition* may be better suited to this kind of work as it permits the discussion of a more extensive notion of the ways that different works are put together. So a term such as *composition* might be more useful than *narrativity* in this context.

'Multimediality' may be regarded as the combination of a number of these qualities. In this sense we wish to consider the multimedial aspect of contemporary performance as the ways in which the work under discussion develops integration, interactivity, hypermediated or remediated content, and immersion in its formal composition. Accordingly, we develop a reading of works which present a combination of these terms as an initial framework upon which to build an analysis of multimedia performance. But it is not simply a combination of factors or a taxonomy of styles that we wish to record here. It is also the trace in our culture of the artists and performers who have re-awakened the old art forms of world performance with the new tools of the digital age.

Figure 2 *S/N*, Dumb Type. Photo © Emmanuel Valette

To take just one spectacular example: in the classic multimedia performance piece *S/N* (1992) by the Japanese group, dumb type, a projected text declares:

> I do not depend on your love/I invent my own love …/I do not depend on your sex/I invent my own sex …/I do not depend on your death/ I invent my own death …/I do not depend on your life/I invent my own life …/where's the imagination to cut across borders?/now at last I let them go.

In the last years of his own life director Furuhashi Teiji focused his company's attention on the AIDS crisis, a disease that would consume him, and the silence from parts of the scientific community that marked its early appearance in Japan and elsewhere. This work is about the interaction between medical technologies and the body but also the power of the creative imagination to produce an independent virtual reality. The performative style of the text confirms this with a constant sense of invention coupled with a continual sense of restriction: 'I do not depend on your death/I invent my own death.' We see slides of naked torsos with '+' or '−' marks superimposed on them. Dancers run for their lives on the floor space above the thrust screens that comprise the stage, before leaping to their deaths again and again, falling off the stage into the void space in the rear. Here the performer is the border crosser tracking the limits of the organic system, dying and re-appearing continually in the peculiar way that theatre enables but with the added sense of the action replay that media provides.

Like a number of dumb type performance works, *S/N* was remediated as an installation work with the title *Lovers* (1994). This would be Furuhashi's last work before he died of AIDS and was produced as a collaboration between Furuhashi and Tokyo's Canon Artlab, who made the technology. It involves timed slide projections onto the walls and floor of a cubic space. Here the bodies of the company's dancers approach the viewer with arms wide open before falling back out of reach, the unattainable virtual body and also the ghost of Furuhashi. As Hood and Gendrich point out, 'technology emerges in dumb type's world as a tangible part of our emotional, spiritual, rhythmic, physical experience; it is linked inextricably with [whom] we have become' (Hood and Gendrich, 20). The strength of dumb type's work lies exactly in its affective power amplified by sound and image. The visual media are deployed to create an immersive multimedia scenography in a way that doesn't neutralise the body's singularities and vulnerabilities but interfaces with the performers in a way which suggests that the cybernetic system of the company's famous 'human/machine interface' doesn't only produce clones but multiplies new differences. The cyborg in dumb type is not just anybody; it's someone very close to each of us. It is who we have become.

Defining multimedia performance

When addressing the current cultural moment in performance we observe a haemorrhaging of nomenclatures: 'Cybertheatre', 'postorganic theatre', 'mixed media theatre', 'intermedial theatre' or 'transmedial theatre', 'video performance', 'networked performance', 'multimedia installation', 'new media performance', and 'computer theatre', 'virtual theatre', 'multimedia theatre' ... perhaps there is no need to settle for any particular one of these. As Packer and Jordan suggest, one of the defining features of multimedia is its inherent mutability (Packer and Jordan, 2001, p. xxxviii), and just as multimedia is constantly evolving and assuming new forms, so the field of multimedia performance is continuously pushing the parameters of existing practice and inventing new modes of performance and prompting new ways of talking about it. This book does not attempt to establish definitively the limits of multimedia performance, but rather to ascertain the emergent trends and outline some basic principles that are manifesting across a very wide field of practice, beginning with some versions of the theatrical and post-dramatic traditions.

Post-dramatic theatre

One of the key concepts used to explain the effect of these creative dynamics and to link different contemporary multimedia theatre practices is the 'paradigm of post-dramatic theatre', as outlined by Hans-Thies Lehmann. Post-dramatic theatre as both a term and a concept is useful in defining the manifestation of postmodernism in theatre. Lehmann discusses the new theatre forms that have emerged since the 1960s, and argues that the one facet in common across this landscape has been the rejection of the traditional dictates of the drama. He argues that the 'spread and then omnipresence of the *media* in everyday life since the 1970s has brought with it a new multiform kind of theatrical discourse' (Lehmann, 2006, p. 22) that he terms post-dramatic theatre. Yet his study of post-dramatic theatre 'does not aim to trace the new theatrical modes of creation to sociologically determined causes and circumstances' (Lehmann, 2006, p. 175). The paradigm of post-dramatic theatre does not necessitate the use of digital media within its domain; however, the field of post-dramatic theatre is relevant in this discussion as many works that utilise filmic or video media alongside the live performer while still maintaining a theatrical dramaturgy fall within the frame of post-dramatic theatre.

Whether used to create a distancing effect, to assume the narrative line, or to create associative layers and depth in the *mise en scène*, the use of projected media within the theatrical frame inexorably disrupts the dramatic representation of a discrete fictional dimension. Karen Jurs-Munby, in her introduction to the translation of Lehmann's book, clearly summarises Lehmann's intention: 'By systematically paying attention to *theatre as performance* (unlike Szondi who reads drama predominantly as literature), Lehmann can show that theatre and drama as such have drifted apart in the second half of the twentieth century' (Jurs-Munby in Lehmann, 2006, p. 3). In his theoretical exploration of post-dramatic theatre, Lehmann addresses an extensive variety of diverse performance genres such as physical theatre, devised performance, dance, performance art, and non-traditional reworkings of classic texts.

He also specifically explores multimedia theatre as a field within post-dramatic theatre and analyses work by practitioners such as the Wooster Group and Robert Wilson, as key postmodern practitioners. He offers the following typology of the types of post-dramatic theatre that involve media:

> We can roughly distinguish between different modes of media use in theatre. Either media are occasionally used without this use fundamentally defining the theatrical conception (mere media employment);

or they serve as a source of inspiration for the theatre, its aesthetic of form without the media technology playing a major role in the productions themselves; or they are constitutive for certain forms of theatre (Corsetti, Wooster, Jesurun). And finally theatre and media art can meet in the form of video installations. (Lehmann, 2006, pp. 167–8)

In his discussion of this form of theatre, where media is *constitutive* of the form, Lehmann refers to the New York-based Wooster Group and argues that in their work, 'video technology tends to be used for the co-presence of video image and live actor, functioning in general as the technically mediated self-referentiality of the theatre' (Lehmann, 2006, p. 168). In his description of the Wooster Group's *Brace Up* (the company's recombination of Chekhov's *Three Sisters* from 1991) he illustrates how 'very casually the illusions of the theatre and the familiar but actually quite amazing equal weighting of video presence and live presence are ... highlighted' (Lehmann, 2006, p. 169). This nexus of the mediated presence and the live presence has been a key focus of multimedia theatre practice and theory in the late twentieth century.

Lehmann's position would appear to support the contention that, in general, the main function of the media presented within multimedia performances is to self-referentially reaffirm the 'liveness' of the performance, and that while the live and the mediated may have 'equal weighting', they are fundamentally discrete. Lehmann elaborates on the nature of the distinction between live theatre and media technologies when he explains that 'The point of theatre, however, is a communication structure at whose heart is not the process of a feedback of information but a different "way of meaning what is meant" (Benjamin's *'Art des Meinens'*), which ultimately includes death. Information is outside of death, beyond the experience of time' (Lehmann, 2006, p. 167).

Lehmann's adherence to the understanding that theatre requires an 'aspect of shared time-space of mortality with all its ethical and communication theoretical implications that ultimately marks a categorical difference between theatre and technological media' (Lehmann, 2006, p. 167) is reflected in his omission of 'virtual' models for theatre within his typology of modes of media use in post-dramatic theatre. Yet, as Gabriella Giannachi argues in her book *Virtual Theatres: An Introduction*, virtual theatre remains a significant site for multimedia performance.

Virtual theatre

Giannachi's discussion focuses on 'virtual art forms', where the viewer encounters either a mediated virtual reality or a technologically altered reality (such as in the case of 'cyborg theatre') enabling the multiplication and dispersal of the viewer's point of view. She analyses the aesthetic dimensions of performative digital arts, framing virtual theatre within the context of interactive arts practices that have developed out of fields such as video art and early computer art. The trajectory of her discussion suggests that virtual theatre is moving towards an 'aesthetic of virtual reality' (Giannachi, 2004, p. 123) where everything is simulated and the live performer has disappeared. Giannachi does not include within the parameters of virtual theatre more traditionally 'theatrical' performance that, while utilising mediated technologies within the frame of live theatre, adhere to a theatrical dramaturgy and still maintain the 'live', the 'real' and the 'here and now'. Nor is virtual theatre positioned within the historical context of experimental theatre practice.

Giannachi offers a typology of **Virtual Theatre** forms using case studies and practical examples to dictate theoretical boundaries. She classifies four main areas of virtual theatre as it moves towards an 'Aesthetic of Virtuality':

'Hypertextualities' ('forms of textualities that are rendered through HTML');
'Cyborg Theatre' ('an art form that uses cybernetics as part of its method and practice' and that is 'primarily concerned with the modification and augmentation of the human'); theatre that involves the 'Re-creation of Nature' through technology; and theatre that is 'Performed through the Hypersurface'.

Giannachi also outlines the potential of Virtual Reality as a platform for performance and describes works by artists such as Jeffrey Shaw, Merce Cunningham and Lynn Hershmann that exemplify an 'aesthetic of virtual reality'.

Virtual theatre has moved beyond concerns of liveness and authenticity and directly manifests the interrelation of information and materiality. Giannachi explains: 'in Virtual Art – both the work of art and the viewer are mediated' (Giannachi, 2004, p. 4). It also extends the evolution of audience participation and hybridisation into the new century, constructed through the interaction of the audience and the artwork, allowing the audience to be present in both the real and the virtual environments. It is this interaction that Giannachi identifies as the most important characteristic of virtual theatre (Giannachi, 2004, p. 11). It is enabled through the hybridisation of the live (the material participant) with the virtual.

Of course, 'virtual theatre' is not an exhaustive category. Multimedia performance practices extend beyond the boundary of mediated production in virtual theatre to include performance that occurs in real space, utilising digital technologies alongside the live performer. Such works utilise and problematise digital media while adhering to the conventions of staged theatre or live art. Performances such as those of Complicité, The Builder's Association, Sydney-based company Version 1.0, and of multimedia dance companies such as dumb type and Troika Ranch, not only innovatively 'stage' technological media but they are part of a field of practice that has heavily influenced the nascent domain of virtual theatre.

Postorganic performance

An augmentation of the proposals in 'virtual theatre' may be found in 'posthuman' or 'postorganic' performance. In his article *Postorganic Performance: The Appearance of Theatre in Virtual Spaces*, Matthew Causey labels theatre occurring in a technologically mediated environment 'postorganic performance', declaring that '(a) "posthuman" culture will create "postorganic" art' (Causey, 1999, p. 186). He describes the way that the ontology of performance is altered when it occurs in the virtual domain and argues that performance in the virtual realm establishes "a para-performative tele-theatrical phenomenon wherein the immediacy of performance and the digital alterability of time, space, and subjectivity overlap and are combined" (Causey, 1999, p. 185). Causey utilises the term 'postorganic' to refer to the resulting aesthetic events, for he sees this term as reflecting the 'transition from the privileging of presence, the authentic aura, the immediacy of the live to the exploration of issues surrounding the circulation of representation' (Causey, 1999, p. 185).

In this article, Causey declares: 'performance theory fails postorganic performance' (Causey, 1999, p. 185). In the virtual environment, the performance is no longer a 'time-dependent disappearing act' for it is no longer restricted to the non-repeatable present. Causey calls for an 'expanded performance theory' that can adequately address the phenomenon of digitally mediated performance. He claims: 'What the mediated technologies afford performance theory is the opportunity to think against the grain of traditional performance ontology, including the claims to "liveness", "immediacy", and "presence"' (Causey, 1999, p. 185). Certainly with regards to audience experience and analysis of virtual and postorganic performance, a focus on issues of 'liveness' and 'presence' is inadequate, for these concepts are limited, belonging to the realm of materiality. With theatre now operating in the digital realm, where everything is mediated and experience is 'hypermediate', where the concepts of 'presence and absence' (the basis of materiality) have been translated into 'pattern and randomness' (the basis of information) as outlined by Katherine Hayles, theatre analysis must adapt these terms from new media theory and expand both understandings of, and ways of talking about, theatrical performance. For, as Causey articulates, '(p)erformance, in the digital medium, has taken on the ontology of the technological' (Causey 1998, p. 187).

New media performance

All forms of virtual theatre, as articulated by Giannachi, involve viewer interaction; 'A virtual theatre is one which through virtuality is able not only to include the viewer within the work of art but also to distribute their presence "globally" in both the real and the simulated information world' (Giannachi, 2004, p. 10). As such, Giannachi does not focus on the field of 'video installation' or 'new media performance'. New media performance often permits the direct physical interactivity of the audience and the media, and is the art form most liable to extend interactivity to include enabling the audience to modify the work. However, new media performance may also be considered as 'remediating' live performance.

The phrase 'new media performance' covers a large terrain of practice, and includes forms utilised by practitioners such as Blast Theory, Jeffrey Shaw, Granular Synthesis, Company in Space, Bill Viola, Gary Hill and David Rokeby. We include within this umbrella title phenomena such as 'tele-performance', 'video performance' and some examples of 'multimedia installation'. The choice to include multimedia installation within the field of performance may be contentious. While many multimedia installations offer high levels of audience interactivity, enabling participants to navigate their own journey through the work, effectively transforming the role of the spectator into that of a performer, works such as those by Granular Synthesis and Company in Space do not offer the audience a high degree of agency, nor, in some works, is a live performer present. On the other hand, in the tele-performance installations of Company in Space there are many layers of interaction between the live performers and the media. For example, performers can interact with each other through a media interface and exhibit agency over the media itself, but there is rarely the opportunity for the audience to participate physically. In this sense interactivity is often limited by the demands of a particular compositional aesthetic or a set of dramaturgical decisions.

It is our contention that such works, alongside the interactive work of Jeffrey Shaw, Rokeby, and Blast Theory, must inform any study of contemporary multimedia performance. The position that media art pertains to the field of multimedia performance is further argued in Chapter 2 through a discussion of the media art of Nam June Paik. Often in such performances the media itself self-reflexively performs, whether it is presented as 'live' video installation (Granular Synthesis) or whether it mediates a live performer (as in the case of tele-performance). Many multimedia installations explore similar modes and means of communication to multimedia performance. They are often immersive, creating a spatial environment, and are inherently post-dramatic. Michael Rush writes that the installation environment 'also allows for greater participation of the viewer in the process of "completing the art object"; to use Duchamp's famous phrase. In many installations, the viewer actually enters the artwork in a literal sense to experience it' (Rush, 1999, p. 148). This highlights how such installations are 'environmental' and unfold not only through *time*, as does cinema, but also through *space*, as in the theatre. They are 'open' works; the experience of the *process* is emphasised, and the works demand a high level of audience interpretation. For these reasons we have chosen to include certain kinds of video installation within the parameters of the performative art work that forms the focus of our study.

Conclusion

The various species of contemporary multimedia theatre outlined in this chapter do not constitute discrete categories; however, they have been identified here as each engages a different platform of practice. Virtual theatre is a prominent form of multimedia performance, but the terrain of multimedia performance is not confined only to performance that occurs in the virtual realm. Multimedia performance also includes post-dramatic theatrical works that stage video or filmic media alongside live performers within the theatrical frame. Indeed, definitions of post-dramatic theatre offered by Lehmann suggest that all multimedia performance may be considered as essentially post-dramatic, yet some performances such as those which occur in the context of televisual popular culture do not refer to the conditions of theatre at all. The field of 'new media performance', including some installations, approaches the condition of theatre but with an entirely distinct institutional context and history. Examples of this form of multimedia performance, such as the work of Granular Synthesis, Bill Viola, and Janet Cardiff, are examined in the following chapters.

Multimedia performance is identified here as theatre or performance that creatively utilises media technologies as an integral component of the overall work, with the media significantly contributing to the content of the production. As established in the next chapter, the poetics of all forms of multimedia theatre are built on the fundamental characteristics of hybridisation, audience participation, and the prioritisation of the performative act over linear literary narrative, characteristics that have evolved as trends in experimental theatre practice throughout the last half of the twentieth century. The qualities of intermediality, immersion, and interactivity, identified above as defining qualities of multimedia performance and discussed in the following chapters, extend these twentieth-century trends.

Further reading

Nick Kaye's *Multi-Media: Video-Installation-Performance* (2006) provides an excellent account of key aspects of multimedia performance in a way which includes the perspective of the artist. More broadly Michael Rush's *New Media in Art* (2005) also offers a useful survey of diverse new media practices in terms of their staging of time and performance. Matt Causey's study *Theatre and Performance in Digital Culture: From Simulation to Embeddedness* (2009) is a demanding but rewarding analysis of the form while Dixon's encyclopaedic *Digital Performance: A History of New Media in theatre, Dance, Performance Art and Installation* (2007) is the obvious resource for scholars and artists interested in extending their reading and understanding of the key elements in multimedia performance.

Chapter 2

The Evolution of Multimedia Performance

It may be tempting to consider contemporary practices such as new media art, video-performance, and 'cyborg-theatre' as a product of the digital revolution of the 1990s. These same practices, however, when framed within the paradigm of performance, may be viewed less as the by-product of a revolution than as the result of a more gradual process of what we might call 'discontinuous evolution'. Steve Dixon notes that the emergence of contemporary multimedia performance owes much to three key periods: the Futurist years of the early twentieth century in Europe (1910s), the 1960s mixed media experiments associated with Fluxus and the American avant gardes, and the 1990s digitally enhanced multimedia aesthetic (Dixon, 87). The new forms of media art that have manifested in the early twenty-first century extend these twentieth century multimedia art and performance practices, which in turn develop and extend the representational and the performative strategies of earlier artists. In this chapter we map the development of the key characteristics that establish the basic framework for the aesthetics of multimedia performance by looking at the first two of Dixon's periods, the 1910s and the 1960s, in the context of earlier developments in integrated performance aesthetics.

In particular we focus on the emergence of a number of key transformations in performance aesthetics: the hybridisation of traditional artistic disciplines (integration), a greater emphasis on performative process rather than product or object (composition), and the development of a more active audience (interactivity). While these dynamics have continued to be developed and refined in the contemporary moment of multimedia performance, in what follows, each of these characteristics is addressed in relation to the historical development of multimedia.

The hybridisation of forms: Towards an integrated aesthetics

There are two strands to this genealogy. The first articulates the impacts of Wagner's theory of total art in the theatre of the late nineteenth century and the second examines the significance of technical advances in photography of the same period. These two strands did not significantly overlap and so are treated separately here. Both engage the notion of the integration of forms but in different ways.

Perhaps the most prominent transformation of theatrical performance in the twentieth century has come through the hybridisation of traditional disciplines. Artists now routinely combine dance, dialogue, photography, film and music to present an aesthetically rich and immersive exploration of concepts through a multiplicity of media. The hybridisation of artistic disciplines has manifested itself in theatrical performance in two prominent ways: either through the integration of media, as has been the dominant aim, or by creating a kind of counterpoint effect among media. The first significant expression of integration in theatre was the Wagnerian idea of the *Gesamtkunstwerk*, or Total Artwork, in which the nineteenth-century composer prophetically envisioned the integration of traditional disciplines into a unified work with the aim of intensifying the audience's experiences of art.

> In 1849 **Wagner** produced the landmark essay, *The Artwork of the Future*, in which he declared: 'Artistic Man can only fully content himself by uniting every branch of Art into the *common* Artwork' (Wagner, 2001, p. 4). Wagner's call, in his essay, for a fusion or 'totalising' of all arts was arguably the first systematic effort in modern art towards such comprehensive integration (Packer and Jordan, 2001, p. 4).

Wagner asserted that the individual disciplines of music, architecture, poetry, dance, and painting should be united, and viewed 'the Drama' as the ideal medium for this synthesis. In the 'true' Drama, 'each separate art can only bare its utmost secret to their common public through a mutual parleying with the other arts; for the purpose of each separate branch of art can only be fully attained by the reciprocal agreement and co-operation of all the branches in their common usage (Wagner, 2001, p. 5). In creating the 'music-drama', he advocated the privileging of the dramatic text over the 'musical text', for previous operas had relegated the drama to a mere pretext for the musical score. He viewed the drama as the 'soul' of the artwork and declared that the purpose of drama is the only truly 'realisable' artistic purpose:

> whatever deviates from it (the drama) must necessarily lose itself in the ocean of things indefinite, unintelligible, unfree. This purpose, however, will never be reached by *any one branch of art by itself alone* but only by *all together*, and therefore the most *universal* work of art is at the same time the only real, free, that is to say the only *intelligible*, work of art. (Wagner, 1998, p. 11)

Wagner also valued the live performer as the most important medium or conveyer of the drama, for the live performer is the vessel in which the art forms of poetry, dance, and music are united: 'It is in him, the immediate performer, that the three sister arts (poetry, music, dance) unite in one collective operation in which the highest faculty of each reaches its highest manifestation' (Wagner, 1998, p. 8).

Wagner's motivation to embrace the complete scope of human experience and to reflect this in his art was continued by early twentieth-century artists Adolphe Appia and Edward Gordon Craig, who also believed that modern experience could not be adequately expressed within the rigidity of traditional disciplinary boundaries. Both practitioners demanded the total artistic control of a director who was both visionary designer and practical stage-director. They too envisioned a total 'organic' artwork and for a synthesis of the arts in theatre and rejected the limitations of naturalism and the drama. Movement was privileged as the ultimate communicator of emotion and meaning, and the creation of space through set design and lighting was key in facilitating the stage movement. In Appia's later writing, as he developed his notion of 'living art', he identified the need for the breakdown of the audience–spectator separation and the creation of a new 'spirit of community' (Brandt, 1998, p. 145).

In the first decade of the twentieth century electric lighting was still a novelty and Craig's innovations in stage lighting to provide effects of three-dimensionality instead of simply using footlights were key to this. While Appia and Craig were revolutionising scenography, the influence of technology and media began to affect theatre practice directly in even more fundamental ways. The advent of the cinema was to significantly alter perceptions of synthesis and 'totality' in art and grew from an entirely separate development in the aesthetics of integration: the experimental photography of the late nineteenth century.

Art and technology: Differential genealogies

Alongside Wagner's innovations and their effects on theatre practice was the evolution of audio-visual (a/v) technology, especially in photography. The observation that new technologies produce new artforms is as old as the medium of a/v itself – it's certainly as old as the camera – and suggests differential genealogies for what we now describe in terms of multimedia. Any history of photography would need to account for the ways that new cameras and photographic film development technologies gave artists a new means with which to explore and defy existing conceptions of time and space. The recent history of Western/European performance is intimately bound up in the exploration of the artistic possibilities brought about by the camera. The most famous of these early photographers to experiment with photography as both a scientific and an aesthetic art were Etienne-Jules Marey and Eadweard Muybridge. Marey, a French physiologist, studied the movement of flight, examining the shape and action first, of insects and then of birds. He proved his theories regarding this natural movement through photography and diagrammatic analysis, introducing the sense of movement in a single frame.

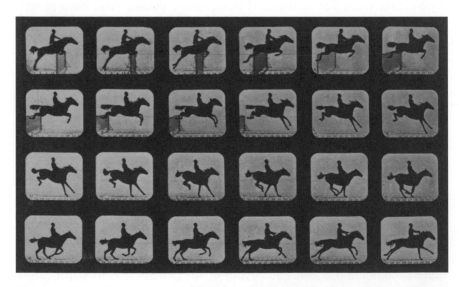

Figure 3 J. Eadweard Muybridge (1830–1904): Muybridge's Horse, 1881. Series of shots used in the newly invented zoopraxiscope, which produced the illusion of moving pictures. London, The National Archives © 2011. Photo: Scala Florence/Heritage Images

Eadweard Muybridge (1830–1904) was the first photographer to freeze action in an image and to enable the analysis of rapid movement. He used cameras in series to capture a continuing motion or action – most famously a sequence in 1872 showing the motion of a trotting horse.

While Muybridge's array of cameras produced images of movement in series, especially the series of the horse trotting showing all four hooves off the ground, it was Marey who really developed the art of capturing time in a single image. Marey was the inventor of *chronophotography* which in turn directly contributed to the development of cinematography (especially slow-motion and scientific film). He used it to study the movements of animals and of human beings without, as he had previously done, attaching recording instruments to their bodies which restricted and changed their movements.

Marey took his chronophotographs at speeds of up to 100 images per second, much faster than anything Muybridge could do at Palo Alto (1878, 1887). The effect of this was that, when projected, the images appeared to move very slowly, distorting the perception of the temporality of movement. Using polygraphs and other unique recording instruments, Marey published a number of his images of the movement of men, horses, birds, and insects in *La Machine Animale* in 1873. These and his subsequent chrono-photographic images would profoundly influence a number of later visual artists such as the Italian Futurists, and Surrealists such as Man Ray and the founder of conceptual art, Marcel Duchamp.

Duchamp took Marey's chronophotography as the literal basis for a new understanding of visual perception in a way which altered the function of his painting. Duchamp explicitly cites Marey as a source for his painting (*Nu descendant un escalier* number 1 or 2, 1911–12), with its accumulation of perspectives on a moving body: 'I saw in an illustration from a book by Marey how he had shown people fencing or horses galloping with a system of dotted lines delimiting the different movements. This gave me the idea for the execution of *Nu descendant un escalier.*' (Cabanne 57)

These nineteenth-century photographer-artists made little distinction between art and science, a perspective which became less prevalent throughout the twentieth century but was kept alive in places such as the Bauhaus school (1919–33). The Bauhaus aimed to synthesise the aesthetics of design with the needs of commercial functionality and mass production. Its aim was epitomised in the images of Laslo Moholy-Nagy,

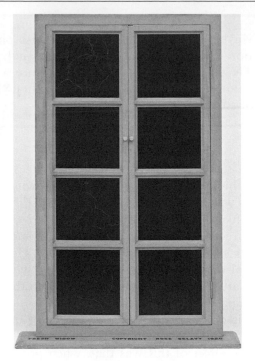

Figure 4   Filippo Tommaso Marinetti (1876–1944), eécrivain italien (futuriste). vers 1920 © 2011. White Images/Scala, Florence

who was particularly intrigued by the impact of mass production on the status of the artwork, and viewed photography as the art form of the future. He predicted: 'It is not the person ignorant of writing but the one ignorant of photography who will be the illiterate of the future' (Mac-Carthy, 2006). His interest in technology was visionary, and he foresaw the impact new technologies would have in shaping cultural values in the twentieth century.

French visual artist Marcel Duchamp had an enormous impact on the art of the 1950s and 1960s and laid the foundation for the experimental practices of figures such as John Cage and Robert Rauschenberg. Duchamp encouraged artists to explore the use of different materials and perceive the everyday and the functional through a new lens. His 'readymades' emphasized the centrality to the artwork of the concept rather than the object and exploded previous notions of what constitutes art. The notion of the reframing of media or technology as readymades reached its purest technical expression in the 'tv art' of Nam June Paik in the 1960s. With his huge arrays of monitors, his TV bras and TV cellos, Paik comprehensively reframed the dominant media of the time – television – as a readymade.

In 1915, the Italian poet Filippo Tommaso Marinetti, in collaboration with Emilio Settimelli and Bruno Corra, wrote the essay *The Futurist Synthetic Theatre*. Their essay articulated a theatre which would reflect the rapid technological advances of the age and directly oppose the historical 'passeist' theatre. In the age of the automobile and the aeroplane they felt a new type of art practice was needed to reflect the changes

Figure 5   Marcel Duchamp (1887–1968): Fresh Widow, 1920. New York, Museum of Modern Art (MoMA). Miniature French window, painted wood frame and eight panes of glass covered with black leather, 30 1/2 × 17 5/8' (77.5 × 44.8 cm), on wood sill 3/4 x 21 x 4' (1.9 × 53.4 × 10.2 cm). Katherine S. Dreier Bequest. 151. 1953 © 2011. Digital image, The Museum of Modern Art, New York/Scala, Florence

that the industrial revolution had inaugurated: a new aesthetic for a new mechanised social and industrial infrastructure. The Futurist Theatre was to be 'synthetic', 'atechnical', 'dynamic', 'simultaneous', 'autonomous', 'alogical', and 'unreal' (Marinetti et al, 1998, pp. 177–80).

Fundamental to Marinetti's concept of theatre was the notion of audience participation, and it was the aim of the Futurist Synthetic Theatre to 'Symphonise the audience's sensibility by exploring it, stirring up its laziest layers by every means possible; eliminate the preconception of the footlights by throwing nets of sensation between stage and audience; the stage action will invade the orchestra seats, the audience' (Marinetti et al., 1998, p. 181). It was the Futurists' intention to instil in the audience a 'dynamic vivacity' and force them out of the monotony of everyday life. In keeping with their ideas of speed and mechanisation and the increased efficiency of movement made possible by the machine age, they constructed performances which tried to 'compress into a few minutes, into a few words and gestures, innumerable situations, sensibilities, ideas, sensations, acts and symbols' (Marinetti, 1998, p. 177). They wanted to reduce all of Shakespeare into a single act. A key concept here lies in the idea of temporalising the artwork, foregrounding its evanescent quality and its transitoriness. The compressed events of synthetic theatre emphasised this aspect of the artwork, which would become central to understanding the conceptual significance of performance art.

F. T. Marinetti wrote *The Manifesto of Futurism* in 1908. It was published on the front page of the French newspaper, *Le Figaro*, on 20 February 1909. He wrote, 'We stand on the last promontory of the centuries! ... Why should we look back, when what we want is to break down the mysterious doors of the Impossible? Time and Space died yesterday. We already live in the absolute, because we have created eternal, omnipresent speed' (Marinetti in Kern, 2003, p. 98).

A prescient aspect of their approach was that they sensed the imminent cultural dominance of the cinema and argued that the theatre should meet the challenges of this new art form with its '*polyexpressiveness* towards which all the most modern artistic researches are moving' (Marinetti et al., 2001, p. 12). They declared that Futurist cinema 'will be painting, architecture, sculpture, words-in-freedom, music of colours, lines, and forms, a jumble of objects and reality thrown together at random' (Marinetti et al., 2001, p. 13). Such an endeavour called for the full integration of technology into the arts; indeed, Marinetti demanded an end to all art that would not embrace the social transformation brought about by technology in the early twentieth century (Packer and Jordan, 2001, p. 11).

The concept of artistic 'synthesis' articulated by Wagner and developed by Marinetti, Edward Gordon Craig and Adolphe Appia, among other figures, proved highly significant in the history of experimental arts practice in the twentieth century. The Futurists' recognition and championing of the social transformation brought about by technology and their demands that this transformation be embraced by artists was perhaps most influential in the field of music practice. Their manifesto entitled 'The Art of Noises' was one of their most influential. It was composed by Luigi Russolo in 1913 and was based on his own performances of noise music. Russolo developed *intonarumori* or noise instruments rather than simply using ambient sound in his work; but the principal of using noise as music to reflect the new industrialised landscape can be recognised in the works of later avant-garde artists such as John Cage, a student of Arnold Schoenberg.

John Cage (1912–92) had studied counterpoint and analysis with Schoenberg from 1934–7. He began to use 'maps' as scores partly as a parody of his old teacher's use of transparencies in denoting serial sets in the 12-tone system of composition. He was a writer, artist, mushroom expert and a composer whose impact on contemporary performance has been profound. His most famous work is *4' 33"*, which is a silent piano work in three movements. It was first performed by David Tudor on 29 August 1952 as part of a recital of contemporary piano music.

Cage produced multi-genre work that seldom complied with the traditional boundaries of artistic practice. In 1952, he initiated an 'untitled event' at the summer school at Black Mountain College which has proved to be a remarkable and highly influential event in performance history. The work was a collaboration between Cage, a musician and composer, and the painter Robert Rauschenberg, the pianist David Tudor, the composer Jay Watts, the dancer Merce Cunningham, and poets Mary Caroline Richards and Charles Olsen. It did not aim for the synthesis of artistic media but rather enabled the simultaneity and counterpointing of various modes of performance.

In his introduction to the piece Cage said that 'no good or bad, ugly or beautiful art should not be different from life but an action within life'.

Numerous artistic forms were employed within the event: as Cage spoke about the 'relation of music to Zen Buddhism', Rauschenberg played records on a gramophone and projected slides and film on the ceiling. Merce Cunningham danced through the audience while Olson and Richards read their poetry and Jay Watt sat in the corner and played different instruments. It was significant that these events/processes/ performances occurred simultaneously, and could be considered equally important, without any mode being relegated to a supportive role. In her article, *Performance Art and Ritual: Bodies in Performance*, Erika Fischer-Lichte explains that although the individual arts were not linked or motivated by a central focus or goal, the various actions were not to be perceived in isolation from one another (Fischer-Lichte, 1997, pp. 22–3). The actions of the 'untitled event' were not causally dictated; however, the simultaneity of events meant that they could be perceived as occurring in parallel rather than as entirely isolated. Performers were given a score which indicated time brackets only – the rest was up to them. The performances were simultaneous events unified by the theatrical frame, and by the audiences' experience.

From object to action

The 'untitled event' at Black Mountain College not only evidenced the hybridisation of artistic disciplines but also epitomised the shift in emphasis from product to process and from dramatic theatre to performance. Despite the obvious disparity between the different components of the piece, Fischer-Lichte finds congruity in the style of their appearance and suggests that the 'union of the arts', the dissolution of the discipline boundaries, was achieved here because all the artistic forms were realised in a 'performative mode' (Fischer-Lichte, 1997, pp. 22–3). The event challenged the borders between the arts, as it

> dissolved the artefact into performance. Texts were recited, music was played, paintings were 'painted over' – the artefacts became the actions.... Poetry, music and the fine arts ceased to function merely as poetry, music, or fine arts – they were simultaneously realised as performance art. (Fischer-Lichte, 1997, p. 25)

This shift of emphasis from the artefact to the action was a defining feature of the broad field of visual artistic practice at the time and had its origins in the work of visual artist Marcel Duchamp, whose 'ready-mades' placed emphasis on the informing concept, undermining the privileged status of the object or product. But Cage was first and foremost a composer, so the shift in the construction of performance work from organisation based on a principle of narrative to a musical notion of composition is significant.[1]

In 1969 at the University of Illinois Cage made *HPSCHD* in collaboration with Lejaren Hiller. This five-hour multimedia performance incorporated the following elements: seven harpsichords playing chance-determined excerpts from the works of Cage, Hiller, and a number of other well known classics; 52 tapes of computer-generated sounds; 6400 slides of visual designs from NASA, projected using 64 slide projectors; and 40 motion-picture films. The piece began before any of the audience had assembled and continued after they had left. The scale of this work has rarely been repeated in the history of multimedia performance and provides a sense of the ambition and vision of Cage's aesthetics. The seemingly random juxtaposition of elements in the piece emphasises the contingency of composition. There is no narrative here, no guarantee of the work's meaning. In *HPSCHD* the principle of composition is floated as an experimental practice in its own right and is fully realised in performance.

Cage's privileging of the active performance over the static score or text developed into a definitive characteristic of avant-garde performance, permanently altering the way visual and performing art was to be consumed and processed. His 'untitled event' triggered the series of events in NYC known as the 'Happenings'. These were also largely unscripted performances in which spontaneous events could take place within a certain frame of time. Though many of them were rehearsed, Allan Kaprow and others organised unscripted events called happenings by the press after a piece by Kaprow from 1959. Fischer-Lichte outlines the manner in which, prior to these events, Western dramatic theatre had under-utilised the performative function of theatre, stressing the psychological realm and motivation for the action, plot construction and scenic arrangements (Fischer-Lichte, 1997, p. 24). The genre of 'performance' developed in opposition to the symbolic hierarchies engrained in a theatre reliant on the narrative text.

The rejection of representation in favour an aesthetic of action in the Happenings was influential in the approach of the Fluxus group of artists (see next section) and is still a significant influence on current postmodern and multimedia theatre. Like the practices from which it has evolved, multimedia performance continues to reject the dominance of the dramatic matrix of character and narrative to embrace aspects of performance that Wagner considered utterly undesirable due to their 'unintelligibility'; 'things indefinite, unintelligible, unfree' (Wagner, 1998, p. 11). This does not necessarily mean that such performance lacks the notion of a driving 'soul', as outlined by Wagner. Rather it is perhaps the expressive exploration of an informing concept, theme, or idea that is at the heart of these works.

From passive to active spectator

One of the boundaries Cage challenged was the line between the artwork and the spectator, who was now required to assume a more active and participatory role in the creation of meaning. Cage changed the focus of the audience from intellectual understanding and subjective engagement with the action to a more immediate and sensorial experience of the performance and an awareness of the collective nature of this experience. As the notion of 'theatre-as-representation' was displaced and the substructure of individual sign systems liberated, the audience were able to realise the performance in real-time and real-space. Referring to Cage's 'untitled event', Fisher-Lichte explains that

> the spectators did not need to search for given meanings or struggle to decipher possible messages formulated in the performance.... Thus looking on was redefined as an activity, a doing, according to their particular patterns of perception, their associations and memories as well as on the discourses in which they participated. (Fischer-Lichte, 1997, p. 25)

The realisation of a performance event in real-time and real-space injected the possibility of 'chance', and as the responsibility for the outcome of the work shifted towards the audience, the level of indeterminacy in the nature of the final outcome was increased.

While certainly the Performance Art of artists such as Rauschenberg, Nam June Paik, Carolee Schneeman and Joan Jonas epitomised a hybridisation of artistic disciplines and the focus on action over object, the shift in emphasis from the audience as passive spectator to active participant was most explicit in the Happenings of Allan Kaprow, Claes Oldenberg, and Jim Dine, which attempted to eliminate the distinction between audience and performer altogether.

> Allan Kaprow studied experimental composition with John Cage at the New School for Social Research in Manhattan between 1956 and 1958. After this Kaprow created site-specific environmental works that expanded Cage's ideas of audience participation to involve the integration of multiple elements of performance – space, time materials, and people – in the happenings. Kaprow's happenings were also influenced by the Dadaists, the theories of Antonin Artaud, and the conceptual works of Yves Klein.

In his essay, *Untitled Guidelines for Happenings*, Kaprow portrays art as a means for enhancing our awareness of life through unexpected meaningful interaction, and calls for the border between art and life to be as fluid as possible, even perhaps indistinct (Kaprow, 2001, p. 280). Theatrical convention is the enemy of the Happening, and Kaprow declares 'that audiences should be eliminated entirely', for this will allow the complete integration of all elements – people, space, the particular materials and character of the environment, time (Kaprow, 2001, p. 285). The Happening was shaped by the actions of the participants, and took place entirely in real or experienced time as opposed to conceptual time.[2]

It should be restated, however, that the Happenings may have appeared as spontaneous and random gestures, but were always planned, timed, and structured sequences of events. The original happening was a fully rehearsed and directed production presented at the Reuben Gallery in New York in 1959. The gallery was divided into three spaces with plastic walls within which the performers, including Robert Rauschenberg, Jasper Johns, and Lester Johnson, performed choreographed sequences of actions such as lighting matches, squeezing oranges and playing instruments. The everyday was transformed into performance and the boundary between world of the audience and the performers was blurred. While Happenings may not have achieved the complete dissolution of the boundary between performance and audience, Kaprow's ideals have continued to resonate throughout the interactive practices of media arts.

Nam June Paik, Fluxus and the performance of media

A prominent descendant in the lineage of Duchamp and Cage, Nam Jun Paik is widely regarded as the 'father of video art' and the inventor of the term 'electronic superhighway'. Paik's work explores the juncture of technology and popular culture and plays with the different ways performance, sculpture, music and video can be combined to challenge the status of dominant cultural media, and the cultural messages associated with television in particular. Paik took advantage of the appearance of the first portable video recorders in the mid 1960s effectively to pioneer the use of video within performance and establish work using these media as legitimate art forms. Through his arrays of videotapes, films, installations and performances, Paik has shaped contemporary perceptions of the temporal image in art. Paik's work impressed George Maciunas, founder of the neo-Dada 'Fluxus' art movement, and Paik became aligned with Maciunas and other Fluxus artists, including Joseph Beuys, Dick Higgins, Wolf Vostell, and Yoko Ono, all working in a suitably diverse range of media. Michael Rush emphasises the cross-fertilisation of artistic disciplines in the development of Fluxus as an 'intermedia movement that flourished in the 1960s and inaugurated several innovations in performance, film, and eventually video' (Rush, 1999, p. 24).

Nam June Paik (1932–2006) was a South Korean-born American artist and also part of Fluxus. In 1963 he began to work with modified TV monitors in installations and in 1965 with the newly released Sony Portapak, the first portable video and audio recorder. As such he is considered to be the first video artist. He worked extensively with performers in developing a video art practice that engaged questions of presence and liveness and made early video art an intensely performative type of medium.

As social space became flooded with televisual images, Paik experimented with various means of altering the image. In 1963, he dismantled a number of television sets and tested ways of affecting the signals and images using magnets and microphones, and created *Exposition of Music – Electronic Television,* perhaps the first video art exhibition and displayed in Wuppertal, Germany. The monitors were scattered around the gallery, with unexpected sound effects and light patterns being projected throughout the space. As the title of the work explains, Paik had shifted focus from music to the media image, and the exhibition also involved four 'prepared' pianos in the style of Cage, mechanical sound objects, record and tape installations, as well as modified TV sets, and the head of a recently slaughtered ox.

In a leaflet for the exhibition, Paik wrote,

> One can say that electronic television is not the mere application and expansion of electronic music in the field of optics but represents a contrast to electronic music (at least in its starting phase), which shows a pre-defined, determined tendency both in its serial compositional method and in its ontological form (tape recordings destined for repetition).

This exhibition not only represented Paik's departure from electronic music but also marked the beginning of a new art form – what is now termed 'video art' or 'video installation'; however, at this stage Paik was yet to work with 'video'. Instead he was modifying secondhand TV sets and using electro-magnets to distort the images being broadcast. Then, in 1965, Sony developed the Portapak, the first mass-market portable

Figure 6 *TV Cello*, Nam June Paik. Photo: Peter Moore

video and audio recorder and, with a Rockerfeller Foundation grant, Paik was able to explore this liberating new technology. At the Café Au Go-Go in New York, a hotspot for performance gatherings, he presented a tape accompanied by a text titled *Electronic Video Recorder*, which established him as the pre-eminent pioneer of video art, 'television's first popular revolt' (Ross, 1973, p. 102).

At this time another early Portapak user, Les Levine, was making his first videotape, simply titled *Bum*. In 1966 at the Toronto Art Gallery, he exhibited one of the first closed-circuit installations that presented images of the audiences on a five-second time-lag. In 1968, Levine presented *Electric Shock*, a room filled with electrostatic energy. With Paik, Levine is one of the first recognised 'media artists', and not only focused on developing the use of technology in art, and technology as art, but also in using such art to question societal norms. He is responsible for the terms 'software art', 'disposable art' and 'camera art' and his book, *Media: The Biotech Rehearsal for Leaving the Body*, is prescient in its exploration of the relationship between media and the mind.

In 1964 Paik moved to New York and developed an ongoing artistic collaboration with cellist Charlotte Moorman. The pair produced a series of works that challenged the way music was traditionally heard and performed. In *TV Bra* (1968) Moorman played the violin topless with two square mirrors strapped over her breasts that reflected the image of cameras pointed at her face. This work followed the scandalous *Opera Sextronique* performed on 9 February 1967 at the Film-Maker's Cinematheque in New York, during the second movement of which both artists were arrested. Moorman had performed this part of the work topless, with Paik's naked back positioned as her cello upon which she bowed. The work explored the potential sexual experience of performing music, disrupting the iconic image of the suited string player.

Another significant performance at this stage in Paik's career was *Concerto for TV, Cello and Video Tape* (1971) which involved Moorman bowing a stack of television sets that sat between her knees. On the sets were pre-recorded and simultaneous images of her performing the same process, bowing the television-cello. Various levels of remediation functioned within this work, with each medium (the televisions, the performer, the 'cello', the music) providing the content of another medium to echo McLuhan's famous words. Moorman's 'live' performance was remediated within the frame of the TV set, which in turn was remediated by the frame of the live performance. The work probes at definitions of liveness, blurring the line between the live and the mediated, as the spectators in these works were asked to negotiate two modes of viewing: the experience of the live presence of the artist and the tele-presence or imaged body.

> Yoko Ono (1933–) is a Fluxus artist famously married to John Lennon. Her early works involved the viewer completing the work, for example, *PAINTING TO SEE THE SKIES Drill two holes into a canvas. Hang it where you can see the sky* (1961 summer). In *Cut Piece* (1965), Ono sat on stage and invited the audience to use scissors to cut off her clothing until she was naked. The book of her performance instructions, *Grapefruit*, first published in 1964, includes instructions that are to be completed in the mind of the reader, for example: *Hide and Go Seek Piece: Hide until everyone forgets about you. Hide until everyone dies.*

By the late 1960s, Paik was at the forefront of a new generation of practitioners creating an artistic discourse out of television and the moving image. Throughout the 1970s and 1980s, Paik also worked as a teacher and an activist, supporting other artists and working to realise the potential of the emerging medium. Along with his influential series of videotapes, projects for television, and live performances featuring collaborations with artists and friends such as Laurie Anderson, Joseph Beuys, David Bowie, Cage, and Merce Cunningham, Paik installations fundamentally changed video, redefined artistic practice, and exemplified the hybridisation of disciplines, the move from object to process, and the shift from passive to active spectatorship.

Joseph Beuys (1921–86). An enormously influential figure in post-war European art. Also associated with Fluxus. Beuys created and carried out 70 actions between 1963 and 1986. During this time, he also created approximately 50 installations, participated in more than 130 solo exhibitions, and conducted numerous interviews, seminars, lectures, and discussions. He developed the idea of performance as a kind of social sculpture in which, as he famously asserted, 'Everyone is an artist'. Performance Works: *How To Explain Pictures to a Dead Hare* (1965), *I like America and America Likes Me* (1974 New York), *7000 Oaks* (1982–7).

There are, of course, a number of ways of approaching work such as Paik's. His video art is often categorised simply as 'installation' and is not often discussed within the frame of performance practice. Yet this is a vital dimension to many of the works not only in terms of their direct engagement with performance but in their vivacity and playful energy. Michael Rush has described them as 'video sculptures' which 'appear more like mechanized organisms than inert monitors' (Rush, 1999). Rush also describes them as 'performative installations'. This slippage of nomenclature is significant and places Paik's work alongside the interactive work of contemporary practitioners such as Jeffrey Shaw, David Rokeby, Gary Hill, Bill Viola, and Blast Theory, all of whom have made important contributions to contemporary multimedia performance.

Multimedia performative installations set up a self-reflexive environment, which as Rush illustrates, 'allows for greater participation of the viewer in the process of 'completing the art object'; to use Duchamp's famous phrase. In many installations, the viewer actually enters the artwork in a literal sense to experience it 'and thereby takes on the characteristics of the performer' (Rush, 1999, p. 148). This highlights how such installations are 'environmental' and unfold not only through *time* as does cinema, but also through *space*, as in the theatre. They are 'open' works; the experience of the *process* is emphasised and the works demand a high level of audience interpretation.

George Quasha and Charles Stein, in their article *Performance Itself*, argue that performance 'is really the heart of the *process* of art, most especially art that sees itself as process' and that 'this sense of process is essentially *performative*' (Quasha and Stein, 2002, p. 75). Their essay details the performative nature of installations by Gary Hill in works such as *Processual Video* (1980), which is described as an 'exemplary instance of the performative simultaneously manifesting a root principle and generating an actual performance piece' (Quasha and Stein, 2002, p. 75). This particular installation involves a white line revolving slowly around the middle of a screen to the accompaniment of recorded spoken text. The audience receive these two elements simultaneously and inevitably interrelate the image with the content of the text. Quasha and Stein explain: 'The meaning of work or image performs itself in the processual interaction of video and speech, and the real location where that performance takes place is in the viewer's mind' (2002, p. 75). The refusal of these works to offer a single perspective, a single channel, combined with the fact that they unfold through time, means that they are not simply transmitting information but are creating an individual experience for the audience. In this sense they constitute new media performances.

While multimedia installation may be related to the field of new media performance, some argue it is beyond the terrain of 'performance'. Gunter Berghaus states that he does not agree with scholars who 'regard video installations as performance *per se*' (Berghaus, 2005, p. 188). Berghaus makes the distinction between 'video performance' and 'video installation' and outlines the latter as 'a sculpted or architectural setting with electronic actors' that maintains the separation of audience and stage (Berghaus, 2005, p. 188). This separation, he argues, creates a similarly cognitive spectatorship to that of viewing a play, painting or sculpture. Berghaus contends:

> Although multi-monitor video installations have often been described as 'electronic theatre' that requires the viewer to be 'operative' and 'subjective' in the site, standing both inside and outside the installation, I would still maintain that their interaction with the display is extremely limited. The performative quality of a piece of sculpture (even if it fits in a whole room and contains electronic images that introduce a time dimension in the arrangement) is different from that of a human actor. (Berghaus, 2005, p. 188)

This is certainly a valid and perhaps even a commonsense distinction. However, performativity is also a matter of degree and the boundary between the realms of multimedia performance and multimedia installation is indistinct. Interestingly, Berghaus concedes that 'The exploration of the frontiers between theatre and fine art is undoubtedly a task that is pertinent to avant-garde experimentation' and he states that he has 'therefore included some borderline cases, such as Paik's *Exhibition of Music – Electronic Television*' in his discussion of video performance (Berghaus, 2005, p. 188).

Some of these 'borderline cases' are in fact central to an understanding of the efficacy of multimedia performance, for they challenge the essential division of the live and the mediated, and emphasise the need for a revision of perceptions regarding the limits of the live theatrical experience or the performance event. German artist Wolf Vostell, who in 1958 was already creating multimedia installations with his structural collage of a group of TV sets in *TV De-collages*, sees multimedia installation in this way, as a 'total event', and connects some of the threads we have been following in his chapter:

> Marcel Duchamp has declared readymade objects as art, and the Futurists declared noises as art – it is an important characteristic of my efforts and those of my colleagues to declare as art the total event, comprising noise/object/movement/colour/& psychology – a merging of elements, so that life (man) can be art. (Vostell in Rush, 1999, p. 117)

This concept of installation as artistic 'event' again places it within the field of performance practice. The efficacy of the work relies on the experience of the process of time in space, rather than on the object, product or narrative. Rush argues 'It is not surprising ... given the influence of Fluxus performance actions and Happenings on the development of late twentieth century art, that "the theatrical" would be embraced in multimedia installation art' (Rush, 1999, p. 148). In this way both interactive and non-interactive multimedia installations share the trends and characteristics of multimedia performance.

Conclusion

Contemporary forms of multimedia performance are both the direct result of the new media they utilise and reflect and part of an experimental performance lineage that has a particular historical process of development. Theatre has always experimented with new technologies in performance and explored the creative potential of the interaction between the live and the mediated. After Wagner's prophetic visions of integrated media in performance, there were three main periods of dramatic change in the way media and performance were imagined.

The ideas of a total art work seeded experiments in the integration of media in the early twentieth-century avant-gardes such as Futurism and the Bauhaus.

These artists were also influenced by the new image technologies developed by photographers such as Muybridge and Marey which enabled time-based art forms such as cinema to develop. This in turn led to a movement away from matrixed codes of performance (complex acting in narrative and character-based productions) in favour of the styles more pertinent to screen acting in which action is broken up into gesture and the meaning to any gesture is attributed by means of post-production. This kind of performance also surfaced in the Happenings of Cage and Kaprow and into the Fluxus movement. These actions resulted in the emergence of the distinctive practice of performance art, which also foregrounds composition over narrative, intermediality over disciplines, action over object-hood, and interactivity over passive consumption. Ultimately, the digital revolution of the 1990s provides the latest and most effective means of integrating different media through computer-based means.

Further reading

Gunter Berghaus provides an alternative genealogy in his *Avant-Garde Performance: Live Events and Electronic Technologies* (2005) while Giesekam's *Staging the Screen* (2007) is a first rate discontinuous narrative of the development of multimedia in the theatre. There are numerous surveys of the history of new media art but some useful material pertaining to performance can be found in Oliver Grau's *Media Art Histories* collection (2007) and Chandler and Neumark's *At a Distance: Precursors to Art and Activism on the Internet* (2005). As in Chapter 1, Dixon's *Digital Performance* remains an important text for the discussion of the evolution of the form.

Chapter 3

The Theatre of Images Revisited

As discussed in Chapter 2, contemporary forms of multimedia perform-ance are not simply the direct result of the new media they utilise and reflect, but are part of an experimental performance lineage that has a specific historical process of development. Theatre has always experi-mented with new technologies in performance and explored the nature and creative potential of the interaction of the live and the mediated. In this chapter we examine the development of a particular mode of post-modern theatre, the 'Theatre of Images', and its subsequent inflection into a multimedia-based theatre that utilises aspects of conventional dramatic structure rather than simply post-dramatic form. In examin-ing the 'Theatre of Images', we argue that the multimedial dimensions of the work overtake the post-dramatic paradigm as the basis for recent developments in performance.

The 'Theatre of Images' developed in the late 60s and early 70s and in its first phase continued the movement away from that matrix of dra-matic structures based on narrative with illustrative *mise en scène* and complex character acting towards an approach inspired by Cage that was based on the idea of composition along very broadly musical principles. The results were technically complex, visually sophisticated multimedia works dubbed by Bonnie Marranca in her book of the same name, *The Theatre of Images*. In this she describes the process by which 'Value came increasingly to be placed on performance with the result that the new theatre never became a literary theatre, but one dominated by images – visual and aural' (Marranca, 1996, p. ix). The use of images, usually in some kind of projection environment, is ubiquitous in multimedia thea-tre work, so this genre of work is deserving of some detailed appraisal.

Gunter Berghaus suggests that the trend of using filmic/video media onstage emerged in the 1920s when attempts were made to 'integrate actors with filmed décor' by practitioners such as Eisenstein and Piscator (Berghaus, 2005, p. 189). However, he argues that the first major theatrical work to utilise the gamut of electronic media fully was the 1979 production of *Hamlet* by Wolf Vostell, which involved actors performing alongside 120 video monitors. Berghaus describes this form of theatre, 'where artists employed video technology to create a bridge between the theatre and the mediatised culture of the postmodern information society', as 'multimedia spectacle' (Berghaus, 2005, p. 189).

> **Sergei Eisenstein** (1898–1948), famous for his pioneering film work and use of 'montage', was originally a stage director influenced by Vsevolod Meyerhold. In his 1923 article 'Montage of Attractions' published in the journal *Lef* he describes theatre's 'basic material' being the shaping of an audience in a desired direction, and suggests that 'the instrument of this process consists of all the parts that constitute the apparatus of theatre' (Eisenstein in Taylor and Christie eds 1994, p. 87).

This chapter briefly revisits this kind of late twentieth century multimedia theatre in which a variety of electronic visual media are combined with elements of more traditional dramaturgy exploring the various phases of practice within the field of the Theatre of Images. We begin in the 1970s and 1980s with Robert Wilson, Laurie Anderson and the Wooster Group then follow the field into the new century, examining case studies of practice that are not only dominated by images but in which the image is accessed via twenty-first-century media technologies. In developing this account, we focus on the immediate dramaturgical context of the work, the influences on its development and composition. We do not explore the political and social climate in which this body of work was made. In many respects this is just as significant to the understanding of this work as the mediated environment in which it is formed, but it is simply beyond the scope of our study.

As in the Happenings, the actions of the performers in theatre based on the image often appear nonsensical when considered from the point of view of conventional narrative theatre. The basis for the movement might be to simply perform a task or explore a visual style in the same manner as dance, rather than simply to emphasise a piece of the story or to make sense of a particular line of dialogue. The performers' actions in this sense are dictated by choreography rather than a script. This means that the movements of the performers might not make sense of a story (X crosses the stage to answer the door) but might make visual sense (X crosses the stage to be in the light). The implication here is that theatre need not concern itself with story, character and text but can emphasise the physical actions of the performers in a different way which, on the surface, has more to do with the history of art than the history of drama. The Theatre of Images unsurprisingly began as a mixed media theatre relying much more on visuals than textual components and reflecting the developments in visual arts in the period of the 1960s in which Fluxus flourished but also reflecting a tradition of performance on stage and an integrated arts practice in the theatre. But what we see in the more recent forms of Theatre of the Image is a return to the matrixed density of character and narrative in dramatic rather than post-dramatic structures. In these works, there is again a concern with motivated behaviours of characters fleshing out the narrative development.

Robert Wilson

When Bonnie Marranca first coined the term 'Theatre of Images', her ideal example was Robert Wilson, whose spectacular, large-scale productions were utterly unlike the comparatively humble 'readymade' staging of the Happenings. Wilson's theatre is primarily visual and therefore has more in common with Tadeusz Kantor and the Bauhaus architect/design/ figures of years earlier than the multisensory experiments of the Fluxus artists. Like them, Wilson's choreographies are based on repetitive gestures and bio-mechanical movements. The difference is that rather than occupying centre stage and the central action, the human body in productions such as *Einstein on the Beach* (1976) forms part of a larger machinic assemblage. Through this Wilson shows the interconnectedness of the human with the post-industrial landscape and how we have adapted ourselves to our own technological developments. The suggestion is that the individual human experience, rather than being the basis for all creativity and the centre of all values as in Kantor, has become marginalised and decentred. Wilson reveals these tensions through the virtuoso manipulation of stage space. It is both measured and *démesurée* (disproportionate); the gigantic with the infinitesimal. The struggle to maintain ourselves at the centre of the action unleashes destructive potentials, as the subtitle to Wilson's planned 1984 LA Olympics piece *the CIVIL warS* suggests: *a tree is best measured when it's down*. Human physical scale is played with, negated, enhanced, and amplified but never entirely finished off. It remains a category, however problematic.

Choreographer and designer Oskar Schlemmer (1888–1943), also the director of the Bauhaus Theatre Workshop, promoted the physical, plastic, and sensory elements of theatre over the dramatic

> elements of story and character, and so may be seen as a forerunner of Wilson and the 'Theatre of the Image'. He also described the role of the artist as a 'synthesiser' of different elements.

Wilson at this time was opposed to the notion of a literary theatre and his defence of a visual theatre still contains some important insights for contemporary theatre artists:

> people are just beginning to return again to discerning visual significances as a primary mode – or method – of communicating in a context where more than one form or 'level' exists. In that sense of overlays of visual correspondences.... See, we're not particularly interested in literary ideas, because having a focus that encompasses in a panoramic visual glance all the hidden slices ongoing that appear in clear awareness as encoded fragments seems to indicate theatre has so much more to do than be concerned with words in a dried out, flat, one-dimensional literary structure. I mean the Modern World has forced us to outgrow that *mode* of seeing. (Wilson in Drain, 1995, p. 60)

The insistence on the image in multimedia theatre reflects this approach; the idea that information can be best processed by a visual rather than literary sensibility is still very much in evidence in recent narrative-based works. In *Einstein* Wilson took a more integrated approach to language and the image, collaborating with Christopher Knowles, an autistic child who became Wilson's most important collaborator of the 1970s and who wrote the libretto for *Einstein* in a way which used language as a form of musical notation, creating images with sound rather than relying on the construction of a universally valid meaning with conventional sentences etc. With Christopher Knowles, Wilson explored the images language can generate:

I FEEL THE EARTH MOVE
CAROLE KING
So that was one song this what it could in the Einstein On The Beach with a trial to jail. But a court were it could happen. So when David Cassidy tells you all of you to go on get going get going. So this one in like on WABC New York...
JAY REYNOLDS from midnight to 6 00.
HARRY HARRISON
So heres what in like of WABC...

Figure 7 *Einstein on the Beach,* 1976. Photo © Byrd Hoffman Watermill
Foundation

JAY REYNOLDS from midnight to 6 AM
HARRY HARRISON from 6 AM to L
I feel the earth move from WABC...
JAY REYNOLDS from midnight to 6 AM.
HARRY HARRISON from 6 AM to 10 AM.
(from 'I feel the earth Move' the middle section of *Einstein on the Beach*)

The libretto is built out of references to media identities of the time but the presentation of these signifiers (the word signs) is fundamentally material which means that Wilson is not interested in the content (the media identities) or even the formal syntax of literary language but the new perspectives provided by the acoustic and visual properties of repetitive verbal forms. The approach here forms what Lehmann refers to as the post-dramatic 'textscape' since the content of the text is less significant for Wilson. The issue is primarily one of perception and Wilson deploys jarringly repetitive forms as the tool for re-ordering the perceptual habits of his audiences. As another critic points out about *Einstein*: 'The fascinated

lingering attachment to the images frozen in repetition frees the performance from linear narrative, from temporality, from rhetorical functions ...
from recognisable references to history ("Einstein"?), from anything in
particular' (Birringer, 1993, p. 187).

Laurie Anderson

The place of the image in politics or history is not something Wilson
deals with in his Theatre. Other performance artists from the 1980s such
as Laurie Anderson, Wilson's contemporary, are more critical, observing
the inevitability of consumerism while revealing its fundamental banality and the way it forces everyone to play the game. You could say Laurie
Anderson deconstructs the opposition between consumer products and
art objects. Her ironic voiceover style parodies adspeak (advertising language and its mode of delivery) while acknowledging its necessary place
in global media (including the arts).

There is an identifiably postmodern performance aesthetic in Wilson
and Anderson which celebrates a super-flat, affectless attitude for the
performer, a focus on the materiality of signifiers (see the Wilson text
fragment above) in the use of text, a use of pastiche in delivery, and in
composition, a celebration of popular culture. We see this in Anderson's
1980s works such as *United States* (a performance 1983, a book 1984,
and a 4 CD set) and her performance *Home of the Brave* from 1984 (also
a CD and a documentary film available on video), both notable for their
use of archetypal 80s iconic objects: power suits; 'synthesisers'; drum
machines; and irony. In her track *O Superman* from 1982 (inspired by
Massenet's *O Souverain*, one of the arias in *Le Cid*) we find lyrics such
as: 'So hold me Mom, in your long arms .../in your automatic arms/your
electronic arms/your petrochemical arms/ your military arms/in your
electronic arms'.

The critic, Herman Rapaport, says that this song is a pleasant 'invita-
tion to consider disaster' and a way of getting people to think critically
about popular culture but, cunningly, the message is itself 'communi-
cated by way of muzak'. This approach to critical muzak is a recognisably postmodern move, an apparent banality which carries its critical
message lightly. Her references similarly offer no distinction between
high and low forms of culture: in discussing her performance personae
Anderson claims to have been influenced by characters such as Bugs
Bunny, Daffy Duck, Yosemite Sam, and Porky Pig. Her stage show, *The
Speed of Darkness* (1997), references Shakespeare, Wittgenstein and
Frank Sinatra, while the music samples wolf howls and bird calls as well
as wristwatch alarms and the sounds of electronica.

In her 1984 concert, *Home of the Brave*, Anderson's song 'Zero and One' explores the cultural meaning of the two numbers, and argues that there is a need for more exploration of the 'space in between' them. Disguised by a full-body suit and facial mask, with her voice distorted electronically, she discusses the significance and the limitations of digital code. As an androgynous figure hidden by, and accessed through, electronic media, in this work she embodies the figure of the artist as cyborg. You may like to access her website http://www.laurieanderson.com/ or view fragments of her performances on Youtube, or even for the media historians, use her interactive CD-ROM *Puppet Motel* (1994).

A quintessential multimedial moment in Laurie Anderson's opus occurs on the *Home of the Brave* video in a piece called 'White Lily', where Anderson asks: What Fassbinder film is it?/The one-armed man comes into the flower shop and says,/"What flower expresses: Days go by/and they just keep going by endlessly/pulling you into the future ...?"/And the florist says,/"White Lily". The silhouette of Anderson holding a white lily remains on the screen at the end of the scene after she has left the stage. It is a beautifully realised combination of projection alongside live performance. The confluence of image and the live gesture and the sudden removal of the live gesture, leaving the projection on the screen, is suggestive of a range of issues from performance ontology (is it essentially live or mediated?) to technological memory and the ways in which memories have become outsourced to images.

The question 'What Fassbinder film is it?' is unanswered in the piece itself, though the answer is probably *Berlin Alexanderplatz*. This is typical of Anderson's kind of bemused postmodernism. The point of the fragment is not given. It is like a joke with no punchline, a zen koan or an advertising slogan. The medium is the message and this medium is the cultural fragment, split off from its grounding moment or text and set adrift to join the other dead images and linguistic pieces that make up the late twentieth-century culturescape.

This remediated scenario in which the scene from the Fassbinder film is reinscribed in the documentary of the Anderson performance is a key to Anderson's own performative development of postmodernism. It functions not simply as an intertextual reference but as a deconstruction of values associated with high and low culture. The contrast of 'Fassbinder film' connoting a high cultural moment with the banal shopping experience in the flower shop produces the characteristic Anderson *frottage*, the friction generated between different cultural modalities gently rubbed together and which produces sparks of humour. The scene of consumer gratification is refigured, the one-armed man wants to talk about a flower that is expected to express something particular – it expresses the passing of time. That there should be an answer to such a question is also a quirk of the scene, which Anderson inhabits in her own way.

Inhabiting public memories, technological memories, both living inside them and outsourcing them to image technologies, is a condition of our time which Anderson's work stages in its play between codes of the popular and the avant-garde and in its rendering of the discontinuities of intertextual performance. In so doing her work picks up a number of voices and reconfigures them with filters and effects to produce an estrangement of the familiar, an uncanny vocalisation which stirs only screen memories and a cultural memory which draws on publicly held image repertoires: 'This is the time. And this is the record of the time' ('From the Air', *Big Science* 1982). These memories are implants, prompted like the memories of the replicants in *Bladerunner*, the groundbreaking film directed by Ridley Scott of the same year, and permit a reading of subjectivity as ineluctably social, necessarily mediated, a reading which is emphasised in Anderson's performance personae. For Anderson, as in much performance of the 1970s and 1980s, the goal of the live performance becomes linked to the performer in a real and present sense, to the revelation of their links to the world: physical, affective and technical. The performer's personality does not disappear in a psychological portrait, nor does their body disappear in a costume. We do not have an aesthetics of disappearance in performance in which the real is blacked out but instead an attempt to stage it.

The Wooster Group

Like Wilson and Laurie Anderson, the New York-based Wooster Group have also explored and deconstructed contemporary media-saturated culture. For more than 35 years, the Wooster Group, under the direction of Elizabeth Lecompte have remained at the cutting edge of post-dramatic multimedia theatre, confusing the boundaries between the theatrical and the media image.

Emerging from Richard Schechner's The Performance Group, the group took up residence at The Performing Garage on Wooster Street in Soho, New York, which the Group own and operate as a shareholder in the Grand Street Artists Co-op, originally established as part of the Fluxus art movement in the 1960s. Founding members of the group were Jim Clayburgh, Willem Dafoe, Spalding Gray (1941–2004), Elizabeth Lecompte,

Peyton Smith, Kate Valk, and Ron Vawter (1948–94). The Wooster Group have been pivotal in forging an experimental contemporary theatre that draws from a variety of disciplines and media and, as Dafoe describes it, aims to create a theatre disconnected from absolutes of text and psychology, theatre that speaks to an age 'where we can talk on the phone, look out the window, watch TV, and be typing a letter at the same time' (Dafoe in Monks, 2005, p. 561). They both use media within their performances and at the same time explore, question, and simply play with the ways in which media alter perspective and influence cultural practice.

A key aspect of the Group's development process is that they use classic texts as 'found' material, as a source that can be quoted, fragmented and entirely redesigned. The final product is a fusion of the original 'play', elements of popular culture and mass media, and personal moments from the group's rehearsal process. The use of media, in the form of television and film onstage, is a consistent feature in many of their works, and the group also 'responds' to the pervasion of media, particularly television, through both the form and content of their works. LeCompte explains how TV has influenced her vision of theatre:

> I never watch something through unless it's an old movie.... I have a remote and I switch through them, pick what I want and make my own stories. That's one of the things I think that was so exciting to me about theatre, that I didn't have to be cut off from all of the media that were available to me.... I didn't think of media as a different thing from theatre. I thought of the television as no different than for Chekov what opening a door and seeing imitation light was outside. The television was there all the time, it was a natural element of our environment, and at the time it was not used in the theatre.... It wasn't used in the theatre because people said, 'if you put the television in the theatre ... everyone will watch TV, they won't watch the theatre experience,' which fascinated me. Why in the theatre ... would they watch the TV image and not watch the performance? (Lecompte on *The Southbank Show*, 1987)

The 1981 production *Route 1 and 9* is a typical example of their approach to multimedia. *Route 1 and 9* was based in part on Thornton Wilder's 1938 play *Our Town*, and involved the Wooster Group actors donning exaggerated blackface and playing the roles of stagehands who must build a tin house onstage. Significantly, video extracts of the original play were shown on overhead TV screens, juxtaposing the onstage performance and creating an underlying tension between the live and mediated content. When the house is built, a raucous party forms in which the cast re-enacts a Vaudeville comedy routine by 'Pigmeat' Markham.

Loudspeakers broadcast real phone conversations of Kate Valk attempting to order fried chicken or ice cream from a series of uptown take-out restaurants. The piece culminates in the screening of two home movies, one of which portrays a journey away from New York City on the New Jersey thoroughfare that gives the piece its title, the second a porno tape featuring Libby Howes, Ron Vawter, and Willem Dafoe.

> 'I've ... always been interested in finding ways of telling a story theatrically that are unrelated to Stanislavsky-based acting. Having studied American comedy for years, I came across Pigmeat Markham in the late 70s and started collecting his records. Using only the records, we tried to re-create the routines as closely as possible. I was interested in the way he improvised his routines on the spot. Out of that idea came the notion of the ensemble constructing the piece at the same time that they performed it' (Lecompte in Holden, 1987).

Some critics denounced *Route 1 and 9* as scandalous and in 1982 the New York State Council on the Arts rescinded the company's funding by 43 per cent, judging the blackface sequences to be 'harsh and caricatured portrayals of a racial minority'. Others understood the work as an effort to expose the racist presumptions hidden behind the stuffy façade of *Our Town*. Wilder's romanticised world is not shared by all. Lecompte herself states, 'people talked about how in *Route 1 & 9* we conjured racism in the room instead of representing the forces of racism and another force of good against racism. That's the way we work – sometimes we become the thing in order to expiate it, to show it' (Lecompte in Shewey, 1983). The production was also controversial in other venues. Kate Valk recalls a violent audience response in Zurich, which had to do with the use of screens on stage rather than their pastiche of blackface performance techniques (Zinoman, 2005).

In the 1984 production *L.S.D. (... Just the high points)*, the company used fragments of text from *The Crucible*, alongside Beat poetry, writing about members of the Beat Generation of the 50s and LSD advocate Timothy Leary, and a re-enactment of a Wooster Group rehearsal. This production blended these various texts with no apparent cohesion or overarching logic, though themes of persecution and paranoia ran as an undercurrent throughout. This production was again received with mixed responses and generated further controversy for the company. Arthur Miller sent the company a cease-and-desist letter for the unauthorised use of *The Crucible* so the company used testimony from the original Salem trials instead.

Various media forms were deployed in the production and for a number of reasons. The actor Michael Kirby was unable to attend the early part of a tour of the production, so he was 'present' in the production as a video image. Later, when he met up with the tour, the video image remained part of the production and Kirby interacted with his own image. In another instance, the Wooster Group performers re-created their own behaviour from videotape, and repeated words while listening to them on a sound recording. Lecompte had video recorded a rehearsal in which the performers experienced the hallucinatory effects of LSD, and the video was then used as the script for part of the final production, as the performers re-enacted their actions from the rehearsal. This use of remediation in their composition process is evidence of how completely the company's approach is immersed in multimedial aesthetics.

The Wooster Group described their 2004 work *Poor Theatre* as a 'series of simulacra'. It is a two-part work, a tribute to and a deconstruction of the work of Jerzy Grotowski and William Forsythe. In Part One, the performers mimic Grotowski's *Acropolis*, which is shown on a tiny television in the foreground. Part Two simulates an interview with Forsythe as Wooster Group performers, playing members of Forsythe's Frankfurt Ballet, throw themselves around the stage, responding firstly to an onstage video of the original dance troupe and secondly to various clips from American Westerns.

The onstage television screen has been an emblematic characteristic of Wooster Group productions, and the relationship between live performance and the televisual is explored on both a thematic and an ontological platform. Phillip Auslander argues that their exploration of the television, their representation of the 'flow of mediatized culture' (1992, p. 83) has constituted the group's key political contribution. Arguing that the Group's work was not apolitical, Auslander asserts that their significant political achievements are their ability to show 'the voiding of historical and political discourses under mediatization' and their capacity to 'enable the spectator to position herself relative to such an environment' (Auslander, 1992, p. 171).

In the production *House/Lights* (1998), the television takes centre stage. This was a reworking of Gertrude Stein's wordplay *Dr Faustus Lights the Lights*, combined with the story of *Olga's House of Shame*,

Figure 8   *House/Lights,* The Wooster Group. Photo: Paula Court

a soft-core bondage and domination movie by Joseph Mawra (1964), in which the leaders of a jewel-smuggling gang of criminals find that one of their own (Elaine) has betrayed them and enlist her to torture other uncooperative gang members. There is an overt connection between main characters – Faust and Elaine, Olga and Mephistopheles, and the notion that identity cannot be taken for granted runs as a theme throughout. The work collages live performance and multimedia, with actors often doubled in real-time via live feeds. Via closed-circuit video cameras, images of the real-time Wooster actors are superimposed into the black-and-white movie, blending them with the light-pornographic action. Live performance is juxtaposed with TV screens that record and transform what is happening on a stage littered with scattered lightbulbs and assorted mic booms.

The emphasis on televisual media in *mise en scène* and the notion that media comprise a part of performance aesthetics at the level of composition and are not simply an aspect of scenographic design has been one of the Wooster Group's most significant contributions to late twentieth-century theatre.[1] They have come to epitomise postmodern theatre, with their use of pastiche, their closed-circuit self-reflexivity and the intertextuality of their compositions. The Woosters have developed the use of text as readymade or found material which forms part of the composition but does not constitute the core of the work. In terms of structure, the company focuses on discontinuity and investigates the ways that the use of different performance elements (dance, song, comedic routines, lectures) and different media (telephony, video, voice filters etc) creatively disrupt narrative cohesion in favour of a sensorial complexity. With their evocative use of sound, film and video, they have been a major influence on our current generation of post-dramatic and multimedia theatre makers.

The members of the Japanese group, dumb type, used to say that their aims were 'to explore ever new dimensions of human system interaction'. A virtual multimedia dance theatre collective, they were formed in Kyoto, Japan, in 1984 by Teiji Furuhashi, then a student at Kyoto Uni of Fine Arts. More so perhaps than Anderson and Wilson, Furuhashi's direction of dumb type's performances involved elaborate technoscapes and technography, a choreography of devices and tools. In 1990 their piece, *PH*, toured nine countries and took as its theme the emergent global 'infobahn'. The prescience of this theme cannot be overestimated as it predates the formation of the world wide web by several years. This piece features precision choreography on a tennis court-like gridded stage over which an enormous electronic boom (actually a metal scanner) sweeps back and forth. The scanner resembles a giant photocopier projecting texts and images onto the floor (the seating is steeply raked to facilitate viewing). One such text is the phrase 'New world order', which morphs into 'New world border', suggesting that the global village is not a utopic projection but contains the dystopic possibilities of an ever-present and metastasising bureaucracy. The message of the piece is that at the threshold of the new world we will have to show our identity documents before crossing over. If Wilson and Anderson incorporate images into their theatre, then dumb type use the image as the space of performance, turning the stage space into a gigantic screen.

Return of the matrix: Revisiting the theatre of images in the twenty-first century

Ironically, perhaps, if we look at a number of more recent examples of Multimedia Theatre, we see a return to character and narrative in a more complex style of matrixed performance. However we might expect

Figure 9   *[OR]*, dumb type. Photo © Emmanuel Valette. dumb type turns the stage into a gigantic screen

the a/v technology in work like this to return to its more traditional illustrative role, there are a number of startlingly different deployments of multimedia in these works. The following section provides three case studies showing how multimedia technologies in theatre have developed and evolved in the twenty-first century in the context of more conventional dramatic structures.

The first explores the 2008 production *Sarajevo Story* by British multimedia theatre makers Lightwork. This piece utilises live feeds, image mixing and projection not simply for aesthetic ends, but as a dramaturgical function to enhance the themes of the text. The second, the 2004 production *Supervision* by The Builders Association, uses projected imagery both as a key feature of its architectural design and as a dramaturgical tool. Under the direction of Marianne Weems, The Builders' Association use the integration of contemporary technologies to extend the boundaries of live narrative theatre. Based in New York, the company blends text, sound, architecture, video, and stage performance to explore the impact of technology on human presence and selfhood and locate the development of character firmly within a multimedia setting. Their staging is organised so that the performers move in and out of virtual and screen-based environments, which multiply perspectives on the characters and the narrative events. The third case study also uses filmic projection to create a fluid environment, but in this instance it is the audience rather than the actor that is immersed in the architecture. In this case study we see how the legacy of the Theatre of Images extends into the arena of new media installation. The iCinema Centre for Interactive Cinema Research, based in Sydney and directed by renowned media artist Jeffrey Shaw, epitomises this extension of theatre into installation. Works such as *Eavesdrop*, which Shaw created in collaboration with theatre director David Pledger, remediate theatre on a 360-degree circular screen, and turn the participant into the performer as they navigate through the cinematic image-scape.

Sarajevo Story – Lightwork

This case study examines the use of the live projection and doubling of the actor within Lightwork's 2008 production *Sarajevo Story*. Interestingly, this production thematises the failure of communication in general, both interpersonal face-to-face communication and electronically enabled communication. Throughout the work the characters utilise voicemail, video-conferencing and other technical facilities to stay in touch with one another as they travel internationally. The staging has a number of cameras positioned at various places around the stage, allowing the actors' faces to be projected on a long strip that runs across the back wall.

Artistic director Andy Lavender formed Lightwork in London in 1999. The company's work attempts to confront issues of love, trust, chance and superstition, and utilizes an array of onstage media such as live feed, microphones and projected imagery to create a 'hypermedial *mise en scène*'. Their previous work *Here's What I Did With My Body One Day* presented the story of a leading genome scientist who follows a series of clues in the hope of unravelling his family 'curse'. The 'genetic detective thriller' is further intersected by ghost stories of three French intellectuals whose deaths all relate in some way to the scientist's family history.

The various media in this work are not designed to effect sensorial dislocation as in the Woosters but are organised around the elements of the story and are in a sense grounded by the narrative. Barbara is an American judge working in Sarajevo, overseeing war crimes cases. Her husband Jeff is an artist who creates sound installations and is working

Figure 10   *Sarajevo Story* 2008, Lightwork. Performer Bella Merlin. Photo: Simon Kane

on a commission to create a piece for the Charles Bridge in Prague. Their daughter back home in America is about to be married to her Irish fiancé. The mediated communication between the characters is an essential element of the story, and a key mode of dialogue. For example, Jeff and Barbara have dinner with each other via Skype. The mediated conversation and action evolves in real-time in the production.

A key theme within the work is the idea that, even with so many methods of communication in today's society, meaning can still be misconstrued, and people will still hear what they want to, rather than what is said. Dramaturgically, the device of having the actors performing via the camera or talking on the phone, as if the *characters* are speaking via live mediation, emphasises the mediation of the individual that is part of everyday life experience. This is also a question of translation and shows the various ways, technical and cultural, in which our behaviours and discourses are translated for the consumption of others.

The process of translation itself is a key theme of the play – verbatim testimony, drawn from the Bosnian war crimes tribunal, is read before the court, simultaneously translated into English for the benefit of both Barbara and the audience. At times the translator has difficulty keeping up.

In other scenes, Barbara is having difficulty communicating with her Bosnian colleagues due to the language barrier. Throughout the work, both thematically and within the staging, the individual is shown as always mediated, via technology, via culture, and via language. Communication is coded, it relies on informational pattern, and it is not always deciphered as accurately as intended.

When the audience is faced with both the actor, and their live, mediated projection within the same space, we see the translation of the presence of the actor into the pattern of information technology. However, these are not separate, the actor is not doubled, and the presence is not erased. Rather, the audience perceives the actor as speaking *through* the media, as communicating simultaneously through material and informational languages. The 'distance' between the moving image and the actor is eradicated as their movements are exactly coordinated. By having the characters speaking via Skype, with the audience party to both the physical actor and their mediated presence, the characters become more layered and the performances become composites of restrained task-based gestures for camera and more fully expressive gestural acting. In this composite style of performance, *Sarajevo Story* underlines the duality of multimedia aesthetics in that it is possible to see how communications media frame our everyday experiences but that we still rely on our own senses and our own physical and perceptual capacities to frame these media messages as meaningful.

The use of Skype is an interesting development in live theatre, but not in this case extending the possible communicative reach of the performer. In *Sarajevo Story* there is no use of Skype equivalent to the use of the phone in *Route 1 and 9*, where it is used to disrupt the effect of 'stage presence' by introducing the liveness of telephony. Instead, the effect is embedded within the matrix of the narrative, where it testifies to the situation of the characters and by implication the audience. Like sightlines, we/they are reliant on bandwidth for our gestures to be meaningful and communicable across differential space–time coordinates. If bandwidth isn't there, the medium becomes opaque and hinders live exchange. When the technology falters, the immersion is broken, the materiality of the frame is emphasised, character is interrupted and presence reappears.

Supervision – The Builders Association

The Builders Association's production, *Supervision*, was created in 2005 in collaboration with multimedia company dBox. It explores the concept of 'data bodies' – the versions of ourselves that exist in data space as the collation of all the data files collected about us. Three intertwined stories of human–computer relationships explore the diverse ways in which digital information technologies record, reflect and refashion human identity. Characters in a range of social and geographic situations interact with the world of information, and their social lives are overtly and inadvertently affected. *Supervision* highlights 'the changing nature of our relationship to living in a post-private society, where personal electronic information is constantly collected and distributed' (www.superv.org) and how in our digitally saturated environment our data-identity is often recognised as more 'authentic' than the physical or subjective self. As in *Sarajevo Story*, this new ontological scenario is played out through fictional devices and dramatic structures.

> The Builders Association was founded in New York in 1994 by director Marianne Weems. They have collaborated on ten large-scale productions that employ a 'blend' of technical devices and feature extensive use of projection and live media (http://www.thebuildersassociation.org/). In such a multimedial *mise en scène*, the stage actor performs to both audience and camera simultaneously; they are both in close-up and in the distance, working various proximities, both live and mediated.

A traveller, a Ugandan citizen of Indian descent, repeatedly enters the US on business. In each of his scenes he must pass through a security check, and as the checks grow more interrogative, the traveller become more frustrated and defensive. In a keystroke the security official can access endless personal details about this 'potentially suspect' visitor and these details appear as swirling information patterns on a large screen that surround the figure of the traveller. In a witty take on a very quotidian experience of technological determinism, the airport security officials believe only what is recorded in the traveller's passport and travel information, disregarding the person standing before them. The patterns of information that create his 'data-body', for all practical and legal purposes, effectively displace his material presence.

In a middle-class Seattle household 'John Snr.' secretly conducts fraud via the Internet, using the identity of his young son to run up credit card debt. The trails of information he leaves behind are recorded and stored and his actions in the virtual world of information have very real impact upon his material existence. Interestingly, John Jnr. is never materially present on the stage; rather, he is shown as a projected image and, as such, the digital information manipulated by John Snr. is just as 'real'

Figure 11 *Supervision*, The Builders Association

as his son; the digital information in this case is not inferior as a 'copy' or representation of the real, but is constructed from the same bits and bytes as the material 'presence' of John Jnr.

In New York, a member of the 'digirati', the burgeoning generation of young technology-obsessed professionals, communicates daily via webcam with her grandmother in Columbia, Sri Lanka. From the other side of the world, 'Jen' is organising her grandmother's affairs while simultaneously building a family history, recording and storing photos and important documents on her computer. As she scans old photographs, the audience watches as the old medium of photography is remediated by digital technology, and as the grandmother in Sri Lanka narrates (via webcam) the memories each photograph evokes, we are reminded of other, older ways of locating one's identity. As the grandmother's mind begins to wander and slowly fragment, we see the import role the technology plays in allowing Jen to 'keep-an-eye' on her grandmother's health and state of mind. At the same time, the projected image of the grandmother's pixellating face serves to remind us that electronic systems too are fallible, they can get their wires crossed, slow their electrical impulses and create misleading patterns in the randomness of data.

Within the three stories presented in *Supervision* we see the relationships between middle-class society and digital technologies manifest in differing ways. We see its positive potential to unite the distanced and enable the monitoring of those that require assistance, we see it manipulated to both commit, and catch financial fraud, and we see its impact upon the boundaries of personal privacy as it is exploited by governments in the name of security. *Supervision* presents the Orwellian omniscience of surveillance in a digital age as unlimited, its impact underestimated.

In an interview (with Klich, 2005), director Marianne Weems explained that the work was created in reaction to other artworks that explore the issue of surveillance, because 'in a post 9/11, post-private culture we all know we're under visual surveillance'. This is not news. Rather, what interested Weems was the idea of 'dataveillance, that invisible form of surveillance that's actually much more omnipresent at this point and much more insidious ultimately', for 'dataveillance' is 'compromising our sense of identity in a way that visual surveillance never will'.

The onstage media architecture and slick sound and lighting effects create the sense of a world where digital technology reigns; digital technology is not only depicted as vital infrastructure allowing communication and access, but it is a fundamental part of the environment. The integration of the live performer and the digital scenery is crucial in developing the themes of the work. In his study, the character of John Snr. sits at his desk surrounded by swirling patterns of information in which he appears completely immersed. Here the live performer does not appear in contrast to the digital environment but rather the scenography shows the virtual, the streams and patterns of information, as emanating from the computer screen and completely encompassing his physical self. While the actor is recognisable as a material form within the virtual environment, the patterns of information that flow over his face and body create the effect that he is only two-dimensional, a shape and not a being. The boundary between his body and the virtual environment seems fluid, insignificant, and potentially permeable. These visual effects create the sense that information is leaking out of the computer-based world and colonising material space.

This work explores the idea that human behaviours are not only mediated by communication technologies, or even simulated within media, but that the potential to become *translated* into digital pattern risks a posthuman scenario in which people are functionally replaced by their virtual counterparts. As the character of the grandmother begins to show signs of senility, the giant webcam image of her face slowly breaks apart. The pixellation of the image suggests that the breakdown of the machine and the gradual injection of randomness within the pattern of the media image may correlate with the disintegration of the human brain and the disconnection of organic electrical impulses.

Figure 12 *Supervision*, The Builders Association

At its heart, this work poses questions about emergent cultural performatives: while we know that human behaviours are more than the accumulation of their statistical information, the emergence of ubiquitous virtual information environments negates the functionality of those differences and asserts that we are now essentially posthuman, in that human beings now function not only *through* technology but *as* technology. Human actions and impulses have the same value as information but less utility, for unlike human behaviour, digital information is recordable, objectively classifiable and almost permanently storeable.

Eavesdrop – Jeffrey Shaw and David Pledger

Unlike the previous examples, the new media installation *Eavesdrop* (2004) is an interactive work for screen rather than stage, but a particular kind of screen. The work was created as a collaboration between Jeffrey Shaw of the iCinema Centre for Interactive Research and David Pledger, founding artistic director and producer of the Melbourne-based theatre company Not Yet It's Difficult (NYID). It was presented at the 2004 Brisbane, Melbourne and Sydney Festivals in the iCinema AVIE screen environment, a 360-degree cinematic landscape (or Advanced Visualisation and Interaction Environment) that invites the user to explore the scene before them from a platform with a control console. The user/director operates this rotating podium in the centre of the viewing space and uses a Nintendo-like console to manipulate the focus of the projection before them, select the scenes for viewing, and to zoom in and out of them. The work consists of nine discrete scenes with continuous narratives rendered as dramatic dialogues.

Not Yet its Difficult was founded in Melbourne in 1995 by director David Pledger, dramaturg Peter Eckersall and lighting designer Paul Jackson. NYID has produced over 40 art projects, including performance works, plays, public space projects, and television and screen-based installations. The company's work is often controversial and develops a strong critique of the apolitical popular media culture in Australia.

On screen, ten characters are positioned at six tables within what appears to be a jazz club staged within a theatre. At each table a small narrative vignette is performed, with the characters sharing intimate conversations that form a nine-minute loop. A band continuously plays soothing background music, and as an audience member uses the console to focus on a particular conversation, the background music fades and they are able to eavesdrop on the private dialogue of the characters. The audience's role is both director and detective as they piece together the interwoven stories. Described as 'part game, part real-time film-making, part spectator sport, part magical realism' (www.notyet.com.au), *Eavesdrop* opens up the borders of the cinema screen and allows users to navigate their own path through the multi-narrative, multi-layered, theatrical terrain.

The setting of the club appears to function as a type of purgatory, as the characters all explore certain moral, spiritual, and psychological conditions. Director David Pledger explains: 'Really the stories are about a middle-class Australia in purgatory which is basically how I see the country at the moment. I see it as in a kind of limbo' (Pledger, 2005). Some characters have clearly been in the purgatorial club a long time, for their gestures and comments depict a comfortable familiarity with the environment, while other characters are only just arriving. Each character's conversation reveals a moral dilemma: A woman discusses her attempts to find identity through cosmetic surgery; an old couple discuss their preferred method of suicide; a middle-aged man suffers the pangs of unrequited love; a radio broadcaster interviews an activist about ethics, choice, and revolution; a young man tries to convince his girlfriend to leave their small-town suburb for the promise of the city; while two other young men drink, smoke, and mourn their lost potential. Shaw describes the work as a 'multi-narrative mediation of psychological states in and around the theme of moral inertia' (www.icinema.unsw.edu.au), which was a prominent issue in Australia during the term of the conservative Howard Government (1996–2007).[2]

As the user moves in to eavesdrop on the conversations, they discover they are able to 'zoom' into the interior landscape of the characters and view their private thoughts. As they zoom in, the participant is able to access the third dimension of the imagery and give the image physical depth. Inside each character is an image or story depicting a repressed emotional state that reveals a hidden agenda behind the surface appearance. The audience assumes the role of an investigator, searching for links and unifying themes. There appears to be no overt connection between the characters other than their patronage of the club and their questionable morality, and yet through their choice of focus the participant

Figure 13 *Eavesdrop* 2004, Jeffrey Shaw and David Pledger. Photo: Greg Ferris

appears to connect the characters as their navigation structures the linear sequencing of events.

The depiction of the club is not naturalistic, but is a manufactured setting within what appears to be a theatre. Behind the band are rows of seats, as if the band is rehearsing onstage in an empty theatre. Drop-curtains and exit-doors behind some of the tables suggest a 'backstage' area. The lighting is theatrical, rather than the enhanced naturalistic lighting of film, and the general effect is very much one of theatrical 'staging'. Although the work is described by Shaw and producer Martin Thiele as 'cinematic' and as multi-linear narrative 'film', the work projects a strong sense of 'theatre on film', of 'mediatised' or 'remediated' theatre. Cinema, as articulated by Lev Manovich, 'works hard to erase any traces of its own production process, including any indication that the images, which we see could have been constructed rather than recorded' (Manovich, 2000, p. 178). The content projected on the screen in *Eavesdrop* emphasises the process of theatrical staging and of the actors' performance 'for the camera'.

However, unlike both cinema and theatre, here the spectators physically direct their focus and determine the shape of the story. The user controlling the console guides the focus of the camera, as if they are themselves the director of the film, editing the stock footage through processes of zooming, jumping, sweeping, and panning. The user is presented with a plot from which they are invited to develop their own unique story. David Pledger explains that the work

> is designed for people to go in at different points and make their own story. You are a detective, and you are putting together a story and trying to find out who is related to whom. The way that you negotiate this is absolutely individual and unique, and no-one else can do it the way that you do. Moreover, when you get on the machine it is at a certain point where somebody has left off, so there is no beginning and no end even though it loops. (Pledger, 2005)

The individual determines their tempo and pace, creating their own unique rhythm as they make narrative links. As the participant in *Eavesdrop* manipulates the interface to navigate a path through the paradigm of images, selecting some footage and omitting or scanning over the rest, the user performs their narrativisation of the environment.

Like the computer user, the *Eavesdrop* participant's process of engagement is a continual performance of choice and identity. However, unlike the computer user who usually performs via media or in isolation, the *Eavesdrop* user performs to a live audience in real space. While only one person is able to interact with the work at a time, the rest of the audience are able to stand within the space behind the user-console and observe the actions of the user. From their pedestal, the user mediates the database of images for the other participants, and as these participants group together behind the user and await their turn in the driving seat, they are able to observe, assess, and compare the individual performances of each user.

> Jeffrey Shaw has pioneered the field of interactive media installation. His work uses electronic media to transform the cinematic experience and create a screen dimension responsive to user participation. His works are both immersive and interactive, presenting the user with a workable interface that allows them to navigate virtual environments and media imagery. They also require a very embodied kind of audience response, as in *ConFIGURING the CAVE* (1996), in which 3-D imagery crosses the visual and affective field of the spectators at an angle determined by a centrally located mannequin figure whose bodily poses, manipulated by a participant, determine the viewing experience for the spectators.

The work enables a sense of shared experience akin to the theatre. Pledger argues that 'The relationships between the person who is using the machine and the people who are both waiting to use the machine or watching what somebody else makes of it is in fact where the theatrical elements of [the work] are' (Pledger, 2005). He contends that a lot of media artworks cannot be experienced in a communal environment, with the interface enabling only individual interaction. In such works, argues Pledger:

> You put a headpiece on and you interact with it, and people watch you but they do not understand what you are doing because it doesn't manifest. Whereas in *Eavesdrop* it manifests for everybody to see; you're turning it, you make a choice that you like that person and you zoom in on them; that conversation is boring you but you think that person's interesting so you turn and go inside their head and then all of a sudden you're in there for five minutes and people are saying 'C'mon, get a move on'. So that is indeed the performance of the work. (Pledger, 2005)

Eavesdrop is designed so that with each participant's individual interaction comes a unique performance of the work, and spectators who observe a number of interactions are able to view different versions of the work over time.

Eavesdrop plays with the ingredients of narrative such as character, language, and setting to create a unique text, the form of which is reconstructed with each user's interaction – they temporally arrange the presentation of these elements in real-time. The inner time of the fiction unfolds in parallel with the 'external' time of the participants' journey. Though the constructed internal space is virtual, there are no discrepancies such as lapses or jumps to indicate that the time of the virtual world is not in accordance with 'external' time. If the work is observed over a period of time, the eventual repetition of the conversations and of the single piece of music played by the band emphasises the temporality of the work as 'looped'.

However, the constant movement of the navigation means that, though the individual episodes may be looped and therefore without temporal progression, the sequence of their showing is never the same. As the user interacts with the work, and in doing so mediates it for the other participants, the performance text unfolds in real-time as the user follows their own pace, whim and intuition. With every new user-interaction, a new text is created, with a new rhythm, a new tempo, and a different sequencing of events. In this way the text is not pre-scripted but rather develops through a process of interaction.

Technically, Jeffrey Shaw's user-platform is a beautifully smooth and user-friendly rotating projector which nods in the direction of cinematic immersion. Shaw states that it is 'intended as a means of achieving a semantic and experiential extension of the cinema's narrative space' (Shaw, *Eavesdrop* Press Kit 2004) In fact, it represents more than this. In Melbourne this work appeared in an exhibition titled 'Sensesurround', which was originally a technology fundamentally connected to the cinema's commercial and technical requirements. However the 'panoramic and interactive augmentation of the image' in *Eavesdrop* is a significant departure from cinema even cinematic narrative space. Its multiple perspectives and subtextual complexity associate more readily with the interactive cave-based installations of Shaw's other iCinema works, which are fully immersive 3-D environments, and with the kind of powerful image-based theatre that the company Not Yet It's Difficult are known for.

Further distancing this work from familiar cinematic formats is the fact that it is completely reliant on audience intervention, connecting it to other computer-based narrative formats and, even again perhaps, post-dramatic theatre. A defining feature of post-dramatic theatre is the open acknowledgement of the audience, and in *Eavesdrop* the user is not hidden behind the interface but centrally raised on a pedestal, openly acknowledged not only as a participant but also as the key performer.

Eavesdrop clearly occupies the territory between theatre, cinema and computer game, and it is in such interactive, performative, new media installations that the legacy of the Theatre of Images is manifest in the twenty-first century.

Conclusion

Bonnie Marranca's phrase 'Theatre of Images' usefully describes a type of mixed-media theatre that foregrounds the visual rather than the textual component of the work, as in the dramatic tradition. This kind of aesthetic, which Lehmann also discusses in relation to post-dramatic theatre, also reflects developments in the visual arts of the 1960s particularly associated with the work of the Fluxus group of artists, where performance became part of an integrated and interdisciplinary arts practice working not in theatres but in art galleries and in public and spaces. Theatre artists such as Robert Wilson, like Tadeusz Kantor before him, and The Wooster Group after him, demonstrate the gradual integration of a mediated visual apparatus into the theatrical frame through a growing emphasis on the visual components of architecture, space, and image. The Builders Association, Lightwork, and media artists such as Jeffrey Shaw extend this dynamic, and in different ways reunite the media image with post-dramatic character and narrative. In the works described above, we find the non-matrixed acting styles of film and television adopted on the stage to cope with an increasingly intermedial scenography. This means that actors in these productions can work in the discontinuous way demanded by other media and by the extended use of video- and screen-based performance on stage. Actors in these works engage in dialogue across media; some on stage, others on screen. In works such as *Eavesdrop* there are no live actors but only viewers interacting with the screen performances and constructing their own narrative from what they see. In the next chapter we explore the meaning of this type of situation in terms of the recent theoretical discussions on liveness.

Further reading

The Twentieth-Century Performance Reader edited by Michael Huxley and Noel Witts (1996) contains material from a number of the artists featured in this chapter including Wilson, Anderson, and Liz Lecompte as does Dasgupta and Marranca's *Conversations on Art and Performance* (1999). *PAJ* is a useful journal to look into as well. To follow up some of the other case studies in this chapter we refer the reader to the various company websites: the iCinema website for information about *Eavesdrop* http://www.icinema.unsw.edu.au and other related projects; The Builders Association pages for further material on *Supervision* http://www.thebuildersassociation.org/; and http://www.lightwork.org.uk/ for information about Lightwork's recent productions including *Sarajevo Story*.

Chapter 4

Liveness and Re-Mediation

As we saw in the previous chapter, the uses of audio-visual technologies in theatre practice tend to fall into two very basic categories. The first is the use of onstage filmic media within staged theatre, as in the 'Theatre of Images', and the second is the remediation of theatre itself in screen-based environments, as in the iCinema project *Eavesdrop*. Both these categories, staged and screened, offer numerous examples of how technological mediation enhances live performance. Both also displace comfortable certitudes about the live experience of performance with questions such as how we know/recognise the performer and how the experience of the spectator is extended and sharpened in multimedia work. After all, in virtual theatre such as the iCinema work there are multiple performances on screen and they are encountered and activated differently by different audiences with the aid of a projection device that enables the suspension of narrative events in favour of backstory or a discussion of the character's motivations.

This approach of technological enhancement for the spectator suggests new possibilities for the composition as well as the experience of multimedia performance work. It begins to explore the ways in which the virtual spaces of digital performance can be utilised as a theatrical tool, but it also asks us to reconsider the question of the live. What, if anything, of a live experience survives the migration of performance into a screen-based environment such as the AVIE in *Eavesdrop*? To discuss this question we first revisit the terms of the live vs mediated debate, then look into the potential of 'intermediality' as a theoretical paradigm. In this task we are guided by the recently published anthology *Intermediality in Theatre and Performance* edited by Freda Chapple and Chiel Kattenbelt and we refer to a number of the essays from this collection in this chapter. We also ask how 'intermediality' responds to the terms of this debate in examining the 'liveness' presented in three key case studies of intermedial performance.

The live vs mediated debate redux

In his influential essay 'The Screen Test of the Double: The Uncanny Performer in the Space of Technology', Matthew Causey explains the root of the problem in these terms: 'the contemporary discourse surrounding live performance and technological reproduction establishes an essentialised difference between the phenomena' (Causey, 1999, p. 383). The polarisation of live theatre and mediatised performance is epitomised in the debate initiated by the differing perspectives of Peggy Phelan (1993) and Phillip Auslander (1999). Whereas Phelan asserts the authenticity of live performance, arguing that performance is *essentially* non-reproducible, Auslander undermines this perspective, arguing that liveness exists only as a result of mediatisation. In his book *Liveness: Performance in a Mediatised Culture*, he questions the status of live performance in a culture dominated by mass media, and explores different instances of live performance such as theatre, rock music, sport, and courtroom testimony. He argues that media technology has impinged on these live events to the extent that they are no longer purely and simply 'live' and that therefore the entities 'live' and 'mediatised' are not *essentially* different but merely operate within dissimilar cultural economies in which the cultural values appertaining to these entities are unequally distributed.

Philip Auslander is a significant theorist of recent performance whose books tend to work the seam of contentious issues in the field through the lens of postmodern thought. In *From Acting to Performance: Essays in Modernism and Postmodernism* (1997) he charts shifts in the notion of theatre as a traditional form based on certain skills and 'crafts' such as acting to an understanding of recent performance culture in terms of more complexly conceptual modes of representation that rely on irony and intertext. He has also investigated the gaps between the ideas of political opposition and effective resistance in *Presence and Resistance: Postmodernism and Cultural Politics in Contemporary American Performance* (1992), while in *Liveness: Performance in a Mediatised Culture* he addresses the effects of ubiquitous media technologies on both society at large and understandings of performance as an essentially 'live' medium. The book's second edition was published in 2008, and has been updated to consider the advances in technology that have occurred over the ten years since it was first written.

In *Unmarked: The Politics of Performance*, Phelan explores the characteristics of 'performance' as a species of contemporary art, and posits the view that the ontology of performance derives from the fact that it is incapable of being reproduced. Performance from this perspective is definitively 'live' and cannot be re-experienced in its exact form and context. Indeed, Phelan asserts that the being of performance, its essential form, is dependent on its 'disappearance'; 'it becomes itself through disappearance' (Phelan, 1993, p. 146). Performance in this theorisation of it is a celebration of that which is non-reproducible; its power and value lie in that which is transient, intuitive, experiential. Phelan makes her case in language which continues to resonate throughout the discipline of performance studies: 'Without a copy, live performance plunges into visibility – in a maniacally charged present – and disappears into memory, into the realm of invisibility and the unconscious where it eludes regulation and control' (Phelan, 1993, p. 148).

Peggy Phelan's writing on performance shows an intense interest in multimedia work from the perspective of representation and reproduction. Her book *Unmarked: The Politics of Performance* features famous readings on photographers such as Robert Mapplethorpe, Cindy Sherman and visual artist Sophie Calle as well as describing the activities of right-wing political activists' 'Operation rescue' and the dance film work of Yvonne Rainer. But her work is possibly best known in performance studies circles through the chapter 'The Ontology of Performance: Representation without reproduction'. This chapter deals with the question of the non-reproducibility of performance, which is the topic of our analysis in this chapter.

This is a noble destination for performance but the increasing insistence on retention and repetition within the visual field in performance cultures everywhere seems to militate against it. Increasingly performance fails to disappear, especially where there is a degree of integration of live and pre-recorded forms within the space of the work. Here it is not the distinctiveness of the different elements (live v mediatised) that matters; rather, it is the real-time interaction and experience of these elements that is key. And this interaction constitutes a live experience of performance, which, however mediatised and pre-recorded, may never be exactly reproducible. When pre-recorded elements are brought into the space of the live event, they become part of a live conversation, and while the components of this event may vary in their degree of liveness, they are part of a larger whole that is complex, multi-dimensioned, and transient. The pre-recorded elements of the production are 'remediated' into a live performance, a notion that will be explored further later in this chapter.

But what happens when this 'live conversation', this performance, is itself remediated? With the advent of new forms of theatre suggested by terms such as 'networked performance', 'video performance', 'cybertheatres', and 'virtual theatres', the notion of performance as essentially 'live' is brought into question. The assumed ontological status of the opposition between 'the mediatised' and 'the live' cannot account for either the variety of new forms of mediatised performance or the experience of them which is basically limited to the audio-visual sensory apparatus of the spectator no matter what the form or content of the work may be. For Auslander, this is partly why the ontological argument, this perceived essential or intrinsic opposition, does not convince. We can see this, for instance, when we talk about 'live tv' (an argument made by Auslander), or when we communicate 'live' via the phone or internet. Online liveness (social co-presence online) and social or group liveness (mobile contact facilitated by sms) are other modes of 'mediated liveness' (Couldry in Auslander, 2008, p. 61). Liveness here simply refers to something that is happening now and is not purely a replay of something that has happened earlier.

So we have live mediated theatre, performed via technological interfaces that translate the performer in real time. Certainly we could argue that live mediated theatre is not the same as unmediated live theatre; but as many scholars now argue (Boenisch, Kattenbelt etc), theatre is itself a medium. Scheer argues elsewhere that even performance art, which in some of its manifestations aims at an experience of the 'immediate', must also be understood as a medium, in which case when we talk about the mediation of performance by technology, we are really referring to the *re*mediation of performance (Scheer, 2006). And the process of this remediation is live; it is in the 'now', but not necessarily the 'here', as another frame is placed between the audience/participant and the performer. Both these new, technologically mediated spaces of performance, and the use of media alongside performers in the space onstage or in the gallery emphasise the need to move away from the notion of the live and the mediated as opposing forces. It is also not where the interesting and productive differences between them are to be found.

Intermediality reconsidered

The framework provided by the notion of intermediality moves away from the theoretical polarisation of the live v the mediated and provides a lens through which to explore the patterns manifesting across media within the theatrical frame. The 'inter' of intermediality implies a between space, and the intermedial exists between previously assumed ideas of medium specificity. It therefore extends the historical dynamic of hybridisation and cross-disciplinary fertilisation outlined in the previous chapters. However, it can also imply a mutual reciprocity, with two or more media coming together in conversation. Intermediality can be both a creative and an analytic approach based on the perception that media boundaries are fluid and recognising the potential for interaction and exchange between the live and the mediated, without presupposing the authenticity or authority of either mode. Most importantly, intermediality relates to a form of audience reception enabled when a presentation is patterned across various media, creating a multidimensional performance text which comes together in the experience a spectator has of the work.

While the objective of reaching a synthesis of art forms within theatre practice has an ongoing history of development, a distinction can yet be made between early visions of integration in theatre, which focused on the collaboration of artistic disciplines, and contemporary understandings of intermediality involving the complex integration of media. As discussed in previous chapters, early steps towards the integration of art forms within theatre taken by practitioners such as Wagner, Yeats, Appia, and Marinetti paved the way for later visions of intermediality, establishing a precedent for the synthesis of artistic disciplines within the theatrical frame. However, these earlier practices were largely based on 'collaborative' forms in which discrete media operate in the same aesthetics space and were not necessarily in a complex relation or a state of interpenetration and were not therefore 'intermedial' in the contemporary sense of that term.

Intermedial theatre subsumes media, uniting both live and mediated elements within the frame of performance. The term is used here to denote the perception that all media and systems of communication can be non-hierarchically integrated within a theatrical performance. In intermedial performance, the realms of the live and the mediated develop reciprocity and are framed as complementary and symbiotic elements of the performance whole, creating what Meike Wagner has described as the 'intermedial *mise en scène*' (M. Wagner, 2006, p. 129). In such instances the audience can experience a merging of the material and the virtual, for these modes simultaneously have an impact upon the audience and develop meaning only in relation to the other.

As recognised by Fluxus artist Dick Higgins in his early discussion of intermediality, the 'intermedium' poses a challenge to the separation of artistic media and embraces continuity over categorisation. In his 1966 treatise *Intermedia*, Higgins asserts the Happening to be the most explicit development of the idea of the intermedium, using the term 'intermedia' to describe work that does not strictly adhere to the 'rules' of an individual artistic medium. Higgins argues forcefully against the separation of media in art practice, as the need to enforce rigid categories does not reflect a contemporary social milieu characterised in the 1960s at least by populism and classlessness (Higgins, 2001, p. 29). The 'intermedium', according to Higgins, does not conform to a predetermined structure or form; the concept itself is better understood 'by what it is not, rather than what it is' (Higgins, 2001, p. 29). He does not view Art that is produced within restrictive traditional boundaries as allowing a sense of dialogue, and he asserts, 'much of the best work being produced today seems to fall between media' (Higgins, 2001, p. 28). Theatre in its traditional form, argues Higgins, is unable to provide 'portability and flexibility', and thus the Happening was produced as the ultimate intermedium, an 'uncharted land that lies between collage, music, and the theatre' (Higgins, 2001, p. 32). In this vision, intermediality exists as the indefinite and ambiguous space between traditionally recognised artistic media.

Richard Higgins founded the 'Something Else?' press in 1963, which was dedicated to publishing 'artists' books' and statements. He also created an 'Intermedia Chart' that maps the various forms of performance and art that can collaborate in the intermedium. As artist and theorist Higgins has significantly broadened our understanding of the role of media in contemporary aesthetics.

While Higgins' understanding of 'intermedia' recognises that this form does not adhere to earlier media-specific conventions, his use of the term 'media' is still reliant on perceptions of medium specificity or 'purity'. Higgins' concept of the intermedium may be summarised as 'that which is not pure'; indeed, he states that the 'ready-made' or found object such as that presented by Duchamp may be considered an intermedium, since 'it was not intended to conform to the pure media' (Higgins, 2001, p. 30). Peter Boenisch explains that it was the original aim of discourse on intermediality such as Higgins' to counter notions of 'media-strategic purity' in the arts. He asserts that most of those involved in the discussion of 'intermediality' at the time of Higgins and the Fluxus movement adhered to the formula 'theatre + (other) media = intermedial theatre', and as such, implicitly propagated the notion of media specificity (Boenisch, 2003, p. 35). In examining a more contemporary work entitled *Circulation Module* (1998) by the Japanese group NEST, Boenisch emphasises its 'non-hierarchical, web-like interlinking of separate elements'

(Boenisch, 2003, p. 35). His explication of intermediality in relation to NEST's production emphasizes the patterns occurring across media and the principles that produce cohesion.

This approach is in synch with more recent uses of the term 'intermedial' to imply the fundamental integration of media and intermedial performance as transcending demarcations of artistic disciplines and media. In his essay 'The Moment of Realised Actuality', Andy Lavender examines excerpts of work by experimental multimedia companies Blast Theory and dumb type and asks the pertinent question, 'Can we still talk at all of two different media – theatre and video – coming together like partners on a dance floor in order to have their spin as separate bodies?' (Lavender, 2002, p. 187). Lavender suggests that in some contemporary performance the media 'intermingle like liquids which colour each other' (Lavender, 2002, p. 187). As colours blend to generate new colours, so too does intermedial performance blend media to generate a new whole.

In this formulation intermediality involves more than the mere collaboration of media, but requires the fundamental integration and blending of different aesthetic modes (colours). This explanation remains somewhat imprecise, for it can be interpreted as positioning intermediality as both a quality and a form, suggesting that it is a matter of degree. Jens Schroter clarifies the potential variations of this term and offers a typology that clearly identifies a number of points along an intermedial axis (Schroter in Chapple and Kattenbelt, 2006, pp. 15–16). First, *synthetic intermediality* refers to the combining of two or more art forms or media into a new art form or medium. The second, *formal and trans-medial intermediality*, assumes that aesthetic conventions manifest themselves in several media. The third is *transformational intermediality*, 'which refers to the representation of one medium within another medium' (Schroter in Chapple and Kattenbelt, 2006, pp. 15–16). And, finally, *ontological intermediality* is 'where a medium defines its own ontology through relating itself to another medium, and raises the issue that it is not possible to define the specificity of a medium in isolation except through comparison with another medium' (Schroter in Chapple and Kattenbelt, 2006, pp. 15–16). The first two forms outlined by Schroter operate at the level of 'collaborative' or 'intertextual' integration, and although 'synthetic intermediality' may achieve media integration, neither of these forms necessitates genuine complex intermixing of media. However, transformational and ontological intermediality offer more complex forms of media integration in which the nature of mediality is perceived as dynamic. Both these forms operate in the field of multimedia theatre, and the relevance of Schroter's typology to the analysis of multimedia performance is referred to within the analysis of case studies later in this chapter.

Intermediality and remediation in theatre

Schroter's description of transformational intermediality as potentially involving a process of combining two or more media into a new medium, or as involving the representation of one medium within another, is consistent with definitions of 'remediation' offered in new media theory. Just as digitalisation translates previously established media into a uniform format, *remediating* converges various means of communication and presentation within a single frame, a process (of convergence) for which theatre provides the historical model. Indeed, the case of multimedia theatre represents an interesting convergence of intermedial aesthetic practices as Brigit Wiens suggests: 'maybe this is the first time in its long history that theatre meets another hypermedium, which also synthesises a variety of signs' (Wiens, 2006, p. 24). As argued above, this meeting of theatre and digital multimedia can itself be recognised as a process of remediation.

Although the nature of remediation was discussed in different terms by earlier media theorists such as McLuhan and Kittler, the concept of 'digital remediation' is definitively articulated by Jay Bolter and Richard Grusin in their publication *Remediation: Understanding New Media*. Bolter and Grusin define remediation as 'the formal logic by which new media refashion prior media forms' (2000, p. 273) and 'the defining characteristic of the new digital media' (2000, p. 45). Remediation does not merely involve the content of one medium presented in another but involves a medium itself represented within another means of mediation. It can manifest in a range of forms that differ based on the original medium's degree of stability.

First, remediation in new media can manifest as the digitalisation of older media objects, where old media are represented but are not challenged and the digital reorganisation 'does not call into question the character of a text or the status of an image' (Bolter and Grusin, 2000, p. 46). Secondly, the digital medium can totally 'refashion' an older medium while still maintaining a certain degree of acknowledgment towards it. Here Bolter and Grusin explain that the work 'becomes a mosaic in which we are simultaneously aware of the individual pieces and their new, inappropriate setting' (2000, p. 47). And, finally, the new medium can completely absorb the old medium so that there are minimal discontinuities between the two. While this involves the total reorganisation of the older medium, it is not completely effaced; 'the new media remains dependent on the older one in acknowledged or unacknowledged ways' (2000, p. 47). Like intermediality, remediation is a matter of degree and processes of remediation in multimedia theatre create different degrees of intermediality. As remediation involves the incorporation of one medium within another, it is inherently more complex than mere 'collaborative' integration and evidences various levels of *transformational* and potentially *ontological* intermediality as defined by Schroter.

Bolter and Grusin assert that remediation is characterised by the two logics of 'immediacy' and 'hypermediacy', which relate to the spectator's level of immersion in the media content and their awareness of an object's 'mediatedness' (Bolter and Grusin, 2000, p. 273). Immediacy occurs when a medium is 'transparent', so that the medium disappears and the spectator becomes closer to the object of mediation. The aim of 'hypermediacy', on the other hand, is to remind the viewer of the medium and so the medium will draw attention to itself and to its distinct form of mediation. While these two logics appear to be in opposition to one another, hypermedia and transparent media are described by Bolter and Grusin as 'opposite manifestations of the same desire: the desire to get past the limits of representation and to achieve the real' (2000, p. 53). As such, both immediacy and hypermediacy may be manifest within the same work, complementing each other in a shared bid for authenticity.

Media can be identified as either hypermedia or transparent media; however, this distinction creates a number of paradoxes. Hypermedia blatantly remediate, and yet they also develop a degree of immediacy through their self-justification: 'With their constant reference to other media and their contents, hypermedia ultimately claim our attention as pure experience' (Bolter and Grusin, 2000, p. 54). And despite the denial of mediation by transparent media, they also remediate, for 'although transparent technologies try to improve on media by erasing them, they are still compelled to define themselves by the standards of the media they are trying to erase' (Bolter and Grusin, 2000, p. 54). As such, they claim that 'all current media function as remediators' (2000, p. 55).

In this sense multimedia theatre also functions as a 'remediator', achieving a degree of intermediality through the deployment of various modes of representation within the frame of the performance. Like new media in Bolter and Grusin's formulations, theatrical performance can be seen as simultaneously immediate (sharing spatial and temporal coordinates) and hypermediate (referencing other media). Kattenbelt argues this position, pointing out that theatre is both a *hypermedium*, providing other media a stage upon which they can perform as theatrical signs, yet also a transparent medium as it 'foregrounds the *corporeality* of the performer and the *materiality* of the live performance as an actual event, taking place in the absolute presence of the here and now' (Chapple and Kattenbelt, 2006, p. 39).

Andy Lavender also recognises the dynamics of hypermediacy and immediacy in the simultaneous presentation of the screen and the stage. While the medium of film, in contrast, often functions transparently,

filmic images presented within the theatre are 'staged' as part of the theatrical event so that the 'screen is folded into the live event and so into
the phenomenal realm of theatre' (Lavender, 2006, p. 65). Within the
space of theatre, all media, including the transparent medium of film and
the transparent medium of the live human performer, develop a level of
hypermediacy in their relation to one another as elements of the total
performance. Through their staging the media are not merely simultaneous but integrated; 'The images are not self-sufficient. What might
once have been separate media are not self-contained. They can only be
decoded in relation to the *mise en scène* – a *mise en scène* that is flam-
boyantly hypermedial' (Lavender, 2006, p. 65). In intermedial theatre,
both live and mediated elements are remediated to form the hypermedial
performance event.

However, theatre is still in some traditions defiantly 'old media' and
some theorists, both defenders of the traditions and proponents of new
media forms, have argued that levels of audience engagement inherently
differ between live and the projected action; that in the same aesthetic
space, the live and the mediated can be perceived as being in competition
for the audience's attention. In 1966 actor Roberts Blossom developed a
series of experiments he called 'Filmstage' that combined projected film
and live performance. For Blossom and his contemporaries, the human
presence paled alongside the opulence and pervasiveness of the projected
media. The performers onstage in the presence of the enveloping film
media became 'but fifty-watt bulbs waiting to be screwed into their source
and to shine with the light that is perpetual (behind them, around them)
but which they can only reflect at fifty watts' (Blossom, 1966, p. 70).

> Roberts Blossom views the use of film on stage as combining the
> unconscious (recorded) with the conscious (present). In his reflec-
> tions on his *Filmstage* experiments he illustrates the limitless value
> and potential of film in theatre, likening it to 'the most highly
> developed imaginations' and proposing, like Bergson before him,
> that the onstage screen, 'if it has taken away tangibility, has
> replaced it with extraordinary powers, *imitating consciousness*'
> (Blossom, 1966, p. 70).

While Blossom's view may be relatively unsophisticated in that it regards
only the simple re-presentation of filmic media within theatre, the relationship between performer and projected media he describes is not dissimilar to the position outlined by Auslander in his brief examination of

multimedia performance in the case of *Poles* by 'Pps Danse' of Montreal. In describing the effect of this piece in which holography is used along-side the dancers, he asks whether there is in fact a juxtaposition or a fusion of the live and the virtual. In answer to his own question he suggests the answer is that 'Dance + Virtual = Virtual' or, in other words, that we now 'experience such work as a fusion, not a con-fusion, of realms, a fusion that we see as taking the place of its raw materials' (Auslander, 1999, p. 38). For Auslander, as we shall see in the next chapter, it is at the location of this 'fusion' of the live and the digital that we see the 'implosion' of the realms of information and materiality. The location of this fusion, however, does not lie within the performance frame but, as for Blossom, at the junction of performance and audience reception.

The set of relations between live and mediated elements that both Auslander and Blossom are describing here is not intermedial, for in both cases the medium they describe is not contingent on the live performer but exists independently. For the medium to be viewed as dominating the live performer, it must be perceived as transparent and self-sufficient rather than as a co-dependent element of the hypermedial whole. In intermedial performance, no single element can dominate the production for they are all contingent, developing meaning only in relation to other elements. Neither can the 'live' and the 'mediated' be viewed as discrete. However, both Auslander's and Blossom's comments indicate that the limits of the intermedial paradigm in performance are located in spectatorial experience since they point to a differential experience of live and/or mediated representations.

Liveness case study: Intermediality and/*as* remediation?

The following case study explores the various levels of mediation in the intermedial *mise en scène*, exploring the manifestations of materiality and information, the live and the mediated, and the process of 'remediation' that occurs in 'live' projection. The production, by Sydney-based company Version 1.0, effectively establishes intermediality in the *mise en scène* as a tool to underline thematic concerns, creating a performance environment within which the live and the mediated are integrated. Yet this work also problematises the boundary between the live and the mediated and addresses the political utility of the media simulacrum.

Wages of Spin was produced and performed by Version 1.0 at the Performance Space in Sydney in 2005. Like all of this company's work, the piece does not present a linear narrative but, in their words, 'kaleidoscopic portraits of the contemporary world we inhabit' (www.versiononepointzero.org). The work questions Australia's involvement in the Iraq war and asks whether or not, as seems probable, the deployment was based on a lie. The performance engages the manipulation of the mass media by government officials and the power of media 'spin' that clouded the facts during Australia's entry into the war. The performance text blends the actual words of government officials with often contradictory video imagery and statistical information as well as surreal movement sequences and fictional text. It critiques the values of a society more concerned with celebrity infidelity (e.g., tennis ace Mark 'the Scud' Philippoussis' alleged infidelity and its effects on his then popstar girlfriend Delta Goodrem) than with the threat to democratic values posed by Australia's participation in the 'coalition of the willing' and the invasion of Iraq on spurious grounds. The performers parody figures such as Australia's then Prime Minister John Howard and then US President George W. Bush, continually moving in and out of various personae that never settle on a particular identity for the performer.

The corporeality of the performers is emphasised from the outset of the work. To get to their seats the spectators enter and traverse a space resembling a film set in which an act reminiscent of the torture scenes from Abu Ghraib is occurring. A blindfolded performer dressed in standard military camouflages is slowly stepping across a long plank of wood containing fierce upturned nails. While the action does not actually represent the Abu Ghraib atrocities, metonymic associations are unavoidable due to the prominence of the blindfold and the military and punitive context. The figure is guided by the instructions of another performer, who offers directions of 'left, right, forward and down'. As the audience take their seats, they realise that towards the end of the path the nails are too close together to fit a foot between. The inevitability of agony, of the body's destruction, is painfully visceral and the audience is confronted with the vulnerability of the material body before them. This sets up a position for the audience from which to read the entire performance.

The intermedial landscape utilises image, sound, movement and dialogue to create rhythms and resonances that rebound within the performance space and have an impact affectively upon the audience. For example, there is a recurring motif of running; at various stages throughout the performance a number of the performers run on the spot, invoking metonymic implications of exhaustion and endurance and literally embodying physical deterioration. The pace and rhythm of the running contrasts with the empty sonority of the political language and offers an affective accompaniment to the relentless casualty statistics that are projected onto the back screen.

This opening act is recorded and the 'live' video transmission projected onto an outsized screen behind the performance area. A level of remediation in the work is thus established from the outset of the performance, as the content of one medium (live performance) has already become the

Figure 14 *The Wages of Spin* 2005, Version 1.0. Photo: Heidrun Lohr

content of another and the same information is simultaneously manifest in two material forms. The demarcation of the live and mediated is blurred by techniques such as having the camera intensify the threat to the body by using the zoom function to highlight and enhance the proximity between nail and foot. In other words, the image on the screen further validates the immediacy and authenticity of the act. Its size, easy visibility and magnifying capacities fulfil our desire for proximity, affirming the event's 'liveness' even as it translates the material into information.

Causey addresses the phenomenon of privileging video subjects by using the example of rock concerts. As we know, rock concerts are 'routinely supplemented by video projections which become the evidence of a live act'. In stadium concerts the 'Jumbotron' video screens are the manner in which audience members access the liveness of the event. He concludes that 'the split video image sourcing from a live feed ... reestablishes the status of the real', and even that 'the video image is more real than the live actor' (Causey, 1999, p. 387).

In *Wages of Spin*, this dialectical relation between materiality (the lived experience of human bodies) and informatics (assemblages of data and the use of data) is constantly raised through the contrasting of the material body and the mediated image, and through the exposure of the processes of production that construct information. While this work creates an intermedial performance space, it actually illustrates the cultural perspective in which information has authority over materiality. The use of video media in this work both affirms this relative 'cultural presence', as Auslander puts it, and is critical of this relation and so stresses the discrepancies and demarcations between the realms of informational pattern and material presence: information is depicted as shaping social reality, but it is also presented as producing a loss of authentic material instantiation.

Wages of Spin illustrates the passivity of the audience's role in the reception of media imagery and reflects on the nature of mass-media imagery that can no longer be considered as transmitting the real but as manipulating the real, editing it, and fabricating a new, authored reality. An alternative version of events is created that resembles the real but fictionally embellishes it, and it is this simulacrum that becomes the authoritative version, disappearing the real, for it is, of course, permanently documented and widely distributed. This work exposes the simulacra as spurious by revealing the usually unseen mechanics of media production. The audience is witness not only to the camera's filming but also to the 'behind the scenes' of the enormous editing desk, which is presented at such an angle so as to allow the audience to see the feeds of all cameras at all times. This focus on the processes of manufacture inhibits the possibility of becoming mesmerised by the illusory capabilities of the videography and forces the audience to maintain a critical eye on the boundary blurring and translation of materiality taking place in the media production. The revelation of the mechanics of production establishes the work as functioning 'hypermedially'; the opacity of the medium is made prominent as the process of remediation itself is placed at issue, and the transformation of the live into the mediated is revealed as completely recontextualising and reconstructing the intended referent. The presence of the material referent does not extend into the informational context, but is replaced by manufactured pattern.

In *Wages of Spin*, this mistranslation is particularly evident in a critical scene where the audience are themselves remediated into the performance frame and are confronted with their mediated other. Early in the work, the audience is videoed madly applauding at the instruction of the performers, and the live feed from a boom camera sweeping back and forth across the crowd is displayed on the screen opposite. Later in the work the audience is confronted with their cheering-mediated double framing media footage of Prime Minister Howard's election win in a year in which his party's campaign slogan was 'We decide who comes to this country and the circumstances in which they come' (an overtly racist message which won the Australian Federal election for the Liberal party in 2001). We the audience feel cheated, in some way betrayed, furious at this misrepresentation of our actions and intentions but, like the election, it is too late and we let it happen. We are also faced with the disorienting experience of identifying the self 'outside the self' and recognising the translatability of our material selves into malleable digital pattern.

In *Wages of Spin*, the audience's experience of witnessing themselves as other certainly evokes a sense of the uncanny. It also generates an unease, a wary mistrust, because the spectators are forced to acknowledge that once their Double has been permanently captured in the realm of information, it is no longer their own and they have no control over its apparent behaviour. The focus is on the process of the production of information and the onscreen simulations can no longer be passively consumed without questioning the effect of this process. This inclusion of the managed projection of the audience within the onstage action further troubles the boundary between the onstage realm of the performers and the world of the audience. The only potentially fictitious 'other' world is the hyperreal content of the media, which becomes the key to understanding the work.

In attempting to expose the dominance of the mass media's effect upon our lives and its prominence in creating our sense of reality, Version 1.0 problematises the distancing effect of this medium in relation to accessing war and violence. As in the American and Australian telecasting of the war, the casualties in *Wages* are represented not as corpses but as statistical information relayed via the detachment of the screen. The dominance of television in shaping our reality is also emphasised as the performers repeatedly present caricatures of media personalities, with the audience witness to both the live performer and the mediated representation. In one instance the performers are involved in a 'television interview' and the actual sequence of events is contrasted with the televised representation of these events. The audience is shown how television dramatically manipulates the nuances and context of the original action through the use of techniques such as jump-cutting between interviewees and the editing out of text. Here we not only see how the projected medium remediates the live, but we also experience the remediation of television by theatre. This process of remediation creates both transformational and ontological intermediality; through the representation of the medium of television within the medium of theatre, theatre defines its own ontology as a hypermedium.

Liveness case study 2: re-enactment + remediation = ?

Taking a very different type of performance as the next example, we now turn to the performance art of the celebrated Marina Abramovic. Performance art is generally regarded as a forceful engagement with presence, a form in which the artist's body directly encounters the spectator to raise issues around aesthetic experience and the lived experience of the body. As part of *Seven Easy Pieces*, performed at the Solomon R. Guggenheim Museum in New York in 2005, Abramovic re-enacted five major works of performance art by Joseph Beuys, Bruce Naumann, and others.

Marina Abramovic, born 1946 in Belgrade, has been working as a performance artist for more than three decades. Her early works, *Rhythm 10, Rhythm 5, Rhythm 2, and Rhythm 0,* performed in 1973–4, explore the limits of the body, the capacity of the mind, and tests the relationship between the performer and the audience. In 1976, Abramovic began a long-term collaboration with German performance artist Ulay, with whom she created performances that explored a hermaphroditic state of being, extreme states of consciousness, and the relationship of the body to architectural space.

This case study examines the status of the 'live' in the process of re-enactment and explores Abramovic's re-enactments as both a means of documentation and a form of 'remediation'. Performed from 9 to 15 November, Abramovic's production began with her performance of Bruce Nauman's *Body Pressure* (1974)[1] and was followed by, in order: Vito Acconci's *Seedbed* (1972);[2] VALIE EXPORT's *Action Pants: Genital Panic* (1969);[3] Gina Pane's *The Conditioning,* first action of *Self-Portrait(s)* (1973);[4] Joseph Beuys' *How to Explain Pictures to a Dead Hare* (1965);[5] Marina Abramovic *Lips of Thomas* (1975).[6] On the final evening of 15 November, Abramovic performed a new work, *Entering the Other Side* (2005). She had planned to re-perform Chris Burden's *Shoot* but as he didn't respond to any attempts to communicate with him, she decided to create a new work instead.

The selection of original works for performance in *Seven Easy Pieces* were made by Abramovic herself based on, as she says in an interview at the time,

'the fact that the pieces had really struck me deeply, but had done so only through photographs and the little documentation that one could find at that time. This has always interested me, and I have wanted to ask how would I deal with them now, in real time?' (Abramovic in Thompson and Weslien, 2006)

This approach raises the question posed by Auslander as to 'whether performance recreations based on documentation actually recreate the underlying performances or perform the documentation?' as in Guzman and Ortega's *Remake* (Auslander, 2006, p. 2).

At a two-day symposium titled '(Re)presenting Performance' to debate these issues, which preceded the performances at the Guggenheim, Peggy Phelan, according to one observer, 'shunned the idea of "re-performing" and instead offered the idea of "performance *covers*," that, like the covers of popular songs, retain the trace of the original while offering a new interpretation through a different voice' (Cesare, 2005). As the reviewer notes, this idea of 'a relationship to music' obtains some of its pertinence through Abramovic's title for the series, with its referencing of Bartok's *Ten Easy Pieces* (1908) for piano, and raises the intriguing possibility of 'scoring' performance art.

Phelan's idea of 'performance covers' is first of all an attempt to negotiate the difficulty this series of re-enactments poses for her seminal theory of performance as something that 'becomes itself through disappearance' (Phelan, 1993, p. 146). As we have seen, for Phelan the determining condition of the existence of performance (its ontology) is that it occurs once in time. Photographs, videos or other documentations of the event are therefore necessarily second-order material. So performance, in this way of seeing it, 'cannot be saved, recorded, documented, or otherwise participate in the circulation of representations of representations: once it does so, it becomes something other than performance' (Phelan, 1993, p. 146).

Re-enactment challenges this logic. As repetition and re-presentation, it presupposes that something in the performance is coded as reproducible, that in its 'strips' (Schechner) of symbolic behaviour, performance anticipates not only its dis-appearance but its re-appearance, either in re-enactment or documentation in video, photography etc., or beyond that, in the cover version. In popular music studies the function of the cover version swings between two polarities. As Auslander argues (in a different context), it has a modernist tendency as the means by which an artist authenticates themselves 'by asserting a relationship, through creative repetition, to an authentic source' (Auslander, 2003, p. 169), or the opposite, in which it operates as postmodern pastiche. It depends on the artist, the song and the historical context.

Similarly, the cover version of performance art does not necessarily diminish the authenticity of the original artwork (whether understood as photograph or action). No-one would argue that either Abramovic or her antecedent artists in *Seven Easy Pieces* were inauthentic artists no matter how theatrical the *mise en scène* at the Guggenhiem. The point is that in using the language of popular music to describe this event, scholars like Phelan are marking the migration of high art performance works into the realm of popular cultural media. The very use of the term in this context suggests that performance art has turned a corner away from an insistence on auratic presence and inimitable authenticity and has taken a postmodern direction similar to the road taken by popular music in explicitly referring to its own history as material.

This would seem to be Abramovic's position as well, that neither re-enactment nor documentation challenges the essence of performance art. When asked about her response to Phelan's position on the essential liveness of performance she replied,

> First, I always wonder how can the theoreticians say this when they never use video to show the performance work? They just read the texts and show the slides or whatever. I found this disgusting. I hate Powerpoint. I mean, how can you ever show the liveness of performance in slides? ... I don't understand, but every single person here in America, I never see them showing video. I only see them showing slides, of something that is not possible to be seen by slides. And then commenting on how representation doesn't work – of course their representation doesn't work. But I can tell you, there are so many pieces for which it works. (Abramovic in Weslienn, 2006, p. 50)

While many performance scholars seem to prefer the grungy, blurred b&w images of 70s body art, in *Seven Easy Pieces* Abramovic made extensive use of video both as an elaborate record of the entire event and as a kind of dialogue with the live presentation. Real-time documentation of the previous evening's performances were replayed during each evening's re-enactments on flat-screen monitors behind the stage. The reviewer of the event for Artforum, Johanna Burton, described the filming of *Seven Easy Pieces* as 'itself a performance, with Babette Mangolte deftly choreographing a fleet of cameras and crew. Indeed, Abramovic effusively claims that her purpose in hiring the famous documentary filmmaker to record every minute of the total 49 hours was to avoid 'repeating the mistakes of the 70s in failing to attend to such details' (in Burton, 2006).

This comprehensive approach to the documentation of re-enactment seems an almost deliberate challenge to Phelan's position. It also represents a form of 'remediation' since new art works are made from restaging old ones in different media. As discussed earlier, Bolter and Grusin define this idea as 'the representation of one medium in another' and 'the formal logic by which new media refashion prior media forms' (Bolter and Grusin, 2000, p. 273). As we have seen, Auslander uses it extensively in his argument that mediated events are often remediated versions of live ones and that this puts into play a feedback loop which leaves both categories looking shaky.

To restate the position we are taking here, Auslander's argument is that the opposition of live to mediated performance is a 'competitive opposition at the level of cultural economy' not at the level of intrinsic or ontological differences. Auslander's view is that 'Live' & 'Mediated' are in fact mutually dependent for reasons that are both historical and experiential: historical (the theatricality of TV, TV as a 'live medium', the ubiquitous use of media in live performance such as dance); experiential (the discourse of 'going live', intimacy and immediacy, interactivity, cinematic vocab of spectators, laughing on cue, stadium concerts and sports events). The argument is that TV remediates theatre and radio and that media always do this. As an aside look at the way aspects of new cultural media in web 2.0 such as the social networking sites Facebook, Youtube and Myspace are becoming intensely performative virtual spaces remediating both TV and cinema.

If we understand a performance work, however vital or improvisatory, as a work within a representational frame, then it can be defined in terms of media, as an event that is mediated by the artistic or institutional context in which it occurs. Therefore it follows that the documentation of such a work in a photographic or video format, and which is constituted as a work in itself, can be seen as a remediation of that work. In this sense the performance can be said to have undergone a migration into a new medium. The notion of the remediated performance work, the endless interconnection of event and document, suggests, more eloquently than the cover version, the end of the concept of live art in Phelan's terms as an ontologically pristine aesthetic entity. This is not to say that live art loses its distinctiveness any more than video art loses its specificity by interrogating liveness – just ask Nam June Paik for instance.

Abramovic's approach in her re-enactments, including her approach to recording the work, is consistent with the argument that '(e)ach act of mediation depends on other acts of mediation. Media are continually commenting on, reproducing, and replacing each other, and this process is integral to media. Media need each other in order to function as media at all.' Yet for her, the issues are perhaps less philosophical and more pragmatic:

We have to be practical. I think that there is no way that millions of people can see one piece. What if somebody in New Zealand wants to see it? Then he should be able to have very good documentation. Documentation is extremely important. So many artists have the attitude that it is not. I have every single piece documented and I honor every video, because I have a very early, very strong feeling for the historical document. That's important. (Abramovic in Thompson and Weslien, 2006, p. 50)

In re-enactment and remediation, Abramovic's newly postmodern performance art locates itself (rather than loses itself) in an ironic play of differences between action and registration, between gesture and trace, between performance and documentation. Ultimately this game may be undecideable, (neither documentation nor performance art) in which case we could say a certain postmodern indeterminacy has arrived to destabilise the ontological certainties of the reception of performance art as a guarantor of presence. As Auslander puts it: 'It may well be that our sense of the presence, power, and authenticity of these pieces derives not from treating the document as an indexical access point to a past event but from perceiving the document itself *as a performance* that directly reflects an artist's aesthetic project or sensibility and for which we are the present audience' (Auslander, 2006, p. 9). The performativity of the document seems counter intuitive but in the broader context of reenactment it begins to make more sense since what is occurring in this kind of transaction is the remediation of the event as document in which the re-enactment itself becomes another document of history, a way of providing a kind of live action documentation to animate the archival record. In this way Abramovic is more than documenting a personal history of live art, she provides a living history of live art. She thereby 'performs a document' in an additional sense to Auslander's idea of the reenactment of historical documents of performance art.

Conclusion

In the discourses of theatre studies, the mediated and the live have been considered fundamentally opposed. Just as notions of authenticity and representation or the original and the copy have a history of cultural polarisation, the live and the mediated too have been positioned by certain kinds of performance theory as discrete opposites. Yet as Auslander has argued, the live only becomes meaningful in the context of media without which there would be no significance to the live. On the other hand the efficacy of multimedia theatre in performance is often based on the viewers' perceptions of the integration and interdependence of the live and the mediated. So when theorising multimedia works it is obviously important to utilise an interpretive framework that does not polarise these aspects of the composition. The notion of intermediality and the associated theory of remediation provides one such framework.

To restate the argument, a high degree of remediation or 'transformational intermediality' is achieved where previously existing media are completely absorbed into a new medium with minimal discontinuities between the two. In such cases, the live and the mediated cannot be perceived as mutually exclusive. For the live and the mediated to 'intermingle like liquids', as suggested by Lavender, there must be a perceived compatibility between the human body and technological media, between the real and the virtual.

Further reading

On the topic of intermediality the most relevant text to follow up would be *Mapping Intermediality in Performance*, Sarah Bay-Cheng, Chiel Kattenbelt, Andy Lavender, and Robin Nelson (eds) (2010). There is some interesting recent research on liveness occurring in media studies especially Nick Couldry's *Media Rituals: A Critical Approach* (2003) in which he develops the thesis that liveness is a construction of media and is emphasised in the way social media brings people together. In terms of the case studies in this chapter, *Australasian Drama Studies* issue number 48 (April 2006) has some articles on Version 1.0 while the Abramovic case study has been extensively analysed, for instance, by Amelia Jones in her article 'The Artist is Present: Artistic Re-enactments and the Impossibility of Presence' in *TDR* Volume 55, Number 1, Spring 2011.

Chapter 5

Framing Media Theory for Performance Studies

Is Auslander's insistence on the cultural frame of media and, by implication, our entire approach here, a form of determinism? Can we still speak of such a thing without oxymoron in the 'information age'? If we accept the accuracy of the popular label for the epoch in which we live, then perhaps we are all technological determinists by default. The 'information age' is, after all, characterised by the commodification of information enabled by the ubiquity of computer technologies and the ready access of users of this information to global networks of exchange.[1] The suggestion that our historical and social 'age' can be characterised by the nature of a particular technology is clearly a form of technological determinism, but this particular variety of determinism has been a highly contentious intellectual position for most of the last century. The idea may be understood as follows: 'that the mere presence of technology leads to familiar and standard applications of that technology, which in turn bring about social change' (Warschauer, 2003, p. 44). So the technology may change but the notion of a determining impact is a constant. In the twenty-first century, certain technological determinations involving the transmission of information and sharing of experience are widely accepted: 'from the production of daily newspapers to the electronic transmission of the latest racing results, the technical forms of mass communication are altering the experiential content of everyday life' (Stevenson, 2002, p. 120).

A more nuanced idea than technological determinism is the concept of 'social informatics', which as Mark Warschauer explains 'argues that technology must be considered within a specific context that includes hardware, software, support resources, infrastructure, as well as people in various roles and relationships with one another and with other elements of the system' (Warschauer, 2003, p. 45). Within this context the technology and the social system refigure and have an impact upon each other 'like a biological community and its environment' (Warschauer, 2003, p. 45). It is important to recognise that there is a 'digital divide' between the technological saturation of predominantly Western conurbations and many under-resourced rural and, of course, Third World communities, and to acknowledge that the subsequent discussion is confined to the context of highly technological Western society. Within this context it is generally accepted that the ubiquity of information media and technologies, and the technical modes of communication and interaction they employ, have an impact on the social sphere and affect the way we perceive and interact with the world. In this sense we have attempted to base our approach to the question of multimedia on a social informatics model rather than a technologically determinist one.

Both in media theory and in performance studies there are those who oppose the perceived domination of media technologies and those who embrace them. Michael Heim addresses these positions, which he labels 'naive realism' and 'network idealism' as a dialectic (Heim, 2000). On the one hand is the 'cyberspace backlash' that opposes the movement of life and culture into digital and virtual spatialities, a position proffered by theorists such as Kirkpatrick Sale, Clifford Stoll, Bill McKibben and Steven Talbott. On the other hand are the idealists who 'celebrate an electronic collective (Heim, 2000, p. 37), the 'digerati' who welcome the 'digital revolution', an outlook which Heim suggests traces back to philosophers such as Leibniz, Descartes and the Cartesian revolution that prioritised mathematical physics and the reduction of thought to rational logic (Heim, 2000, p. 34).

It should be mentioned that the effect of technology upon the senses had been discussed by **Henri Bergson** as early as the turn of the last century. Bergson suggested that modern technology was negating the affective dimensions in human experience. He argued that science was reducing human experience to the function of calculation and called for the re-establishment of a focus on the affective and sensorimotor experiences of the body. His work has greatly influenced later theories of affect and subjectivity in cinema and new media.

Whether resisted or celebrated, the idea that media fashion our perspectives and alter our subjective engagements with the world is certainly not a new notion, nor is it a perspective unique to digital media theory. Media theory throughout the twentieth century has focused on the impact of new technologies on culture and subjectivity, and how in turn this has fashioned developments in technology and new media. Contemporary theory regarding the effect of mass media upon society and culture may be considered the legacy of Walter Benjamin, who addressed the reciprocal impact of media and culture in his writings of the 1930s. He examined the effect of technical media such as photography and film upon the mythical status of art in society, emphasising their technical processes over their aesthetic values, and recognising the role of media in translating our historical circumstances into bodily experience.

> In his *Illuminations*, Walter Benjamin describes how photography, the reproducibility of the image, has resulted in the loss of the 'aura' of fine art. He describes the 'aura' of art as something that is inaccessible, a 'distance, however close it may be' and argues that mechanical technologies have forced the artwork to lose its 'cult value'. Jay Bolter, in his 2006 article *New Media and the Permanent Crisis of Aura*, applies Benjamin's concept of aura to digital media and mixed-reality technologies, which he suggests allow the invocation of aura in new ways.

Following in the footsteps of Benjamin, the Canadian pioneer of media theory, Marshall McLuhan, has been seminal in enabling an understanding of how the dissemination of cultural forms has an impact upon perception. McLuhan asserted that the most significant characteristic of media does not exist within the issues relating to cultural content but in the technical processes of mediated communication: 'the medium is the message.' A groundbreaking facet of McLuhan's work was his analysis of what he termed the 'Gutenberg Galaxy'. Johannes Gutenberg's printing press, invented in the late fifteenth century, allowed ideas and perspectives to be circulated across space in a short period of time and shaped a new cultural paradigm. McLuhan illustrates the cognitive features that underpin this paradigm and suggests that print culture produced a standardised way of thinking that replaced the unpredictable play of oral culture. He argues that 'print is the technology of individualism' for it is a privatised mode of reception (McLuhan, 1962, p. 158). Alternatively, in a modern electronic culture, reception is passive and unavoidable as cultural forms 'pour upon us instantly and continuously' (McLuhan and Fiore, 1967, p. 16). As print culture was displaced by electronic forms, modernity became characterised as the 'unceasing relocation of information in time and space' (Stevenson, 2002, p. 125).

Taking the lead from McLuhan, Jean Baudrillard emphasises the role of technical media of communication in establishing a postmodern and 'postindustrial' media culture. Baudrillard provides the most provocative and sophisticated critical assessment of the role of mass communication in consumer culture. His later writings have been highly influential and his writings on 'simulation' and 'hyperreality' have laid the foundations for the building of contemporary theories of 'virtuality' and social processes of 'virtualisation'. *Simulation* involves the mistaking of the media image for the real, a process by which the signs of the real replace the real. For instance, automobile simulators for the US military make use of virtual worlds in real vehicle chassis to reproduce exactly the bodily experience of using a military vehicle without actually negotiating battle situations. Flight simulation training devices are used for similar purposes in civilian aviation training situations. In musical composition a sample performs the same function as a simulation, in effectively substituting for the real sound.

A simulation is 'different from a fiction or a lie in that it not only presents an absence as a presence, the imaginary as the real, it also undermines any contrast to the real, absorbing the real within itself' (Poster in Baudrillard, 1998, pp. 5–6). Fiction or mere pretending leaves the principle of reality intact. Baudrillard argues that here 'the difference is always clear, it is simply masked, whereas simulation threatens the difference between the '"true" and the "false", the "real" and the "imaginary"' (Baudrillard, 1994, p. 3). For Auslander, the theory of simulation is the one which 'best describes the current relationship between live and mediated' forms of performance (Auslander 1999, p. 37). There is no one true version and the copy is as authentic and legitimate as the originating act.

Hyperreality is thus produced when reality is simulated and the representation of the real becomes reality. The effect of simulation in hyperreality, as in virtual reality, subverts conventional concepts of time and space. The subversion of time and space into non-linear and unstable frameworks is a feature of postmodernist thought and is explored in postmodern art and performance, but it is not entirely dependent upon digital cultural forms. Baudrillard's particular genius was to predict cultural forms arising from technical developments before they became available to the consumer market.

Baudrillard explores the disassociation of the image from reality. In *The Gulf War Did Not Take Place* he argues that the first Gulf War was accessed only via media; it existed only in its imagery. It was a war of intelligence images and news images which replaced the reality and consequences of the violence. This perspective is explored in Blast Theory's 1999 work *Desert Rain*, discussed here in Chapter 7.

There is a specific restructuring of time and space pertinent to virtual reality that is directly related to the form of computer technologies and digital media. Paul Virilio addresses the contraction of time as a result of new technologies and how 'With the interfacing of computer terminals and video monitors, distinctions of *here* and *there* no longer mean anything' (Virillio in Leach, 1997, p. 360). For Virilio, technology is focused on speed and efficiency. The immediacy that new technologies of communication enable means that in hyperreality, cyberspace, and virtual realities, we 'arrive' at information and images on cue. The interval of time is eliminated as we see 'the beginnings of a *"generalized arrival"* whereby everything arrives without having to leave' (Virillio, 2004, p. 60). As we experience the hypertextual interfaces we arrive at a new destination with each click of the mouse without having to wait the duration of the journey. Virilio's theories of speed and the 'death of distance' are useful as an introduction to the analysis of human–media interaction, and his writings on mediated spatialities may also be useful as a basis upon which to build a discussion of the disappearing gap between the audience and the artwork in multimedia performance.

However, Virilio offers a sceptical perspective, emphasising the less progressive aspects of the developments in new communication technologies, and his writing has been considered as 'a warning as to where technological change might lead rather than as offering a balanced account of the effects of technological development' (Stevenson, 2002, p. 206). He argues that the notion of a 'culture of interactivity' is mostly false and that 'euphoric technological determinism' is creating cultural impoverishment and leading to the eradication of our phenomenological faculties. His is a one-sided view of technology, bordering on 'technophobia'. He asserts: 'The development of what Virilio calls a political economy of speed is such that at times he sounds as though the only way of resisting the totalitarian ambitions of technology is through technological abstinence' (Stevenson, 2002, p. 207).

While the arguments in this book build upon the key ideas of a number of theorists, we would not wish simply to endorse one view over another but to lay out the existing debates for readers to navigate in their own way. We would not simply deny the influence of a/v and computer technologies on the development of contemporary performance culture, nor would we advocate the total abandonment of real 3-D space for virtual environments. There is no extended discussion of gaming or second-life environments in this book because they sit on the far side of the virtual frontier. Perhaps our basic position relates to Heim's 'virtual realism', which he describes as a 'delicate balancing act [that] sways between the idealism of unstoppable Progress and the Luddite resistance to virtual life' (Heim, 2000, p. 41).

Heim suggests that we must be realistic towards virtuality, both suspicious of the idealism and commercialisation in which it is embedded and at the same time affirming that which is real and functional as our culture begins to inhabit cyberspace:

> it is important to find a balance that swings neither to the idealistic blue sky where primary reality disappears, nor to the mundane indifference that sees just another tool, something that can be picked up or put down at will. The balancing act requires a view of life as a mixed bag, as a series of trade-offs that we must discern and then evaluate. Balancing means walking a pragmatic path of involvement and critical perception. (Heim, 2000, p. 42)

In this investigation, it is our intention to be good virtual realists and to maintain the balance upon the tightrope between idealism and scepticism, neither rejecting nor advocating the influence of information technologies on community, culture, and the live event.

Society and virtualisation

At the 1995 Ars Electronica Festival titled 'Welcome to the Wired World', Pierre Levy offered the following declaration:

> Listen to what could be the sensible message of this art, of this philosophy, of this politics: human beings, people from here and everywhere, you who are caught in this great movement of deterritorialisation ... you who are caught in this immense event of the world that never stops returning to itself and recreating itself again, you who are launched toward the virtual, you who are taken in this enormous jump that our species accomplished nowadays upstream in the flow of being, yes, in the very heart of this strange whirlwind, you are at home. Welcome to the human race's new house. Welcome to virtualisation. (Levy, 1995)

For well over a decade we technology-saturated Westerners have inhabited this 'house of virtualisation', holding our heads above 'the sea of information' in which we become enveloped either as vulnerable and susceptible consumers or as critical beings experiencing new forms and qualities of knowledge. We now live not only in a 'wired world' but in a digital world in which the translatability of information has altered our social, economic, and creative practices.

'Virtualisation' is emerging as the defining cultural paradigm of our historical present, manifest in the breakdown of the duality of actuality and virtuality in everyday life. Virtualisation has been built on the foundations of postmodernism and may be characterised by the condition in which the virtual is experienced as the real, and the real as virtual. We now exist in the 'the Desert of the Real', as articulated by Slavoj Zizek (echoing Baudrillard), who explains: 'Virtual Reality is experienced as reality without being one. However, what awaits us at the end of this process of virtualisation is that we begin to experience "real reality" itself as a virtual entity' (Zizek, 2001, p. 11). It is as if cyberspace has leaked out of the computer-bound realm and contaminated, or perhaps diluted, our immediate reality. Or perhaps users, upon exiting computer-generated environments, never really leave 'virtual reality'.

The shift into a state of 'virtualisation', though gradual, may be viewed as a cultural shift embedded in our cognitive and social processes. As performance is an arena for the manifestation and exploration of such conditions, both trends and experiments in performance may be placed within the context of this cultural shift. To understand their significance they should be viewed in relation to the principles of this informing cultural paradigm, and as potentially affirming or challenging its values. As such, the discussion in the following chapters aims to identify the nature of these 'trends and experiments' and also to address how they are manifesting, reflecting, and perhaps resisting the cultural paradigm of virtuality.

Theory and its double: On-screen performances

Theorists of intermediality such as Peter Boenisch explain that, 'for the ones who perceive, whether they are reading books, attending theatre, or playing computer games, the perceptions created by media, that is, the effect on their *sensorium* of all the signs and symbolisations staged and performed – are always ultimately *real* ... they are always "authentic" in the observer's experience' (Boenisch, 2006, p. 113). The degree to which the live and the mediated are experienced as equally authentic and real can be most clearly articulated in the instance by which an object or a subject appears both as a live and a mediated presence at the same time. For instance, when the actor is mediated by a live feed using onstage cameras and projectors, a situation occurs by which the audience is confronted with both the original actor and their live image within the same space.

Force Majeure is the company founded by Australian choreographer and dancer Kate Champion. Her work *Same, same But Different* (2002) blends the spoken, physical, musical and cinematic

texts to present an aesthetically dynamic exploration of the vicissi-
tudes of romantic relationships. It is an absorbing work, the world
of the performance is richly elaborated (the immediate), and yet
the audience members are also made aware of this immersion as
if from the perspective of an outsider (the hypermediate). The
interaction between the live performers and the filmic imagery is
also intricately done; projected versions of the dancers perform
movement sequences in synchrony with the real performers, and
the audience encounter the 'doubling' or 'mirroring' of the live
dancer. The performers become part of the cinema-scape, moving
in and out of the flat surface, while the virtual performers seem to
step out of the frame as if materialised. The projected performer
is very much a part of the 'live' performance and the interaction
between the performer and their filmic self is certainly 'live' and
yet, by incorporating the recorded aspects into the performance,
the nature of theatre not as a 'medium', but as a 'hypermedium'
was revealed. Theatre here is not merely live performance, but the
framing of various interacting media.

Figure 15 *Same, same But Different* (2002), Force Majeure/Kate
Champion. Photo: Heidrun Lohr

There are different ways of understanding this increasingly common experience of the performer's virtual double. Causey attempts to demonstrate how questions of virtuality and the real are being played out in both live and mediated performative work. He specifically questions how we understand the processes of performance which converge with mediated technologies of representation and warns: 'It would be a mistake to imagine that what we experience in the theatre and recorded media is the same experience. It is the same, only different' (Causey, 1999, p. 384). Causey isolates a critical moment in new media performance works when 'a live actor confronts her mediated other through the technologies of reproduction' (Causey, 1999, p. 385). He explains: 'The screens of mediated technologies, now ubiquitous in live performance ... construct the space wherein we double ourselves and perform a witnessing of ourselves as other' (Causey, 1999, p. 386). Causey then examines how this technical doubling of the self reflects the psychoanalytic notion of the uncanny and presents a visual metaphor of split subjectivity.

Causey develops the notion associated with the work of Jacques Lacan that the mediation of the Real, in its reflection and transmission, becomes an embodiment of the Lacanian Imaginary, which involves the 'specifically human act of (mis)recognising exact images' (Kittler, 1997, p. 139). The subject is refracted, split, and simultaneously exists in the realm of the real and the virtual. In mixed-media performance, the screening of mediated imagery often includes a 'doubling' of the live performer, so not only is the live actor confronted with their 'mediated other', the audience is confronted with the 'uncanny' experience of recognising both the real and its double. Friedrich Kittler describes the image of the body in film as 'celluloid ghosts of the actor's bodies' (Kittler, 1997, p. 96). In reference to the bodies deployed by early silent films, he states, 'Every one of them is the shadow of the body of the one filmed, or in short, his Double' (Kittler, 1997, p. 93).

French psychoanalyst Jacques Lacan (1901–81) developed three orders of reality: Real, Imaginary and Symbolic:

> *'The Real' is that which cannot be accounted for in symbols or representations or language. Like Phelan's notion of performance (from which it in part derives) the 'Real' loses its reality in representations or when it is put into words'.
> *'The Imaginary' is the virtual space in which we project our self-image, which is often a false image. It is the realm of associations and meanings. A commonly used metaphor for this notion is 'the cinema'.

> *'The symbolic' is the space of language and is associated with the social, cultural and linguistic networks into which we are born and which shape subjectivity.
>
> Lacan also developed the idea of the mirror phase to describe the experience the child has at around 6–18 months of age, when the child sees itself for the first time as an *other*, a double, an image in the mirror. This phase is linked to the acquisition of language, the rejection of the maternal 'Real' and acceptance of the paternal 'symbolic' order of reality.

The filmic medium presents a similarly 'Imaginary' space in Lacan's sense, an illusory state which projects a copy, a double of the real world. Kittler examines the phenomenon of the 'Double' both within its extensive history of literary representation and within psychoanalytic discourse. The Double is 'the phantom of our own ego' (Kittler, 1997, p. 87) and Causey argues that it is the confrontation with the Double, the 'recognition of yourself outside of yourself' that presents the 'technology triggered uncanniness of contemporary subjectivity' (Causey, 1999, p. 385). This experience of identifying the self as 'other' proliferates within technology, through interactive computer software, through video recording, to a voice on the answering machine.

> E. T. A Hoffmann's story 'The Sandman' first brought the idea of the uncanny to the attention of the psychologist Ernst Jentsch through his character of Olympia the automaton. Freud quotes Jentsch at the start of his own enquiry into the uncanny, in his essay 'Das Unheimliche' (The Uncanny) from 1919 he defines it as 'doubts whether an apparently animate being is really alive; or conversely, whether a lifeless object might not be in fact animate' referring to 'the impression made by waxwork figures, ingeniously constructed dolls and automata' as Jentsch's key examples (Freud, 1953, p. 219). The idea is subsequently developed by Freud to indicate the appearance of the strange within the familiar. Freud argued in an extensive etymology of the terms *'heimlich'* (homely, familiar) *and 'unheimlich'* (eerie, strange) that the most frightening experiences we can have are based on those moments of uncertainty when something familiar to us has been made strange and secret through repression, and then returns.

Another theory of the 'double' that captures the nature of the 'live' image of the actor in performance is Gilles Deleuze's understanding of the time-image, or 'the crystal- image'. In her essay 'Memory, Space and Actor on the Mediated Stage', Thea Brejzek explains the integration of electronic media on the stage through Deleuze's crystal image, an image that unites the past presented in recorded media with the immediacy of its viewing (Brejzek, 2006, pp. 157–73). The crystal-image is a film shot that unifies what Deleuze calls the 'virtual image' and the 'actual image'. The virtual image exists in the past and is remembered, but can be brought to life by the actual image, which is immediate, objective and viewed. The 'crystal image' exhibits time itself, showing it as a constant two-way mirror that splits the present into two directions, 'one of which is launched towards the future while the other falls into the past. ... Time consists of this split, and it is this, it is time, that we *see in the crystal*' (Deleuze, 1989, p. 79).

Deleuze's area of enquiry here is the film image; however, the image of the 'time that we see in the crystal' may perhaps explain the texture of temporality when the actor performs alongside their mediated self. When the mediation occurs in real time, via a live camera feed, the past unfolds in the present – the original (the actor) and the image are not distanced. In fact, with effective technology, the lack of time lapse removes the 'recording' process altogether. Nonetheless, the mediated image is located in the realm of the virtual, in the past, while the live body exists in the now: it is the unification of these images, the 'crystal image', with which the audience is presented.

Gilles Deleuze (18 January 1925–4 November 1995) was one of the most influential French philosophers in the second half of the twentieth century. He wrote and published works which reflect an experimental sense of the world and that the purpose of thinking is creative rather than descriptive. In his two books on cinema, *Cinema 1: The Movement-Image* (1986) and *Cinema 2: The Time-Image* (1989), Deleuze charts a fundamental shift in the presentation of time from pre-WW2 to post-WW2 cinema, suggesting that cinema moved from a primary concern with motion to a more overt concern with time itself.

Deleuze's assertion that the present consists inherently of both actuality and virtuality is certainly made visible via this performance of mediation. This image of the live performer projected in real time presents a visual metaphor for the blurring of the boundary between the real and the virtual that, for scholars such as N. Katherine Hayles, has become a foundation of contemporary existence. To understand the nature and significance of the virtual as a theatrical device we cannot separate it from its cultural context of production, a context defined by the interaction and even the indiscernability of the real and the virtual or, as Hayles identifies, of materiality and information. Hayles defines virtuality as 'the cultural perception that material objects are interpenetrated by information patterns' (Hayles, 2000, p. 69). For example, molecular biology has constructed the understanding that human physicality is 'encoded' as information in genes. This form of cultural intermediality is one of the key developments in the discourse of post-humanism, which we discuss in Chapter 9.

For the present discussion, the importance of these ideas is that the double disrupts the notion of a singular undivided self. It therefore problematises the basic conception of character as a single, consistently defined entity that is still such a feature of some forms of theatre and film. Deleuze's theory of the image and Hayles's notion of the virtual go further in identifying the forms of displacement of the self, both informational and temporal, that produce and represent multiple selves. In the case of theatrical performance this means that when the audience is faced with both the real actor and their live, mediated projection within the same space, we see the translation of the presence of the actor into the pattern of information technology and Phelan's 'maniacally charged present' divides into alternating temporalities.

> Steve Dixon is a leading commentator on media and performance and a practising artist. In his *Digital Performance: A History of New Media in Theatre, Dance, Performance Art, and Installation* (2007), the definitive history of this field, Dixon unpacks Causey's understanding of the uncanny nature of the relationship between the body and its mediated version in terms of a variety of doubles: as ghost, as reflection, as mirror image, as alter-ego, as spiritual emanation, as manipulable mannequin, as avatar, and as puppet. Each of these figures describes a particular manifestation of the mediated doubling of the actor on stage.

Rethinking the virtual body

Anna Munster's writings about media and embodiment are useful in this context as they enable us to think about the kinds of connection and disconnection that the new forms of media can create with bodies. Munster argues that particular information technologies and particular new media art works must be considered in terms of the ways in which they engage the perceptions and senses of performers, participants and spectators. In her account, neither body nor technology is considered as the point of origin in new media works; it is rather that 'embodiment is produced through the relations between the participants' bodily capacities and the operations and limitations of the particular information technologies' (Munster, 2006, 4).

Australian media artist and theorist Anna Munster writes not only about understanding the range of possible connections between virtual systems and human bodies but also about the differences that such terms conceal. Her emphasis is on the relations between body and technology and their capacities and functions rather than on their external appearance, their identity, or some other feature. She is resistant to the idea of cyborgian fusion and insists on the significance of the gaps between all the interconnections.

In any human–machine interface there are points of connection and moments of separation or disjunction so that the idea of a 'flesh-machine fusion' returns in Munster's own terms to the realm of 'reductive cyberfantasy' (Munster, 2006, p. 9). Munster points out that this combination of discrete entities involves 'a kind of a graft', the mark of connection and difference. It is the graft itself, the mark of the embodied connectivity where the digital and the corporeal fold into each other, which is elided in the cyborg fusion fantasy. Munster calls the site of this graft 'digital embodiment', a recombinant notion in which the digital is not pure code nor the body pure physical extension. She argues for a more rigorous discussion about art and media in relation to the body:

If our relations to corporeality are made different through our encounters with digital technologies, it is not through a cyborgian assimilation to the machine. Computers offer us multiplications and extensions of our bodily actions: cursors that glide across the screen interface, then stagger abruptly at its edges; three-dimensional *animé*-styled dancing characters that direct us to clumsily mimic their stilted disco moves in the 'Dance, Dance Revolution' rides that populate gaming arcades; a gaze that swoops and dives over terrain in simulated game landscapes yet frequently crashes into pixellation as machine processing speeds lag behind gamers' actual movements. These multiplications by no means provide seamless matches between body and code; the mismatch characteristic of divergent series triggers the extension of our corporeality out toward our informatic counterparts. (Munster, 2006, p. 33)

So the body is opened out by the technological, not cancelled out but enabled to experience things that might escape normal sensory perception. Think about the way slow-motion images can reveal aspects of a gesture or a movement that would not be evident to the naked eye.

To take this a little further, think about the way that motion capture enables the very style of an individual's movement to be observed and manipulated. The digital thereby enables a properly relational experience of the movement of the body. Munster suggests that this kind of experience is not 'of itself corporeal' but comprises a 'capacity for being affected by the diverse speeds, rhythms and flows of information' (Munster, 2006, p. 33). This is typical of the way that Munster negotiates the apparent gaps between conventional ideas about these notions in the culture of new media art practice as well as critical practice and is useful in this study to assist us to think about the subtle ways that performing and spectating bodies are newly connected with and disconnected from one another through technical interfaces.

Munster consistently challenges the accepted terms of the debate, the 'quagmire' (as she puts it) of 'virtual/real, mind/body and informatic/material that characterizes digital thinking about virtuality' (Munster, 2006, p. 17). In this context the virtual becomes less a dematerialised abstraction and is instead conceived of as 'a movement that passes from the abstract incorporeal spaces of information to the concrete actuality of the body' (Munster, 2006, p. 17). Timothy Lenoir, in his forward to Hansen's *New Philosophy for New Media,* goes further to argue that '(t)he source of the virtual is thus not technological, but rather a biologically grounded adaptation to newly acquired technological extensions provided by new media' (Lenoir in Hansen, 2006, p. xxiv).

This move is significant as it opens up the virtual to include its encounters with the corporeal rather than excluding them. Munster also considers technological entities as 'concrete actualizations of the virtual capacities of both the digital and the human bodies' (Munster, 2006, p. 17). This kind of thinking about what the virtual is and what the role of technology can be extends what can be thought of as the combination of live bodies and virtuality in performance such as in Auslander's formulation of 'dance + virtual = virtual'.[2] This kind of media theory enables performance studies scholars not only to engage with intensely physical performance practices such as dance *and* new media at the same time but also to theorise the relations between things like dance and virtuality as a dialogue between two entities the boundaries of which are not fixed. Not only are the boundaries in play but, in Munster's thesis, virtuality itself arises from an interchange with the experience of the corporeal. 'Dance + virtual' therefore involves the further mixing of already hybrid entities. In this sense there can be no meaning to the notion that this kind of multimedia performance could result in a diminution of the potentials of the one or the other form. The recombination of Dance + virtual recodes the notion of form and of cultural media.

Jennifer Parker-Starbuck's *Cyborg Theatre: Corporeal/Technological Intersections in Multimedia* (2011) uses the concept of the cyborg as a framework to examine the implications of new media on the live body in performance. Her article 'Becoming-Animate: On the Performed Limits of Human' (2006) further develops these topics through the theoretical concept of 'becoming-animate', a triangulation among concepts of human, animal, and technology, and highlights possible affiliations among the three terms.

Mark Hansen's research in *New Philosophy for New Media* explores a similar concern with the phenomenological aspects of multimedia and especially how new media artists foreground what Tim Lenoir calls 'the shift from the visual to the affective, haptic, and proprioceptive registers' (Lenoir in Hansen, 2006, p. xxiv) for the artists themselves, the participants in the work, and the users and viewers. The basis for this argument is in his contention that the digital image, rather than simply being apprehended as a mirror, frame, or window onto the world, is instead a place where the body comes together with a technology for viewing and produces the form for the information that makes up the digital image. Hansen says 'the image can no longer be restricted to the level of surface appearance, but must be extended to encompass the entire process by which information is made perceivable through embodied experience' (Hansen, 2006, p. 10).

From the very origins of the image in digital culture, Hansen suggests, the body is providing a frame for making these photographic, cinematic or video images, meaningful as shapes formed from the flux of information. They must reflect the demands of 'embodied human perception' or risk meaninglessness as total abstractions (Hansen, 2006. p. 8). Hansen's position can be summarised in his claim that '(b)eneath any concrete "technical" image or frame lies ... *the framing function* of the human body' (Hansen, 2006. p. 8). Bodies literally render the virtuality of the digital into comprehensible 'framed' images. In this way Hansen represents another counter-pole to Auslander since in his reading it is the body of the viewer and not the 'cultural frame' of the medium that grounds the experience of the work.

Conclusion

As we have indicated above, the study of social informatics and virtual cultures and the studies of affect have become central to the debates about the place of media in contemporary life. Media theorists and historians of multimedia such as those we discuss above bear witness to the ongoing impacts of media on all aspects of the practices of everyday life, as well as more broadly and abstractly on thought and being. Some, like Virilio, warn of the impoverishments to culture and experience wrought by the ongoing virtualisation of reality. Others such as Benjamin argue that we are well prepared for these shifts, that our media culture itself has enabled a thorough rehearsal of the shocks to human sensory systems. Heim's 'virtual realism' plots a course between a full-blown loss of spatio-temporal coordinates in virtuality and the firm, hard ground of realism.

Postmodernists such as Baudrillard and Deleuze unleash the forces of the hyperreal in their every sentence, performing the very effect of simulation that Baudrillard so eloquently identified. But this has done nothing to banish the modernist ghost of Artaud's double in media discourse, especially as it relates to theatre. If anything, this notion of the double is simply the historical precursor, in the language of fiction, to the media discourse of hyperreality. Causey and Dixon both investigate the status of the screen performer as a double in Artaud's sense of an entity, the ontology of which is entirely indeterminate. Simulation – or Deleuze's crystal-image in which actual and virtual imagery are superimposed to prevent any effective differentiation between them to occur – describes exactly this status which for Auslander also describes the relation between the live and the mediated.

Ultimately these theories return to the question of the place of the body in mediated culture. For Hayles this body is already virtualised, encoded and informatic (think of the language of DNA, for instance). For Munster and Hansen, the question of embodiment is about the interaction between material bodies and virtual and informational systems.

Given that the key questions posed by media theorists return to the place of the body in media culture, it is vital for theorists of performance to respond by using these ideas as indicators to position the discussion of multimedia performance in relation to these more complex arguments around bodies and virtuality and to move beyond the rhetorics of presence which have until recently defined and delimited performance theory, especially in Theatre studies. Multimedia performance is one of the key aesthetic spaces for the development of a critique of naïve presence as the basic value for the experience of performance. It is also where the alternative art forms are developed in ways that reflect the massive technical, experiential, and subjective shifts in the wider society that media theorists have discussed in relation to media and which we examine in terms of the various displacements of the self, of the body, of presence in recent performance work.

Further reading

The area of media theory explicated for performance studies scholarship is relatively new; however, some aspects of media theory have been more extensively covered in performance studies than others. One example is the notion of the cyborg which has already produced a number of responses from performance studies scholars (see Giannachi in Chapter 1). Jennifer Parker Starbuck's research into the figure of the cyborg in *Cyborg Theatre: Corporeal/Technological Intersections in Multimedia* (2011) provides another helpful way into this territory alongside texts such as Joanne Zylinska's *The Cyborg Experiments: The Extensions of the Body in the Media Age* (2002) which focuses on performance art as a vehicle for the development of the cyborg.

Chapter 6

Dance + Virtual = Multimedia Performance

Late twentieth-century machines have made thoroughly ambiguous the difference between natural and artificial, mind and body, self-developing and externally designed, and many other distinctions that used to apply to organisms and machines. Our machines are disturbingly lively, and we ourselves frighteningly inert. (Haraway, 1991, p. 152)

An important context for the exploration of the transfer between real and virtual elements in a performance can be found in contemporary dance and dance theatre. Contemporary dance companies are now routinely placing the moving body alongside 'disturbingly lively' machines and media systems. In this sense dance represents an intriguing site for exploring the ambiguities listed by Haraway above as both elements are vying for liveliness. In the discussion on liveness and remediation in Chapter Four we argued that this intermedial componentry is an essential feature of multimedia composition. In this chapter we develop this argument in relation to dance by taking as our point of departure an observation made by Auslander in his study of liveness (1999, 2008). In a section of the book dealing with dance, Auslander states that the addition of digital media projection to live dance means that the audience watch the projection and not the dancing body. He says that '(r)ather than a conversation among distinct media, the production presents the assimilation of varied materials to the cultural dominant. In this sense Dance + Virtual = Virtual' (2008, p. 42). His position seems to be that dance remains dance no matter how much media you throw at it and the mediated aspects of the dance in a multimedia performance environment render the dancing body somehow invisible. This idea is significant and deserves detailed discussion because it operates against the grain of much of Auslander's research and contradicts much of our own argument in the present context.

To us, Auslander's equation seems to be based on two equally untenable positions: (i) that cultural media such as dance, song, music video are permanent cultural constructs, perhaps cognitive structures as well, and don't hybridise or transform, and (ii) new media forms in digital culture tend towards an effect of disembodiment which, here, would result in rendering the dancing body literally immaterial. In this chapter we outline some examples of practice that refute Auslander's theoretical position by working towards a radical interweaving of the virtual with the live choreographic elements. We examine a small section from this broad spectrum of dance and media, including the following works: *BIPED, Loops* and *Ghostcatching* by the Openended group with Merce Cunningham and Bill T Jones respectively (1999, 2001 and 1999 respectively); and Chunky Move's *Glow* (2007), an interactive dance with an overhead projection triggered by the dancer's movements. We will confine ourselves to works that feature dancing bodies in direct referential relations with an audience, so either in the context of live dance or motion captured dancing bodies.

We also show how recent developments in new media theory suggest quite a different picture to the one Auslander paints; in particular we look at readings of media which suggest that it is not media that frame the body but the other way around, that if we move beyond a discussion of cultural presence and look at the materials of sensorial presencing in the body, we find that just the opposite is the case: that digital media make sense only when downloaded by embodied entities equipped to decode digital information as a/v material.

Johannes Birringer's position is a useful counterpoint to this in that his view is based on his work as a practising experimental multimedia choreographer and as a theorist. He suggests that, in practice, '(m)aking dances for the camera has become not only a cinematographic alternative to theatre-dance, but has motivated choreographers to re-conceive the aesthetics of dance for the theatre' (Birringer, 2002, p. 87). Birringer's argument is further explored later in this chapter.

The Auslander equation

Auslander's arguments have already been rehearsed in this book, but this aspect of his thinking requires a little more unpacking as it seems to undermine the overall logic of liveness. In an interview in 2005 he explained his thinking as follows:

> [D]ifferent media therefore do not interact with one another as equals. I said in the book that if you have live bodies and projections on the same stage, most people are going to look at the projections. This is partly a perceptual matter: the projected images are usually larger and brighter and therefore attract more attention. But it also has to do with the cultural dominance of the screened image at this historical moment. What I meant when I said that 'Dance + Virtual = Virtual' is that because video and digital media currently possess greater cultural presence than live bodies they become the framing elements of any performance that incorporates both. The live elements will be perceived through that frame – they will be seen in terms of the video or digital media, not the other way around. (Auslander, 2005)

This statement about the framing role of media in contemporary cultural space can be read alongside Hansen's argument in the previous chapter about the body framing media images. Hansen's perceptual frame can be contained within the larger cultural space which Auslander describes, but it also suggests a different emphasis. Auslander's argument is problematic in another sense, however, as it endorses a static model of cultural media in which the basic structures of the media of cultural performance (here it is dance) are not subject to the same forces which change the culture of technology, in this case, holography. Cultural media like dance and performance are also shaped by changing social and cultural forces, so just as we will have to re-examine the list of old cultural media (drama, song, prayer, recital) to see what new forms have emerged in recent years (multimedia) so the cultures of dance must also be tested for their response to social changes. It's not just technology that changes; dance also changes, and the application of virtual elements to dance does not mean that it is only the digital media environment that has been affected.

The area of 'dance film' is also responding to technologies and social change. An interesting example of such work is Gina Czarnecki's 2005 work, *Nascent*, a collaboration with the Australian Dance Theatre's Garry Stewart that creates traces of movement to create an effect of animated images on screen composed of hundreds of dancing, writhing bodies. *Nascent* takes original footage of improvised dance and reworks it using digital compositing techniques in post production.

Figure 16   Nascent (2005) Gina Czarnecki. Single channel video with two channel sound. Produced by Forma and Australian Dance Theatre, Commissioned by Forma and Adelaide Film Festival. Sound: Christian Fennesz

Auslander makes his position explicit:

> My analysis supposes that multimedia technologies have not destabilized the definitions of traditional media and forms very much: to speak of interactions among cultural media assumes that they retain individual identities. I believe that dance, music, theatre, and other forms basically retain identities rooted in modern definitions. (Auslander, 2005)

While we can concede that traditional media certainly continue to exist, it is important to recognise the ways in which new cultural media form alongside them and often through them in response to shifting social and cultural conditions. What Auslander's argument does not acknowledge is this latter development and the dynamic cross-fertilisation of forms that is the characteristic feature of much new media art and culture.

Birringer also contests this view by taking the example of dance from the perspective of the composition of dance work and considering how it has been affected by developments in video technology. He says that the effects are evident in two ways: 'Video has thus effected a transition in two directions, opening up a new screen space for movement images (concurrent with the evolution of music television), as well as bringing new modes of digital image processing and nonlinear editing to the practice of composition and scenography onstage' (Birringer, 1999, p. 362). If we look at a number of works in each category, we can begin to see how Birringer's argument plays out in screen-based new media work and on stage.

One of his key examples here is *Escape Velocity*, produced and performed by Company in Space. This company was founded in Melbourne, Australia in 1990 by John McCormick, a computer design and operation specialist, and Hellen Sky, a dancer and choreographer. Their aim was to 'explore the intersections of virtual and actual worlds' and to 'create dialogues between … visual, aural and kinetic perceptions' (http://www.companyinspace.com). *Escape Velocity* was first created at Opera Australia Studios in Melbourne in August 1998. In this version the dancers, Sky and Louise Taube, with shaven heads, began the performance by coming up from beneath the stage and then being suspended in harnesses while walking backwards up a wall and balancing on a perch. This was done to an electronic noise track (Garth Paine) at ear-splitting volume and within a mobile virtual environment of word projections that seemed to embrace the dancers' bodies. Onstage video camera operators captured their movements and threw the images onto walls and onto the dancers themselves so that the live videography of the dance formed part of the

Figure 17   *Escape Velocity,* Company in Space

projection environment and the recording fed back into the composition of the work. For Peta Tait 'the movements of virtual and physical bodies seem(ed) interchangeable' (Tait, 2002). This approach to composition, in which the documentation of the work forms a part of the work, enabled some truly unique developments of mediated performance.

The work was remade at Arizona State University for the International Dance and Technology festival on Saturday, 27 February 1999. This time one of the dancers, Hellen Sky, performed before a live audience in Arizona with one camera operator, Luke Pither, while Louise Taube remained in Melbourne with the rest of the technical production team. In this version the non-matrixed roles of the videographers, Pither and Kelli Dipple in Melbourne, became crucial to the effect of the piece as the dancers were able to perform a kind of duet with the other's image, similar to the previous versions of the work in which both dancers shared the stage. However, in this production the addition of the virtual element, ISDN teleconferencing systems, to the dance enabled an entirely new form of duet across the spatial and time-zone differentials separating the US from Australia. In one scene, as the video in Melbourne zoomed in on Taube, the projected image of her upper body appeared, in Arizona, directly mapped onto the head of Sky. This moment is captured in a famous photograph from the production, which can be seen on the company's website (http://www.companyinspace.com) and has become an iconic image of the aesthetic potentials of dance + virtual. The sonic elements of the work are equally interesting, with the ingenious Paine using MIDI software VNS and Max to 'sense the video image of the choreography and create a layer of interactive sound', a live sonic effect which was then fed back into the mix with 'pre-structured material' (http://www.companyinspace.com). Other sounds were generated by an audience member at IDAT. The composition of *Escape Velocity* was in every sense cybernetic, creating feedback loops between live and pre-structured elements across audio and video channels.

After this ground-breaking project, Company in Space continued to make work which tested the boundaries of dance and new media by conducting a number of choreographic experiments with optical motion capture systems. They presented some of their ideas in unfinished essay-like pieces such as *CO3*, performed at the Capital Theatre, Melbourne in September 2001. In *CO3* Sky wore a Gypsy motion capture suit or 'wearable exoskeleton' as she moved through the physical space. The exoskeleton was a little restrictive on the movement and the phrases were truncated and spasmodic as a result, but the overall effect was again in the direction of a cybernetic servo-mechanism, a machine for staging feedback loops. In this performance, the motion capture suit was working in real time in creating 'movement files' based on live performance. On this occasion these files were used to animate an avatar projected onto the side of a building across the street from the space.[1] The projection was enormous, but the potential of motion capture to enhance choreography was not fully realised in this work – while *CO3* sketched some ideas in space, it did not fully embody them. In the next section we discuss the ways in which artists from the Openended group along with Merce Cunningham and Bill T Jones have more fully explored the virtual as a primary tool within the work itself. In works such as *Loops*, *Ghostcatching* and *BIPED* the motion capture formed a fundamental aspect of the composition of the work and enabled the blending of the physical and the digital in innovative ways.

Motion capture

Motion capture (mo cap) systems are combinations of computer hardware and software that together enable the production of 3-D digital representations of actual recorded moving bodies. Owing to the high degree of referentiality in mo cap, the recording sessions are obviously quite important to the process and involve the 'placement of markers or sensors in strategic positions on the performer's body' (deLahunta, 2000). These are then tracked by arrays of multiple cameras surrounding the performer. The resulting information is then consolidated into a single data file, which can then 'drive the movement of simulated figures on the computer, where they can be merged, connected, resequenced and mapped onto other anatomies' using an animation program such as *Character Studio*' (Birringer, 1999, p. 364).

The OpenEnded Group are based in the US, where they have pioneered the use of motion-capture in performance in creating digital artworks for stage and screen in galleries, museums and public spaces. The group's three collaborating artists – Paul Kaiser, Shelley Eshkar and Marc Downie – have backgrounds in film, dance, drawing, writing, computer graphics, and artificial intelligence, a mix of disciplines and skills still evident in their work to his day. Kaiser and Eshkar have collaborated on numerous installation and dance projects since the mid-1990s, including *BIPED* (1999) and *Ghostcatching* (1999). Downie joined them in 2001 to work on the *Loops* project, a continuation of their collaboration with dancer and choreographer Merce Cunningham.

In the early 1990s Kaiser made *Visionary of Theater* (1994–7), a multimedia study of Robert Wilson's processes and works, as part of which he shot a video of Wilson performing his principles for stage movement before a blue screen This is an effect which completely despatialises the gestures and makes them available for different media environments, a development that the key figure in the Theatre of Images could only dream of back in the 60s, when he was creating the formal and aesthetic mechanisms by which this newer kind of work could be understood. This project with Wilson led to a meeting with William Forsythe, a meeting that influenced Kaiser's future work in interesting ways. Kaiser writes with great sensitivity and empathy about his encounter with Forsythe:

> As he described his methods, he began drawing imaginary shapes in the air, using all the parts of his body – not only his feet and hands, elbows and knees, but also his skull, shoulders, butt, and even his ears and chin. He talked and moved rapidly, building up a complicated and invisible geometry of dance that I had no ability to visualize or follow. (Kaiser, 1999)

The selection of terms here is significant: it was the 'invisibility' of the 'geometry of dance' that Kaiser could not 'visualize' that was at stake in this meeting and which defined the nature of the challenge that Kaiser set himself and his collaborators thereafter. The objectives of much of their work in the period following this encounter would be to over-come this invisibility and to permit the geometric features of the poetics of human movement to be discerned by other 'non-dancers', as Kaiser describes himself.

William Forsythe has also created choreography for multimedia work such as *Synchronous Objects,* a joint project with Ohio State University's Advanced Computing Center for the Arts and Design (ACCAD) and the Department of Dance. This work presents a visualisation of the underlying structures and proxemics in Forsythe's *One Flat Thing, reproduced* (2000). The *Synchronous Objects* interactive website maps Forsythe's choreography using algorithmic techniques, 2-D and 3-D graphics and animation, and visual dance scores in a complex and subtle remediation of the previous work.

The other important influence on Kaiser's artistic trajectory was his experience in 1986 teaching art to learning impaired 12-year old chil-dren, which shaped the place of collaboration in his practice and his focus on the importance of drawing as a meaning-making act with multiple

Figure 18 *Synchronous Objects Project* (2009), The Ohio State University and the Forsythe Company

Figure 19 *Synchronous Objects Project* (2009), The Ohio State University and the Forsythe Company

outcomes. As he says in a description of this period in the catalogue essay to *Ghostcatching*:

> The art of collaboration was first taught to me by my students at a school for the learning disabled. So directly did their lessons lead to

Figure 20   *Ghostcatching* (1999), Bill T. Jones, Paul Kaiser and Shelley Eshkar

the later *Ghostcatching* work with Shelley Eshkar and Bill T. Jones that I shouldn't skip over this unlikely origin. Not only did these children teach me the power arising from unusual collaborations, but they also helped me discover two ideas – *drawing as performance* and *mental space*. These ideas continue to guide my work with others.... Watch children drawing and you'll see this for yourself: they are *performing*, though mostly for themselves. Their strokes are dramatic gestures tied to dialogue, narration, and song (the soundtrack may be sub-vocal, but notice the moving lips). As the drawn improvisation develops, new lines are scribbled in, and old ones erased or crossed out, one scene following another. (Kaiser, 1999)

This expanded concept of drawing as performative technology is clear in the work which immediately follows the Wilson project (as it connects with Wilson's own methodology as an artist) and which began with Merce Cunningham viewing the hand-drawn animations that had been made from Wilson's own sketches. As Kaiser describes it, 'he played it through several times, nodded his head, and paused. "Yes, yes," he said, pointing to a small figure lightly sketched in the background, "but can you make that figure move?"'(Kaiser, 1999). They made it move in ways that would regenerate Cunningham's career as a dancer and challenge the ontological status of dance as a form based on live human presence.

The result of this was *Hand-drawn Spaces* (1998) a virtual dance installation work 'conceived purely for the computer' but one in which the computer would not shape the movements, only the appearance of the moving figures. The figures were hand drawn by Shelley Eshkar and their movements were captured from performances by Jeannie Steele and Jared Phillips based on Cunningham's choreography. The hand-drawn figures were then animated by these digitally recorded movements in a new digital dance in which the resulting phrases were 're-sequenced and re-combined' by Cunningham. This new digital dance re-combines specific gestures of the dancers' bodies, but in new ways. For instance, the 'differences between the two (dancers) in size and sex and style were annulled as Merce combined their captured phrases freely, making long passages in which one dancer's movements alternated frequently with the other's, both mapped to the same hand-drawn figure.' In this sense the addition of virtual elements to the dance created a genuine recombination of elements.

Figure 21 *Hand-Drawn Spaces* (1998), Merce Cunningham, Paul Kaiser and Shelly Eshkar

In the same year as *Hand-drawn Spaces* was completed, Cunningham invited Kaiser and Eshkar to collaborate on a new piece, working title *BIPED*, telling them and the composer (Gavin Bryars) 'that it was "about technology" and would be like "flicking through channels on TV"' (Kaiser, www.openendedgroup.com).[2] This, perhaps 'off the cuff', remark insightfully offers a way into reading the intentions of the work. It suggests that Cunningham saw it primarily in terms of pattern and randomness, in the way that flicking between channels is never purely random but is factored by preferences for genre and builds a kind of metanarrative connecting entirely different sequences of image and narrative. Kaiser and Eshkar, working alongside Cunningham's lighting designer, Aaron Copp, used a large, transparent scrim to cover the entire stage from the front. The projections were designed to use the full scale of the scrim and were made up of a variety of figures redolent of those from the *Hand Drawn Spaces* work. Kaiser describes these 'virtual anatomies' as conforming to three types: 'We had dot bodies (from the dots seen in motion-capture), stick bodies (inspired by the yarrow sticks cast by I Ching practitioners like Cunningham and Cage), and cubist/chronophotograph bodies (our nod towards Marey and Duchamp)' (Kaiser, www.openendedgroup. com). These different anatomies were arranged into animation sequences of motion-captured movement 'ranging in length from about 15 seconds to four minutes' (Kaiser, www.openendedgroup.com).

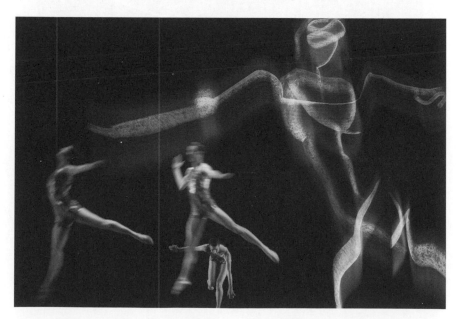

Figure 22　*BIPED* (1999), Merce Cunningham, Paul Kaiser and Shelly Eshkar. Photo: Stephanie Berger//Time Life Pictures/Getty Images

The fourteen dancers in the piece move behind the scrim, sometimes working without projections and on other occasions dwarfed by the gigantic moving figures. Cunningham's choreography in this work is abstract and technical, affectless, and produces an effect which matches the projected movement. A reviewer of the finished installation, Ann Dils, describes the effect as a kind of mutual enhancement in which '(t)hrough the images and environment they create, Kaiser and Eshkar finalize a transformation that Cunningham begins in his choreography: the human body as biped, as stripped down to moving, two-legged being' (Dils, 2002, p. 95). This description suggests that the addition of the virtual elements, the projections of the virtual dancers, enhances the sense that Cunningham's own impersonal choreographic performance has given the dancers in this piece.

A further collaboration between Eshkar, Kaiser and Bill T. Jones, another prominent American dancer, would bring out the same kinds of issue of impersonality in virtuality, but with quite different results. The motion capture session they recorded with Jones for their next installation piece occurred by chance in the same week that they were recording Cunningham's dancers at the Biovision studio in San Fransisco. Jones was not as enthusiastic about the concept as Cunningham had been. Kaiser remembers him saying 'I do not want to be a disembodied, denatured, de-gendered series of lines moving in a void,' hardly an endorsement of the concept. Jones's style of dance is also more muscular than Cunningham's, making the capture by the camera of the movements of his body less substantive as an account of the actual movement, more differentiated from the dance itself. This was reinforced in the recording session as Jones began to work the sequences and started to sweat, so that some of the twenty-four markers slipped off his body. Jones likened the procedure to trying to catch a ghost, which is the origin of the title of the work.

Ann Dils was intrigued to note that the stills of the process of motion capture show Jones with a sensor on the end of his penis. However, Dils observes that no movement of this part of his body is discernable in the finished work. This absence operates as a kind of index in her essay for what is lost in the process of motion capture. She writes about the depletion of meaning in these works as the facts of the body's appearance are transmuted by the motion capture and bodily characteristics such as skin colour and sex are conjured away. In fact, there were two recording sessions with Jones: one in which the dancer was naked and the other in which he wears the more complete motion capture exoskeleton. This second session was in an enclosed space using more formal improvisations based around an imagined central figure described by Jones as 'a being searching for an acceptable state, trying to perform an impossible task. He is trying on modes of being, knowing that they have to change' (Jones in Kaiser, 1999). The sense Dils perceives of a kind of loss in the installation is perhaps deliberate rather than accidental and a function of the choreography as much as the technology.

Dils's analysis rests on the assumption that these media works are somehow replacing the moving body rather than augmenting it, providing another vehicle for it and another way of seeing it and appreciating it. Ultimately, however, she affirms just this kind of reading, describing the experience of seeing *Ghostcatching* as

> a bit like being invited into the home of a very formal colleague, the outward manifestations of the person's identity fall away and something less public, more vulnerable, and closer to personality than identity becomes apparent. *Ghostcatching* is about a person, rather than a personality. (Dils, 2002, p. 100)

The creation of a sort of intimacy with the dancing figure is a surprising achievement of the work and underlines the basic argument we are making through these examples, which is that dance and virtual elements combine to make multimedia performances that are not always reducible to the components of the composition, here the dance, the cameras and the mo cap suits and software.

Another important contemporary group working the interface of dance and technology is Troika Ranch, a collaborative partnership between artists Mark Coniglio and Dawn Stoppiello. Troika Ranch combine dance, theatre and media, presenting live performances, interactive installations, and digital films. In works such as the recent *loopdiver* and *16 [R]evolutions*, performers move across a highly mediatised stage, their actions triggering real-time media systems that generate 2-D and 3-D imagery. The software 'brain' behind Troika Ranch productions is 'Isadora', a 'graphic programming environment that provides human control over digital media', created by Co-Director Mark Cognilio (www. troikaranch.org/technology).

Ultimately, however mobile and vital the movements which engendered them, the motion captured in both *BIPED* and *Ghostcatching* remains the same, quite unlike the bodies of the dancers themselves, unchanged by environment, unaffected by circumstances or even developments in technology. In this sense they could be read as moving 3-D portraits, or

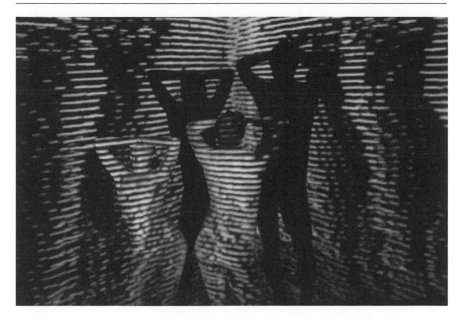

Figure 23   *16 [R]evolutions* (2006), Troika Ranch. Photo: A. T. Shaefer

understood in terms of filmic notions of abstracted performance where there is no longer any stake in the live moment at all apart from the reception of the image itself. Responding to this condition of fixity, the Openended Group created a version of Merce Cunningham's solo dance piece *Loops* in which the presentation of the captured material can be remixed and newly blended with each performance. *Loops* is the name of a work Cunningham made for himself in 1971 and continued to perform until 2001. One of the unique features of this dance is that while it was originally conceived as a dance of his entire body, Cunningham eventually focused its movements into the fingers, hands and arms.

The Openended Group's digital version of *Loops* was commissioned by the MIT Media Lab in 2001 for the 'ID/Entity' show. This version consisted of a recording of Cunningham's arms and hands in the performance of *Loops* in a motion capture studio in August 2000. The installation reveals the skeletal outlines of the hands as points of light flickering on the screen. Yet *Loops* was created within an artificial intelligence program that produces different outcomes every time it is run. So it is a newly made live production on every 'playback' of the piece. Both the Openended group and the Merce Cunningham Dance Company insist that both forms of the work constitute a live performance. The piece was also remade twice with a sound score remade for Ars Electronica in 2005, while in 2007 it was re-created in tryptich form and its underlying

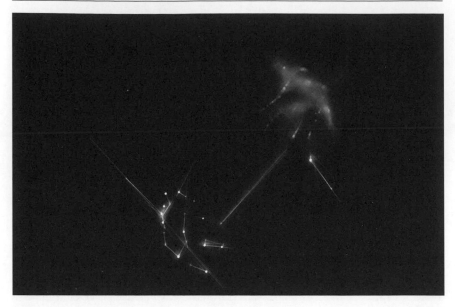

Figure 24   Still frame from *Loops* (2011). Courtesy OpenEndedGroup –
Marc Downie, Shelley Eshkar and Paul Kaiser

code released as open source. In the Tryptich, the central screen shows
Merce's hands directly in front, while the flanking screens give sideway
views from the left and right respectively.

The *Loops* soundtrack is similarly run in real time and has two
elements. The first is Cunningham reading from his diary entries from
his first three-day visit to New York City in 1937 at age 17. The second is
a musical response on a virtual prepared piano to the sounds and rhythms
of the narration as well as to the shifts occurring on screen. This second
element is based on the premise of John Cage listening and responding
to his old friend and collaborators reading. Both image and sound in
this work participate in the 'set of interacting processes' that continually
present and recast both the motion of Cunningham's virtual hands, and
the sound of his voice in the narration.

On the occasion of the public release of the *Loops* Choreography online,
(under an intellectual property licence in the Creative Commons to ensure
open access) accompanied by the release of the digital artwork *Loops*, as
open source software on 26 February 2008, it is possible to see how this
unique artwork provides a vision of the way that dance and virtual components will recombine in future multimedia performances. For instance,
the press release notes that '[s]ince the internal structure of *Loops* is
revealed completely in its visibly open source, re-implementations of it
can go far beyond the present-day practice of "remixes," which operate

only on the surface rather than on the structure of the original work' (Cunningham, 2009). In *Loops* we can identify a radical form of remediation in which the possibilities of a motion capture recording of a dancer's body as a kind of open source for experiments in choreography and in visual arts practice are limited only by bandwidth and the user's ability to reprogramme lines of code. But perhaps we have not come very far from the Auslander equation? Are dance and the virtual the same as a result of this interaction?

Dance + Virtual Theory

In the postscript to her book *Materializing New Media: Embodiment in Information Aesthetics*, Anna Munster describes *Loops* in terms that resonate with our reading of these works. Munster argues that the 'potential of new visualization technologies for the continual manipulation and tweaking of data into patterned flows ... allow the production of an entirely different kind of portrait, an image of the self or body no longer based upon appearance but instead expressed through motion and across time' (Munster, 2006, p. 179). We might add that, in addition to portraiture, the same logic applies for the visual document or the remediated performance. Portraiture is certainly a clear example of a practice the base function of which we might characterise as the production of accurate representations of features. This practice itself becomes volatilised or put into play again in a digital aesthetic context so that the features to be represented may not relate to external appearances but to internal organic componentry, the chemical and muscular construction of the outward physical appearance.

Munster's reading of *Loops* shows that it is not simply a question of the addition of a new virtual element to a pre-existing (dance) element but rather a development of the potentials of both forms:

> The internal discreteness and connectivity of the dancer's muscular skeletal system, trained and refined through years of choreographic experience and experiment, is traditionally presented as a total and externalized form in the spectacle of dance. But in *Loops* we gain visual access to the intensive deformations and twists of contracted and protracted bodily movements that animate the energy of dance. The fact that these now appear to us in a visually pared-down form – as monochromatic lines unfolding and transforming through time – foregrounds the temporal and *topological* propensities of information visualization. What we are seeing then, is a doubling and amplification by data of intensive bodily activity. (Munster, 2006, p. 179)

The thrust of Munster's argument here and elsewhere in her study is that new media, especially in their performative dimensions, activate new aesthetic potentials beyond existing genres and cultural media. In her argument corporeality and information are the broad polarities within which we may discern the outlines of 'dance' and 'the virtual'. The challenge, as Munster says, 'is to move beyond the twin premises of disembodiment and extension in space that continue to qualify both information and corporeality' (Munster, 2006, p. 179). The instances of the capture of the kinaesthetic activity of dancers' bodies by motion sensors in developing work like *Loops* or its predecessors *Ghostcatching* and *BIPED* provide perhaps the most eloquent examples of this new hybrid cultural media in operation and also the most comprehensive refutation of the Auslander equation.

Glow: Embodiment as frame/framing the body

But what about new media work which more overtly encodes existing modes of cultural media, for instance the performance of dance with projection? If we consider the case of Chunky Move's *Glow* (2007), an interactive dance with an overhead projection triggered by the dancer's movements, would we say that we are still looking at dance as a distinctive entity? Would we still agree with Auslander that 'multimedia technologies have not destabilized the definitions of traditional media and forms very much...'? *Glow* is a 'choreographic essay' developed by Chunky Move's artistic director Gideon Obarzanek and interactive software creator Frieder Weiss. It is very different from the previous works we have been discussing in that it makes no use of virtual reality effects and there is no mo cap or use of ISDN links to destabilise concepts of presence. It is a choreographic encounter with a disturbingly lively projection environment in which the interactivity occurs between the performer and the image rather than between the spectator and the work.

Glow features a single dancer working on a horizontal axis in which the body's extension and its compression are two poles of the choreography. Like inspiration and expiration, systole and diastole, the dancer's movements are hunched and then elongated, twisted and mutated across the plain white reflective rectangle of the performance space. The body is tracked by a powerful projector situated overhead. As Obarzanek explains:

In *Glow*, light and moving graphics are not pre-rendered video playback but rather images constantly generated by various algorithms

Figure 25   *Glow* (2007). Collaboration between Gideon Obarzanek and Frieder Weiss. Performer: Kristy Ayre. Photography: Rom Anthoni

responding to movement. In most conventional works employing projection lighting, the dancer's position and timing have to be completely fixed to the space and timeline of the video playback. Their role is reduced to the difficult chore of making every performance an exact facsimile of the original. In *Glow*, the machine sees the performer and responds to their actions, unlocking them from a relationship of restriction and tedium. (Obarzanek, 2010)

The projection environment is 'disturbingly lively' in relation to the performer and 'varies from being an illustrative extended motion of their movement, a visual expression of internal states, and also a self-contained animated habitat' (Obarzanek, 2010). Obarzanek's description of it as a 'choreographic essay' is apt in relation to the first of these as there is something writerly about the dancer's inscription of their own movement onto the surface of the performing area. In this first section of the work, the dancer's body leaves a slowly dissolving smudge behind to indicate exactly where the pressure points of body to surface were situated. Reviewing the premiere in Melbourne, on 5 September 2006, Stephanie Glickman describes this section, performed by Sara Black (and then in turn by Kristy Ayre and Bonnie Paskas), 'Revolving on her back, Black appeared to draw circles with her toes and fingers. In perfect synchronisation, geometric webs of diagonal lines enclosed and expanded around her body' (Glickman, 2006). In a sense, the projection environment, created by Fliess, enables the dance to return to its origins in choreographic design and spatial arrangement.

Perhaps because of the relentless horizontality of the dance and the apparent surveillance of the dancer's body by the tracking system and infra-red camera, the work develops a strange intimacy with the audience. Glickman describes the effects of this: 'On two sides of the room, audiences look down on the action in a white rectangle on the floor. We hear every breath and muttering from the lone dancer ... Towards the end, we even see smudges of blood gradually staining the white surface from a scraped ankle' (Glickman, 2006). In this way *Glow* also works to foreground the physical in its relation to the virtual. They are, for Glickman, 'visually ... impossible to separate'. The system is designed so that the dancer's movements produce the shape and texture of the projection and frame the digital graphics as intelligible shapes and lines on the ground. The movements produce the response from the system in a way that recalls media theorist Mark Hansen's notion of 'the *framing function* of the human body' (Hansen, 2006, p. 8). This idea (see introduction) develops the notion that the photographic, cinematic or video images, which saturate the contemporary cultural space in Western societies are meaningful only insofar as they reflect the demands of 'embodied human perception' (Hansen, 2006, p. 8).

Hansen's position is that only human embodiment can render the virtuality of the digital image into comprehensible 'framed' images distinct from the noise of unrendered code. This does not mean that the work becomes magically comprehensible in the combination with new media systems, just that these systems do not exist themselves independently of the human capacity to perceive their effects. In *Glow* we see this situation literalised as the dancer produces the response from the tracking and projection system which traces and tracks her moves and provides an image to accompany the movement. Although framed by the projections, the body here is clearly productive of the specific shape of its immediate digital environment. It's an obvious point but the dancer is not superfluous to the virtual components of the work but provides the occasion for this environment. It is her movement which triggers the image field. In this sense it performs the function of the frame in Hansen's sense of making the image intelligible as such, as a pattern emerging from random ambient digital noise.

Glow constitutes a great example of the ways artists have found to reconfigure virtuality itself so that it can be seen to arise from an interchange with the experience of the corporeal. Auslander's equation of

Dance + Virtual therefore involves the further mixing of already hybrid entities. In this sense there can be no meaning to the notion that this kind of multimedia performance could result in a diminution of the potentials of the one or the other form. The recombination of Dance + Virtual recodes the notion of form and of cultural media.

Conclusion

The other side of the equation is the traditional form of dance, which some have argued is threatened with invisibility in the new media work. One reading of Auslander's provocation is exactly this: that the dancer becomes an ornament to the serious work of making digital images and the body therefore becomes an embellishment, an epiphenomenon of the artwork rather than its focal point. Yet new media theory also provides a useful counterpoint to this position. Anna Munster's suggestion that in this context 'embodiment is produced' through the relations between the body's capacities and 'the operations and limitations of the particular information technologies' (Munster, 2006, p. 4) suggests that there is more to the body than its separate and distinctive occupation of space. Her work encourages us to see that dance and virtual components working together show the body's 'capacity for being affected by the diverse speeds, rhythms and flows of information' (Munster, 2006, p. 33).

Merce Cunningham's various collaborations with the Openended group are certainly evidence of this especially in the case of *Loops*. The more one considers the place of the dancer's body in this work, the more it becomes a matter of rematerialisation and recombination rather than dematerialisation and disappearance. His own body is no longer capable of performing the work, but the digital version of *Loops* will continue to provide access to Cunningham's own highly eccentric hand and wrist rotations to anyone who wants to experience them. The ghost may have been captured but it has also been allowed to live another day.

Further reading

In addition to the references made within this chapter, Johannes Birringer's numerous publications should be the first point of call for research into dance and technology. In particular, his *Performance, Technology and Science* (2008) explores the aesthetic implications of the technologies driving computer-mediated performance. Another important theorist in this field is choreographer and academic Scott Delahunta, who explores the choreographic potential of technologies such as motion capture and interactive real-time software. There is an interesting discussion between Delahunta and Mark Coniglio of Troika Ranch regarding the software 'Isadora' in the *International Journal of Performance Arts and Digital Media*. The book *Performance and Technology: Practices of Virtual Embodiment and Interactivity* (2006), edited by Sue Broadhurst and Josephine Machon, also provides a number of essays and case studies relevant to this discussion.

Chapter 7

Immersion

As we have seen in the examples of works such as *Loops* and *Escape Velocity* (Chapter 6) the field of multimedia performance emphasises perceptual responses from its spectators in certain ways. *Loops* focuses the attention on the micro gestures of fingers and hands whereas *Escape Velocity* constructs an experience for the viewer that merges virtual and actual corporealities. This merging effect describes, but does not name, an important element of audience experience which these works provide and to which we now turn: the experience of immersion. As mentioned in Chapter 1, immersion is a key characteristic in understanding the efficacy of intermedial, post-dramatic, and virtual theatre, as well as new media installation.

The audience experience of immersion cuts across all aspects of performance and especially in the visual arts practices of video installation and time-based art. Immersion can relate to experiences that are both mental and physical, so this chapter first clarifies the modes and means of both cognitive and sensory immersion. We then describe the feeling of immersion in multimedia performance in terms of Bolter and Grusin's concepts of 'immediacy' and 'hypermediacy'. As discussed in Chapter 3, these terms relate to the audience's level of immersion and their awareness of the process of mediation, and correspond to the two concepts of 'cognitive immersion' and 'sensory immersion'. The nature of immersion is then further explored in a series of case studies that highlight different aspects of the theoretical discussion. We argue that an emphasis on visceral immersion in multimedia performance is creating new modes of reception, embodiment, and contemplation.

The concept of immersion can be seen to operate in a range of art forms and has an extensive history in theatre practice. In their overview of immersive art, Packer and Jordan discuss a kind of dramatic immersion, which they describe as 'driven by a vision of the theatre in which the audience loses itself in the veracity of the drama, creating an immersive experience' (Packer and Jordan, 2001, p. xxxi). In this vision, immersion involves a process of disembodiment, with the audience projecting themselves into an alternative world. The perception that immersion in theatre involves 'losing' oneself in the drama, that is, an understanding of immersion as a purely cognitive faculty, is limited as it disregards the potential for a sensory, corporeal experience such as that which a spectator might have in ritual or contemporary performance art or perhaps even in post-dramatic theatre.

In this regard we can read Oliver Grau's assertion that 'staged media' are not appropriate to the study of immersion (2003, p. 14) as an exemplary case of the misrecognition and reduction of performance to dramatic theatre. Post-dramatic theatre and multimedia performance reject the portrayal of a discrete fictional universe and aim to create physically immersive environments that viscerally engage the participant. Immersion in multimedia performance manifests both as a cognitive and corporeal phenomenon and offers an experiential process that fuses information with materiality as the body is used as host organism to access text, image, and sound.

Cognitive immersion

Representational art aims to achieve audience immersion through the convincing depiction of a detailed reality, and theatre has traditionally been considered a site of immersion in terms of its capacity to create virtual reality. Marie-Laure Ryan, in her detailed examination of the poetics of immersion in digital literature, describes immersion as 'the experience through which a fictional world acquires the presence of an autonomous, language-independent reality populated with live human beings' (Ryan, 2001, p. 14). In traditional theatre, the staged fiction creates a discrete alternative world, and the house lights are blackened so as to help the audience forget their physical reality and become part of the fictional realm. The audience's 'suspension of disbelief' is their mindful attempt to make the level of the staging invisible and to transport themselves emotionally into the depicted drama.

> The practice of darkening the house was pioneered by **Richard Wagner**, who in 1876 darkened the Bayreuth Theatre. He also did away with anything that could distract the audience – such as foyers, boxes, plush furniture, and even aisles – to ensure their immersion in his operas.

In dramatic theatre, immersion manifests as a cognitive experience, with the spectators projecting themselves into an imagined world. For the audience members to achieve belief in the fiction, they must transcend the practical limitations of their physical presence. Elin Diamond refers to Bert O. States's reflection on the moment of 'opening' in which the 'lights dim' and the process begins which 'radically shifts the ground and conditions of our perception of the world' (Diamond, 1997, p. 143). This process of transportation into another world requires the audience to forget their immediate physical location and enter another through an active process of imagining. To be within this space, one cannot be separated from it by the boundaries of mediation, so here the audience's level of immersion may manifest as the degree to which the medium of communication fades into invisibility; the disappearance of mediation heightens the sense of immediacy and authenticity. Oliver Grau articulates this concept when he defines immersion as being when 'a work of art and image apparatus converge, or when the message and the medium form an almost inseparable unit' (Grau, 2002, p. 3).

This kind of cognitive immersion is reaching its artistic potential in the field of computer-generated virtual reality (VR). Michael Rush explains that in VR 'the still passive aspect of watching a screen is replaced by total immersion into a world whose reality exists contemporaneously with one's own' (Rush, 1999, p. 208). Three-dimensional worlds can be accessed via a head-mounted display so that the limitations of the interface are negligible and the medium seemingly disappears. This form of cognitive immersion still relies on the participant's 'suspension of disbelief'; while this suspension may be almost inescapable due to the level of detail in the illusion, the participant may still remain conscious of the fact that the fictional world will disappear when the headpiece is removed. Though computer-generated VR may apprehend the user's entire sensory system to facilitate transportation into the simulated environment, the immersion is still located in the mind; the material world is bypassed as the mind engages directly with the realm of information.

Virtual Reality was a buzz phrase of the 1990s; however, it has a longer history. The term was first used in the 1930s by Antonin Artaud to describe his Theatre of Cruelty. In the late 1960s, computer generated VR was pioneered by Ivan Sutherland, who produced a primitive head-mounted display. In the 1970s, computer graphics replaced video, and by 1979 the American air force were creating elaborate 'flight simulations'.

The media and literary theorist, Marie-Laure Ryan, has developed a typology of manifestations of immersion in art. She identifies three forms of immersion – spatial, temporal, and emotional – which are specifically associated with the narrative elements of setting, plot, and character (Ryan, 2001, p. 16). Immersion in literature and electronic media, as suggested by Ryan, is explicitly bound to representation, presupposing the audience's relationship to a fictional world (Ryan, 2001, p. 15). Ryan's arguments are married to the idea of immersion as a purely cognitive state involving a sense of transportation into a virtual reality. Ryan acknowledges that hers is 'a fundamentally mimetic concept of immersion' but argues that it 'remains faithful to the VR experience, since the purpose of VR technology is to connect the user to a simulated reality' (Ryan, 2001, p. 15). Because it is based on a concept of representation, Ryan's descriptions and typology of immersion may also apply to immersion in dramatic theatre. As with immersion in VR, immersion in dramatic theatre presupposes the audience's relationship to a fictional universe, which in theatre is not merely imagined but is brought into being via the stage. The fictional world is performed, which means that it is conveyed not only through the literary text, but also through the 'performance text'. This dimension of the 'performance text' opens up the potential for different manifestations of immersion in theatre, immersion that is not merely cognitive but corporeal.

Emphasis on the performance text over the literary text is the defining characteristic of post-dramatic theatre and most postmodern performance practice. Hans-Thies Lehmann makes the distinction between the '*linguistic text*, the *text of the staging and mise en scene*, and the *performance text*, and describes the performance text as constituted by, 'The mode of relationship of the performance to the spectators, the temporal and spatial situation, and the place and function of the theatrical process within the social field' (Lehmann, 2006, p. 85). According to Lehmann, the performance text in post-dramatic theatre 'overdetermines' both the linguistic text and the text of the *mise en scène*:

> [P]osdramatic theatre is not simply a new kind of text of staging- and even less a new type of theatre text, but rather a type of sign usage in the theatre that turns both of these levels of theatre upside down through the structurally changed quality of the performance text: it becomes more presence than representation, more shared than communicated experience, more process than product, more manifestation than signification, more energetic impulse than information. (Lehmann, 2006, p. 85)

When theatre becomes more presence than representation, more process than product, the site of immersion shifts. No longer is an imaginary world established into which the audience project themselves, but the focus is placed on their immediate reality and their physical presence within the space. The following section addresses the nature of immersion in the performance text as a sensory experience rather than a purely cognitive one.

Sensory immersion: The most ambitious project

Oliver Grau's *Virtual Art: From Illusion to Immersion* presents a definition of immersion as 'characterised by diminished distance and increased emotional involvement' and requiring

> the most exact adaptation of illusionary information to the physiological disposition of the human senses. The most ambitious project intends to appeal not only to the eyes but to all other senses so that the impression arises of being completely in an artificial world. (Grau, 2003, p. 13)

This statement of the aims of immersive art intends to engage the entire sensorium, an achievement which continues to elude artists in any field. Although Grau suggests that theatre and staged media leave the observer 'outside' the work and 'do not overwhelm the senses' (Grau, 2003, p. 14), his argument is based, as we have said, on a dramatic model. Post-dramatic theatre and performance, especially live art, also place the audience in the same location as the images, and appeal not only to the eyes, but to the entire sensory apparatus. As such, immersion in performance shares some similarities with the nature of immersion in 'ambitious' VR projects.

Performance and new media installation have the potential to immerse the audience sensually, not in an artificial world, but within the immediate, real space of the performance. In post-dramatic theatre, where there is no clearly demarcated alternative reality, there is still potential for the audience to experience a high degree of immersion, not immersion in an alternative world, but immersion in the spatial 'here and now', an enhanced state of being in relation to the surrounding space and responding to immediate stimuli. Here the concept of immersion relates to the audience members' level of sensorial stimulation at any one moment, and their awareness of being within the present of the performance and its capacity to engage them emotionally and corporeally (heart racing, hair-raising, sweating and fidgeting).

This distinction between cognitive and sensory immersion is of course not absolute but recognises two potential forms of audience immersion in both virtual realities and multimedia performance. Cognitive immersion in a fictional world may also involve sensorial engagement but is inherently based on a 'suspension of disbelief' while sensory immersion does not disengage cognitive functions but describes the enhancement of the participants' perception of their immediate 'here and now'. The difference between these modes of engagement can be envisaged spatially: the former involves 'plunging into' an alternative space, whereas in the latter the artwork may be viewed as reaching outside its frame to create a sensory experience that builds on the immediate moment, and that does not require the forgetting of the self nor, importantly, a sense of disembodiment. Cognitive immersion is an effect established through the presence of a fictional reality, whereas sensory immersion can be created through the corporeal and material dimension of performance. While the former requires the dislocation of materiality and involves immersion in an imagined space founded on patterns of textual information, the latter forges the material and virtual to create an embodied experience of pattern and presence within real space.

Throughout the twentieth century the theatrical avant-garde has attempted to create an immediate experience of immersion in real time and space. In the 1920s Bauhaus practitioner Laszlo Maholy-Nagy called for a Theatre of Totality to collapse the fourth-wall and immerse the audience in the same space as the performers. Antonin Artaud developed even more radical ideas in his Theatre of Cruelty which really only came to fruition in the Happenings of the 1960s, which attempted the ultimate breakdown of the audience and the performance. Allan Kaprow, in the style of Artaud, Cage, and others, argued that the 'line between art and life should be as fluid, and perhaps indistinct as possible' (Kaprow, 2001, p. 308). Indeed, he took this concept of integration further when he suggested that audiences should be eliminated altogether: 'All the elements – people, space, the particular materials and character of the environment, time – can in this way be integrated' (Kaprow, 2001, p. 313). With the dying of distance between the audience and the event, the greater is the degree of immersion.

Laslo Maholy-Nagy (1895–1946) – as a painter, sculptor, filmmaker, industrial designer, photographer, typographer, and theorist – embodied the different cultural media of the time. He envisaged a radical type of theatrical immersion in the Bauhaus Theatre: 'It is time to produce a kind of stage activity which will no longer permit the masses to be silent spectators, which will not only excite them inwardly but will let them *take hold and participate* – actually allow them to fuse with the action on the stage at the peak of cathartic ecstasy' (Maholy-Nagy, 2001, p. 25).

This form of audience immersion does not negate interaction, as can often be the case with cognitive immersion, where audience intervention disrupts the illusion of the autonomous fictional world. Rather, audience interaction can further enhance sensory immersion, with the audience included in the process of the performance but contributing to the performance text. Performance artist Marina Abramovic (see Chapter 4) frequently involved the audience as instigators of the performance, especially in some of her early works. In *Rhythm O* (1974), Abramovic provided 72 objects – including a pen, scissors, an axe, chains, and a loaded pistol – and invited the audience to use these objects on her body as they desired. Over the six hours of the performance, the audience become the force that acted upon her body to create the performance text. In such works, the audience are immersed within the world of the performance, because this world inhabits the same temporality and spatiality as their own. Though there is a specifically demarcated performance space, there is no attempt to transport the perceptual experience of the audience to an imagined different location. The audience's level of immersion is based on the degree to which they feel a part of the performance, and the intensity of their emotional and visceral engagement. In this case the immersion proved dangerous as some of the participants became too enthusiastic in their use of the weapons and the event was discontinued.

While it's true that live art has a high potential for achieving sensory immersion, this form of immersion is not restricted to the kind of unmediated performance style often associated with this genre. New media installations that do not attempt the representation of an alternative world order also have the potential to create sensory experience in real time. While representational film often attempts to transpose the viewer into the fictional world, for video artists such as Bill Viola 'the moving image becomes less about representation and instead is a medium that, through its temporal qualities, has a connection to human consciousness and perceptual experience' (Pettard, 2002). So it would seem that the difference between the nature of immersion experienced in representational art and the immersion experienced in non-representational art is not determined by media boundaries. Rather, the different forms are characterised by whether the audience is immersed in real time or projected into an alternative time frame.

Immediacy and hypermediacy

Different forms of immersive audience engagement can also be addressed using Bolter and Grusin's understanding of 'immediacy' and 'hypermediacy', as outlined in Chapter 4. Immediacy and hypermediacy relate to the audience's awareness of an object's 'mediatedness'; immediacy requires the transparency of the medium, whereas the aim of 'hypermediacy' is to remind the viewer of the medium, and so a hypermedium will draw attention to itself and its distinct form of mediation. There is an interesting correlation between the modes of cognitive and sensory immersion identified here, and the qualities of immediacy and hypermediacy as outlined by Bolter and Grusin. While these two sets of terms are by no means interchangeable, the language of immediacy and hypermediacy allows for the further exploration and articulation of both cognitive and sensory immersion in multimedia theatre.

Cognitive immersion, which is based on the presence of a fictional or virtual world, occurs as a result of the transparent mediation of content. Sensory immersion, on the other hand, can be enabled via hypermediacy. Bolter and Grusin explain the different effects of transparent media and hypermedia: 'Transparent digital applications seek to get to the real by bravely denying the fact of mediation; digital hypermedia seek the real by multiplying mediation so as to create a feeling of fullness, a satiety of experience, which can be taken as reality' (Bolter and Grusin, 2000, p. 53). In dramatic theatre, as in digital media, transparent mediation enables the audience to suspend disbelief and become cognitively immersed in the virtual environment. Alternatively, an emphasis on the specific form of mediation, which in theatre is the dimension of the performance text, enables sensory stimulation and a 'satiety of experience'.

Theatre is a 'hypermedium' with the potential to synthesise sensory perceptions. This essential quality of theatre makes it an important inclusion in a history of immersive art, and post-dramatic theatre continues to pioneer means of sensory and corporeal immersion. George Landow and Paul Delaney describe the ideal hypermedia system as 'engaging all five senses':

> Hypermedia takes us even closer to the complex interrelatedness of everyday consciousness; it extends hypertext by re-integrating our visual and auditory faculties into textual experience, linking graphic images, sound and video to verbal signs. Hypermedia seeks to approximate the way our waking minds always make a synthesis of information received from all five senses. Integrating or (re-integrating) touch, taste, and smell seems the inevitable consummation of the hypermedia concept. (2001, p. 212)

Just as computer-based hypermedial systems offer multi-sensory synthesis, so too theatre offers the potential for sensory saturation.

VJ-ing or VeeJay-ing specifically targets the audience's emotional and visceral engagement. The 'vj' is a live performance artist who 'mixes' various pre-existing video and live-feed clips, which are projected onto screens for the audience. Originally born in the New York nightclubs of the 1980s, particularly in the work of Merrill Aldighieri at the club 'Hurrah', VJ-ing is now common practice in many clubs and galleries. The vj (video jockey), like the dj (disk jockey), creates a live art experience around the spectators, who are immersed in music, images, and the communal space.

Whereas cognitive immersion creates 'immediacy', and manifests as immersion in the mediated fiction, sensory immersion is consistent with 'hypermediacy' and involves immersion in the media itself, the performance text. However, sensory immersion does not negate immediacy. Hypermedia, while anti-illusionary, still evoke immediate reactions and authentic emotional responses. Bolter and Grusin articulate this concept in relation to Modern painting, arguing that

> By diminishing or denying painting's representational function, they [Modernist painters] sought to achieve an immediacy of presentation not available to traditional painting, where immediacy had been achieved by concealing signs of mediation. ... Although the real and the representational are separated in modern art, modern art is not therefore less immediate. Modern painting achieves immediacy not by denying its mediation but acknowledging it. (Bolter and Grusin, 2000, p. 58)

Multimedia performance also acknowledges the circumstances of its own mediation and aims to achieve an immediacy of presentation. Elements of staging are not designed to represent an alternative reality, but are used to shape a certain experience of the immediate space and time of the performance. As such, sensory immersion manifests as a simultaneously immediate and hypermediate experience. The potential for the simultaneity of immediacy and hypermediacy is recognised by Bolter and Grusin. While these two logics are clearly divergent, hypermedia and transparent media are 'opposite manifestations of the same desire: the desire to get past the limits of representation and to achieve the real' (Bolter and Grusin, 2000, p. 53). As such, one form of mediation does not preclude the other, and both may exist within the same work in a combined attempt at stimulating authentic experience.

The CAVE

One example of where both immediacy and hypermediacy simultaneously exist within the same work is in the Cave Automative Virtual Environment (CAVE). Initially designed by media artist Daniel Sandin and engineer Thomas DeFanti, the CAVE projects a virtual environment onto the walls, floor, and ceiling of a small room of about three cubic metres. Packer and Jordan explain that the immersive experience of the CAVE was designed as an allusion to Plato's cave; 'its multiple screens and surround-sound audio evoke the metaphor of a shadowy representation of reality, suggesting how perception is always filtered through the mind's veil of illusion.' The space is simultaneously real and virtual since the actual architecture is overlayed by a virtual texture, so that the audience is physically immersed inside the work. As this 'architexture' is primarily virtual, the audience can potentially suspend disbelief and become cognitively transported into an alternative space, while physically remaining immersed in the 'here and now': 'the CAVE immersant does not experience dislocation and disembodiment, but rather is viscerally aware of his or her physical presence "on stage" amid the animated imager and orchestrated sound.'

Immersion cannot be measured within the design of the work, or in the intention of the creator, as it is a subjective experience that can be measured only by the participant. It is a form of awareness in the eye of the beholder, the degree of which reflects the intensity of their cognitive, emotional and sensory connection to both the content and the form of an artwork. The following case studies examine the nature of the immersive experience in relation to three very different examples of multimedia performance. The first two studies examine audience immersion within the gallery space, addressing two installational works that heighten the audience's perception of their immediate environment. Bill Viola's *Five Angels for the Millennium* is a new media installation that uses digital imagery to explore thematically the idea of immersion and create a space that saturates the senses. Janet Cardiff's sound installation *Forty Part Motet* uses different means of creating an immersive experience that is simultaneously cognitive and sensory. The third study examines immersion in the 'mixed-reality' created in Blast Theory's *Desert Rain*, which combines all previously mentioned modes of audience immersion.

Immersive video – Bill Viola's *Five Angels for the Millennium*

In *Five Angels for the Millennium* (2001) five individual video sequences show figures descending and ascending through water. The room and corridor are pitch black and the five large-scale projections are dispersed throughout the space. Ambient sound washes throughout the room, building into a rumble, and finally climaxing as a figure on one of the screens bursts through the water surface, leaving behind a trail of bubbles. The videos utilise Viola's trademark effect of extreme slow motion to manipulate the passage of time.

Viola describes the origins of the work:

Five Angels came out of a three day shoot in Long Beach that I had undertaken for several other projects. All I knew was that I wanted to film a man plunging into water, sinking down, below, out of frame – drowning. A year or so later, going through this old footage, I came across five shots of this figure and started working with them – intuitively and without a conscious plan. I became completely absorbed by this man sinking in water, and by the sonic and physical environment

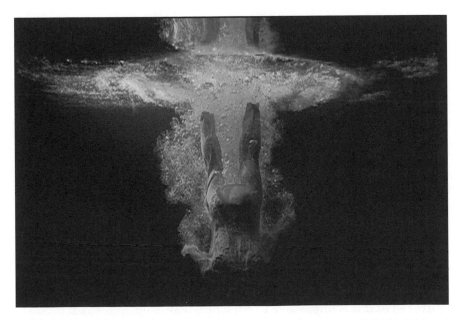

Figure 26 Bill Viola, *Five Angels for the Millennium* (2001). Video/sound installation. i. 'Departing Angel'. Performer: Josh Coxx. Photo: Kira Perov

Figure 27   Bill Viola, *Five Angels for the Millennium* (2001). Video/sound installation. ii. 'Birth Angel'. Performer: Josh Coxx. Photo: Kira Perov

I had in mind for the piece. When I showed the finished work to Kira [Perov], my partner, she pointed out something I had not realised until that moment: this was not a film of a drowning man. Somehow, I had unconsciously run time backwards in the five films, so all but one of the figures rush upwards and out of the water. I had inadvertently created images of ascension, from death to birth. (Viola, 2003)

In *Birth Angel* a figure shoots up through the water surface through the frame in a cold aqua light. *Ascending Angel* presents a figure bathed in blue light, face down as though drowned, but the water surface is beneath him and his body is aimed down towards it. In *Creation Angel*, the water surface is vertical as though we are looking down into a pool, and a figure with outstretched arms evokes an image of crucifixion. *Departing Angel* shows a figure floating into view, rushing through a swirl of bubbles and through the water's surface. And in *Fire Angel*, an eery blood-red glow backlights the outstretched figure. The line of the water surface forms a mirror so that it is impossible to tell which way is up and which is down. The figures hang suspended so close to the surface that perspective is obscured and the angle of the spectator's viewpoint is ambiguous.

There is no linear narrative and the space depicted in the imagery is not governed by familiar universal laws such as gravity and the progression

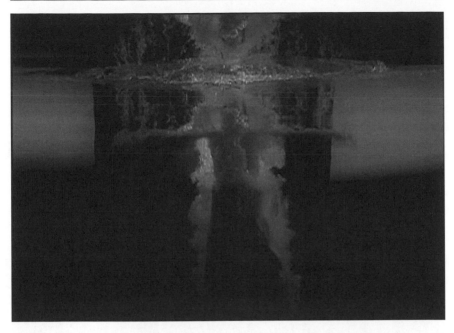

Figure 28 Bill Viola, *Five Angels for the Millennium* (2001). *Video/sound installation. iii. 'Fire Angel'.* Performer: Josh Coxx. Photo: Kira Perov

of time. The 'angels' are simultaneously human and inhuman. Tiffany Sutton comments 'that, since they are called "angels", these figures are, in fact, symbols, but of what? They are rendered nearly tangible, more than symbolic paintings can make them, anyway, for here they loom before one, life-sized, moving, and audible' (Sutton, 2005). The sensuality and totality of the figures' immersion is emphasised and the audience identify with their physicality. As such, the audience experience is one of immediacy. Yet there is also hypermediacy, for the unnatural colours and texture of the films, and the manipulation of temporality via editing effects, remain prominent and draw attention to the specific nature of the media in the work.

The spatial arrangement of the work facilitates both the audience's visceral immersion and their empathetic, immediate experience of the figures' immersion. The darkened gallery space is dominated by the scale of the imagery, and the fluctuating colour and flickering light patterns create a heightened awareness of the immediate environment. Sutton explains:

> In the darkened gallery, unlike a movie theatre, one becomes aware of the 360 degree moving arc of one's eyes, then head, then body, contemplating the relations between the projections; and it is difficult not to be aware of one's body, softly illuminated, in relation to the

Figure 29   Bill Viola, *Five Angels for the Millennium* (2001). Video/ sound installation. iv. 'Ascending Angel'. Performer: Josh Coxx. Photo: Kira Perov

> life-sized angle projections before one. Without question, one con-templates these figures and the work's meaning with proprioceptive awareness. (Sutton, 2005)

Sound washes over the body like liquid; this immediate sensation height-ens the audience's awareness of their own corporeality. Like undulat-ing, sparkling water, the sound ripples through the space, punctuated by escaping air pockets, by drips and the chirping of insects. The low-frequency soundscape slowly builds through sonic layering, until it reaches a crescendo at the same moment a figure leaps whale-like from or into the bubbling water. Once the spectator has succumbed to the rate and rhythm of the images, then they too are caught in the sensations of sur-prise, the shock as the body encounters a new element, the accompanying sense of renewal; we experience the waves, the pull and push of water.

While the climaxes occur seemingly at random, rhythm accumulates and time seems to slow. The effective use of pitch and punctuation com-bined with the hyper-slow motion of the video imagery encapsulates the viewer in another time zone, immersing them in a space of 'liquid

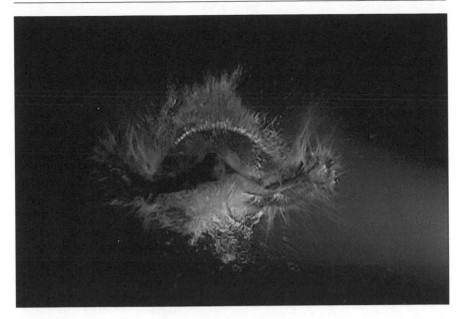

Figure 30   Bill Viola, *Five Angels for the Millennium* (2001). Video/ sound installation. v. 'Creation Angel'. Performer: Josh Coxx. Photo: Kira Perov

architecture' (Novak) constructed of rhythm and flow. Lucinda Ward explains:

> Viola insists on substantial investments of time: only by adjusting his or her schedule to the pace and subtlety of the works will the viewer share the power and complexity that is human emotion – in intimacy and silence, and on a far grander stage. (Ward, 2005)

As the viewer's inner rhythms and pace slowly adjust, their breathing slows and they are immersed in near-frozen time. Sensory immersion is perhaps intensified by the viewer's lack of agency, and the work requires the audience's complete submission to the aura of the imagery. Zsuzsanna Soboslay writes: 'There is no sense of the possibility of our making a contribution to the image, no way we can intervene and assist ... we are left merely to "share" or not in the experience of what is presented' (Soboslay, 2005). To 'share in the experience of what is presented' is to share the immersion of the figures and so engage with the work at an immediate level, and yet the spectators are not required to forget their physical selves and cognitively engage with an alternative world. Rather, the hypermediate work viscerally immerses the viewers in real space, heightening their corporeal awareness through sensory stimulation.

Robin Petterd, in his discussion of his new media project, *Liquid Sensations*, describes the heightened corporeal awareness experienced through immersion in water:

> when entering water the body seems to meld into the substance surrounding it ... Swimming is not an activity where the surroundings disappear, it is an activity where the environment is the focus, the corporeal sensations of it all-encompassing. It is also an environment in which swimmers are isolated and alone. They are unable to communicate normally and are separated from people outside the water and other swimmers in the water. (Petterd, 2002)

It is this same interaction between the environment of the artwork and the body of the audience member that creates the efficacy of *Five Angels for the Millennium*. When submerged in water we are both in control of our movements and at the mercy of the water, and the viewers of this installation are required to negotiate this same balance of control as they are both active and passive within the space. They are both immediately immersed and hypermediately aware of their immersion.

A pioneer in the field of film and video art, Bill Viola uses sound and image to explore universal themes of birth, death, memory and the unconscious. As a child of ten Viola had a near death-by-drowning experience and images of submergence and water, often employed in religious symbolism on both a ritual level (Christianity) and metaphysical level (Hinduism), are repeated in many of his works, such as *The Passing* (1991), *Nantes Triptych* (1992), *Deserts* (1994), *Stations* (1994), *The Messenger* (1994), *The Crossing* (1996) and *Five Angels for the Millennium* (2001). These works depict the slow dynamic of immersion and emergence, of birth, death and reawakening, of climax and renewal, of resurrection. For Viola, birth and death 'are mysteries in the truest sense of the word, not meant to be solved, but experienced and inhabited' (Tate online).

The imagery of five submerged and swimming bodies provides a visual illustration of the various passages and conditions of perception associated with sensory immersion. The figures' immersion, while complete, remains dynamic. The videos emphasise the idea of immersion as *movement* through a very particular environment. This world apprehends the senses entirely, altering them, assaulting them. The figures are suspended, floating as the water buoys them up and washes over them. Movement into further immersion is achieved through the increase of depth. At a certain point, immersion must reach its extreme and result in either the drowning of the body as it is claimed by the liquid world or the emergence of the body from the water. This idea of 'emergence' is at the heart of Viola's work (and is the title of one of the works in the *The Passions* series). The 'angels' are continually passing through the film of the water surface, entering and exiting the other realm. They are bound in these cycles of entrance and emergence. Implicitly suggested is the idea of transition, the process of altering states, with immersion being the osmotic movement from one state to another.

As the video sequences do not show the figures in a static place of departure or place of arrival, it is the process of transition that is emphasised. We see the process of potential transformation that occurs as one 'passes through' something; the allusion to the process of purification associated with water immersion is apparent. The saturation of the senses offers the potential to experience a kind of transcendence, where one is both immersed in the material world whilst simultaneously exceeding it. Like the figures in the videos, the audience too may potentially emerge from its immersion, having experienced some kind of transportation. Immersive multimedia works offer a kind of sensory bath in which the audience are utterly submerged and at the mercy of the pace and rhythm of the work. Sensory perception and immersion in Viola's artwork are intended to become a conduit to self-awareness, clarity, and knowledge.

Immersive audio – Janet Cardiff's *40 Part Motet*

This installation also creates an immersive experience that is simultaneously cognitive and sensory, and which also aims to provide the audience with a transformational experience via immersion. This example is different in that it creates immersion not through visual imagery, but solely through the use of digital sound.

Janet Cardiff's new media installation *40 Part Motet* remediates the live performer and exhibits the simultaneous existence of both immediacy and hypermediacy. In this work, however, the human performer is re-formed not as a visible pattern, but as an aural presence. *40 Part Motet* is installed in its own separate gallery. Around the periphery of the room, 40 individual six-foot-high speakers face inwards, surrounding the spectator from every angle. From these speakers come forty individual voices performing the breathtakingly beautiful 'Spem in Alium' composed by Thomas Tallis during the sixteenth century. It is a magnificently ethereal

Renaissance arrangement and its harmonies resonate around the walls of the spacious room, creating an immersive sound chamber that expands the space and encompasses the listener.

Cardiff recorded the Salisbury Cathedral Choir performing in Sussex, England, with each chorister's voice individually recorded onto a separate track and then played back through a separate speaker. The spectators may enter the space at any time as the work is looped, but it has a discernable 'beginning' and 'end'. At the beginning of the work we hear the choir members chatting and warming up their voices as they prepare for their performance. The speakers are all arranged at ear-height and as the spectator moves from one to the other they hear the individual hums and whispers of each chorister. Then, suddenly and loudly, the singing begins, and is shockingly majestic. It is so overwhelming, so sublime that the spectator may find themselves momentarily in need of a seat.

On sitting, the spectator is able to experience all the reverberation and resonance of a cathedral hall packed into the room around them. All 40 individual speakers are aimed at the centrally positioned seats and surround them completely. While Tallis's polyphony is magical, there is an almost threatening intensity as if the choir is closing in towards the middle of the space. But the work is created in such a way that at times certain voices are quiet, so that the body of sound moves in waves through the room, pushing out the boundary of the space and thickening the air. Justin Davidson suggests that 'One way to experience the 14 minute piece is to plant yourself on the bench at the centre of the room and let those motley points of vocal tone resolve into a luminous, reverberant cloud' (Davidson, 2006). If you move around the room, the various levels of counterpoint playfully sparkle and pulse as you move past.

Davidson illustrates: 'the motet changes hue with each step. It's like inhabiting a kaleidoscope' (Davidson, 2006). The experience of the work becomes just as much an experience of spatial immersion as sound. Robin Petterd states that 'Hearing is a tactile sense and sounds are spatial' (Petterd, 2002). He quotes Sean Cubitt, who, when discussing sound design for the moving image, states 'Sound is physical: it can only be heard. It occupies, and in occupying it creates spaces ... skin produces and receives sound; it is the intimacy of body on body' (Cubitt in Petterd, 2002). In *40 Part Motet* the sound becomes syrupy and amplifies the proprioceptive relation between the body and the room.

However, if the spectator tunes out of the overall composition and listens instead to the individual speakers, a somewhat different experience is available. The balance of harmony breaks down as individual voices become dominant and each is revealed as possessing an individual identity. The voices begin to form a kind of spectral presence. Placing your head near a speaker creates the eerie sensation that you are close to the face of the singer; you hear their breath and feel the effort of their projection. In this way, the digital music becomes more than an experience of sonic quality but the product of human voice and persona. As the spectator is less aware of the mediation, the singer is endowed with an immediate presence, and a sense of intimacy develops. This creates an almost uncanny experience, for there is no evidence of this presence and the spectators can find themselves communing with a large, black speaker box. The role of the speakers as technologies of mediation is explicit and to this effect the work develops a level of hypermediacy.

Yet immersion in the music is inescapable. The tides of sound ebb and flow throughout the room and create a fluid framework that dissolves and coagulates as one moves through it. While music by its very nature is always mediated, the immediacy of sound is undeniable. That the mediation here is recorded and replayed makes the music no less immersive or immediate. And with your eyes closed there is no evidence of technological mediation. It brings to light issues of authorship; can we really attribute this work as Cardiff's creation, or are we listening to the recorded mastery of Tallis as we would any other recording played on a domestic surround-sound system? If the music is viewed as defining the frame of the work, and the work is mediated by the speakers, then this work of art is immediate and persuasively real. Mediated by the staged event, however, the work is clearly constructed and artificially produced; it is hypermediate.

Andy Lavender, in his discussion of filmic imagery within the theatrical frame, suggests that the mediated imagery is not self-sufficient but 'contingent upon other frameworks – notably the live event, the moment of performance, the three-dimensional scenic space and the theatrical gaze' (Lavender, 2006, p. 57). In *40 Part Motet*, this relation is inverted so that we experience the music content as contingent upon its existence within the framework of its mediation and its presentation within the space. While the music may be mediated, and this mediation may be mostly transparent, the music also exists in the time–space continuum of the performance. Here the medium itself is 'staged'.

The effect of this staging is to create a space in which a fictional world and material reality exist simultaneously; the audience are sensorily immersed in real space, and are also cognitively projected into an imaginary world. At one level, the audience experience spatial immersion within the soundscape. At a more imaginative level, they experience the presence of the choir, the referent, the object of remediation. There is also the potential for the audience to access cognitively the original renaissance context; the style of the music has ritualistic incantations and the music

Figure 31   *The Forty Part Motet* (2001), Janet Cardiff. Photo: Atsushi Nakamichi/Nacása & Partners Inc. Courtesy of the Fondation d'entreprise Hermès, 2009. Courtesy the artists, Galerie Barbara Weiss, Berlin and Luhring Augustine, New York

kindles the aura of a cathedral interior. This work uses both immediacy and hypermediacy to allow the audience to experience immersion at many levels. The audience is simultaneously immersed in the virtual realm of the absent choir and aurally, spatially, and corporeally immersed in the immediate present. The use of digital technology does not efface the performance but intensifies it in its remediation.

Janet Cardiff is a Canadian audio-artist who first became famous for her 'audio walks' in 1995. She has continued to create these walks, often in collaboration with her partner, George Bures Miller. These walks are similar in style to an 'audio-guide' as they instruct the listener to navigate a space. Cardiff's walks also offer a layered soundscape that is blanketed over the actual world, creating a new world for the listener. Her work often conjures ghost-like presences that cohabit the spaces she creates alongside the audience.

Desert Rain and the 'Desert of the Real': Composite reality and spatial immersion

The production *Desert Rain* by the British multimedia theatre company, Blast Theory, produced in collaboration with Nottingham University's 'Mixed Reality Laboratory', originally premiered in 1999. It is based on the events of the first Gulf War. It explores the implications of society's reliance on the technologies of representation to access the real and offers a disturbing engagement with understandings of warfare in contemporary society. The key inspiration for the work was Baudrillard's assertion that the Gulf War did not actually take place as it was a virtual event. The company cites Paul Patton's observations (about Baudrillard's speculations) that

> while televisual information claims to provide immediate access to real events, in fact what it does is produce information that stands in for the real.... As consumers of mass media, we never experience the bare material event but only the informational coating which renders it 'sticky and unintelligible' like the oil-soaked sea bird. (www. blasttheory.co.uk)

According to the Blast Theory web pages, *Desert Rain* was designed to examine the significance of the simulacra 'in informing our view of the relationship of the real to the virtual ... especially in its assertion that the virtual has a daily presence in our lives' (www.blasttheory.co.uk).

In experiencing *Desert Rain*, the participants are immersed in both the physical and the mediated dimensions with the agency to interact with both, and as such the work facilitates both cognitive and sensory immersion. The work is part game, part installation, part performance and constructs a series of immersive hyperrealities which the audience are invited to navigate. Six audience members at a time are sent on a mission in a virtual world. They enter individual pod-like spaces and, standing on a moveable footplate, navigate through a world of deserts, motels, and underground bunkers that is projected onto a wall of water droplets. After successfully navigating the virtual world, participants are led through the wall of water spray, over a giant sand dune, and into the final room of the production, where imagery depicting a generic hotel room is projected on the blank walls. In this hotel room each audience member enters a card into a terminal and watches a video presentation by their target from the previous virtual world on a television screen. The targets – two soldiers, a journalist, a peace worker, an actor, and a tourist – have each been affected by the Gulf War in some way. They talk about their relationship to the events, their proximity to them and how 'real' it felt. On leaving, the participants collect their belongings and, at a later point, discover a small box concealed in their coat or bag containing approximately 100,000 grains of sand and a quotation from Colin Powell in which he states that the number of Iraqis killed 'is not a number that interests him'.

Desert Rain focuses on political events that for most people, apart from the protagonists themselves, were accessed only through the mass media image. *Desert Rain* addresses the new ways in which the simulated and the real are blurred and, 'in particular, the role of the mass media in distorting our appraisal of the world beyond our own personal experience' (www.blasttheory.co.uk). In *Desert Rain* the participants are immersed in a composite reality, constructed of both real and virtual elements. They are given the agency to engage with the simulated world and with the mediatised version of others within this space. Within the first world projected onto the wall of water spray, the immediately real (the live performers, the wall of water, and the participants) merges with the virtual to explore the questionable 'realness' of historical events.

In *Desert Rain* the participant immersion creates a fusion of the real and the virtual, for both frameworks form a part of the inhabited space. The virtual world is projected onto something tangible and permeable in the wall of water. The participants are able to communicate with one another through headphones and mouthpieces and these real voices blend into the virtual environment, though all voices are, of course, 'digitalised' and so work as another element in the overall hypermedia system. In the final room of the production, projected imagery on the walls makes the space look like a real hotel room, though it is an illusion; the material space in which we are located develops familiarity only through the mediated information. This becomes significant when the characters on the video appear to be sitting in the same hotel room that is projected around us. Hypermediacy is established as we become aware of our assumption that the video is transmitting the real, re-presenting a real space, real people, when in reality the video content is perhaps just as much a constructed illusion as the hotel room we are standing in.

Overall, however, Blast Theory creates a world of illusion and does not readily reveal the mechanics of production. The work is primarily immediate, and this illusory world does bear some resemblance to the symbolic realm presented through classical mimesis. The process of transportation into another world is manifest in *Desert Rain* but it differs from classical mimesis, as the virtual worlds of the digital projections do not represent an alternative time-frame but offer an openly structured space to be experienced in the immediate temporality of the audience. In *Desert Rain*, by creating the world of illusion out of both real and virtual elements, the participant's experience of the world is grounded in real-time, intrinsically focused on the absorption of the now.

The experience for the participants is deliberately disorienting. Whereas the virtual world exists only as information, the participant is physically connected to it through the moveable footplate and the headphones that become mediated extensions of their physical boundary. The virtual reality has an impact on the participants as though 'real', creating physical and emotional reactions. Giannachi summarises:

> The participants were taken through a journey, from the real to the virtual and then back again, only to find out that what appeared as virtual could in fact be real and hence also leave a real trace (of sand) in the viewer's lives. Likewise, what appeared to be real was mainly performed and thus, in other words, simulated. (Giannachi, 2004, p. 119)

Blast Theory creates facilitative space shared by the performers and audience in which the processes of the production take place in real time. Within this space, the live and the mediated, the real and the virtual are not clearly demarcated and, although the contrast of the real and the fictional has thematic significance within the works, the works remain inherently intermedial, for this thematic significance is distributed across

Figure 32 *Desert Rain* (1999) © Blast Theory. *Desert Rain* is a collaboration between Blast Theory and The Mixed Reality Lab, University of Nottingham

all available communication systems and is visually, aurally, and viscerally received by the audience. The organisation of communication systems promotes non-hierarchical contiguity and although traditional text is utilised to different degrees, it is but one of many elements within the overall intermedial system and develops significance only in relation to other media and modes of communication. Indeed, meaning is derived individually, through engagement with the textual and physical landscape.

This landscape utilises image, sound, movement, and dialogue to create rhythms and resonances that rebound within the performance space and have an affective impact on the participants as they navigate their way through the space. In the projected virtual world the natural rhythm of the falling rain contrasts with computer-generated sound rhythms to create a layered soundscape that is both natural and artificial, immersing the players in the composite reality. This rhythmic immersion is continued through the use of colour and the patterns of light that surround the individual player, first coming through the rain curtain and then projected onto it, creating a science-fiction atmosphere that enhances the sense of space as being immediately real and simultaneously 'other'. The repetition of images and statistics develops more fractured rhythms, mirroring the fractured landscape of the virtual Iraq and confronting the players with fragments of war.

Reflection

These devices are, of course, operating upon the spectator's or participant's entire sensorium. In these examples of intermedial performance, all modes of communication and representation, both live and mediated, are invoking rhythm, repetition, movement, and stillness to involve the audience in the co-creation of meaning and to create immediate immersion. Within the performance space there is no demarcation between those elements that are 'actual' and those that are 'virtual' and the facilitators utilise both real and the fictional components to realise a sensory journey in real time. The live and the mediated are fused, received simultaneously as merged elements of a larger whole. They are connected through the audience's experience, and it is this experience that is the focus of the works addressed. Spectators are continually reminded of their own presence, and the power of these works lies in the capacity of the spectator to live in, live through, and experience the work, rather than simply witness a performance.

Yet the feeling of immersion is a subjective process, so it is difficult to generalise about the nature of immersive experience. While all immersion must be considered spatial, it is more than mere topographical navigation.

And while immersion may involve empathy and emotion, it is more than mere escapism. Immersion is primarily a state of sensory saturation, yet it is more than physical bombardment. In the works discussed here, immersion is both embodied and mindful.

Tiffany Sutton, in her discussion of what she calls 'video environments', suggests the existence of an 'immersive mode of contemplation'; the video environment, she says, 'gives rise to a form of contemplation – one involving *immersion* – that is, if not unique to this genre, certainly demonstrated by it' (Sutton, 2005). She suggests this form of contemplation is enabled when video art is placed in the context of the 'museum effect', so that the everyday is made unfamiliar and experienced as separate and special. In describing this immersive mode of thought, she claims:

> we find what Descartes could not have considered, contemplation without bodily dissociation, contemplation that is possible only in an immersive state; immersion, again, not in the sense of drowning out the senses in pure thought about thought ... nor in the sense of looking at something through something else ... but rather in the sense of being inside the chamber of the camera obscura experiencing the ontological difference between the image on the far wall and all else that the chamber contains, including one's bodily self. (Sutton, 2005)

In works such as Viola's video installations and Cardiff's sound installations the audience can experience, as Sutton describes it, contemplation through embodied reception. In Viola's video installation, the audience's sense of being 'within' the work is not achieved through a process of mental projection by which the disembodied mind escapes into the world of the imagery, but through the recognition that the video imagery unfolds as a phenomenon within the real world. The gallery space becomes 'like the chamber of the camera obscura' within which the audience experience a sense of being in a 'proximal relation' (Springgay, 2002, p. 34, discussed in Chapter 1) to the image, and are conscious of their physical relationship with the space around them. Through their encounter with the immateriality of the image, the audience are prompted to contemplate the ontology of the body and the subjectivity of their sensory awareness. Contemplation evoked by these works is an immersive, embodied process of intuitive reflection.

Conclusion

As more is both demanded and offered by the artwork, the audience members are no longer allowed the distance space of mere contemplation and instead experience a kind of oppressive immersion that may or may not lead to contemplation, but which offers a reflexive experience that can be distinguished from more familiar modes of reception and spectatorship. The facilitation of immersion treads a fine ethical line between efficacy and tyranny, and all immersion plays with dynamics of control, for immersion is a totality. Yet it may be argued that such viscerally immersive works are no less ethical than monologic drama, which aims to capture the mind in an illusion and predetermines meaning.

The examples of multimedia performance examined in this chapter illustrate how immersion in multimedia environments can be addressed in terms of cognitive and sensory engagement, and in relation to immediacy and hypermediacy. In these works, the modes of hypermediacy and immediacy are simultaneously evoked to create sensory immersion in real time and space. Sensory immersion is a state of being in which one develops an awareness of the self through proximal experience of the other, osmotically absorbing and intuitively responding while simultaneously reflecting on this process. The embodied reception initiated by these works presents an ideal model for the relationship of humans to technology and digital media, where information does not subjugate materiality, but where the synthesis of body and mind, of presence and pattern, produces new modes of awareness, creativity, and contemplation.

Further reading

Oliver Grau's *Virtual Art: From Illusion to Immersion* (2003) provides a history of immersive art and investigates the relationship between the artist, the image, and the viewer in light of digital technologies. He does not address theatre or performance art, but his discussion of the position of the spectator holds relevance for our field. We reference Bolter and Grusin's *Remediation* a number of times here, and recommend you visit the original source text for further explanation and examples. Marie-Laure Ryan's book *Narrative as Virtual Reality: Immersion and Interactivity in Literature and Electronic Media* (2001) directly explores the connections between immersion in virtual worlds and immersion in theatre, and Frank Popper's book *From Technological to Virtual Art* (2007), while focusing on the developments of immersive, interactive new media art, offers thought-provoking philosophy about the relationship of humans and technology.

Chapter 8

Forms of Interactivity in Performative Spaces

Characteristics of multimedia aesthetics such as intermediality and immersion are not discrete components of multimedial systems but the complex of effects resulting from the negotiation between a participant and the configuration of elements within the work. This negotiation between work and participant is the basis of interactivity, and is therefore a key to understanding as well as experiencing the dynamics of multimedia performance.

Experimental multimedia explorations of performance going back to the Futurists foreground a constant process and offer themselves as unfinished, with the threads of meaning yet to be woven and the shape of the form yet to be drawn. In this type of performance it falls to the spectator to enter into a conversation with the work and, in doing so, complete it, forming a continually evolving complex system. Interactivity in this sense is not a new phenomenon, but there are different degrees and modes of interactivity. As soon as an audience member has the agency to alter the work or elicit a reaction to its assertions, the relationship between the viewer and the work can be classified as interactive.

This chapter situates the discussion of interactivity in contemporary multimedia performance and particularly in relation to the production of new performative spaces where a combination of virtual and real worlds is developed. The various works examined in this chapter move away from the passive audience model and towards a complex and dynamic relational model. These works transform notions of space, overlaying the everyday with the virtual and creating 'mixed realities'. As an audience encounters these 'liquid architectures' (Novak) we find new modes of spectatorship in which a relationship to the space is performed as spectators navigate the hybrid terrain. In performances manifesting more complex digital effects, the possibility is enhanced for the event to be hacked and remixed in a more extreme form of interactive engagement.

153

Steve Dixon describes four categories of interactivity organised in ascending order of complexity: navigation; participation; conversation, and collaboration. Taking his taxonomy as a point of departure, we begin with the most basic form of audience interactivity in performance, which occurs when spectators are invited to conduct their own navigation of the object or environment, individually controlling their speed and path through or around the work. This base-level navigation can often provide the basis for more sophisticated forms of interaction, and is established when the boundary between the space of the performance and the exterior space of the audience becomes fluid. This new physical relationship with the object, performance environment, or performers then has an impact on an audience member's affective or interpretive engagement with a work.

Navigation

Navigation suggests movement through space, and the viewer's degree of control over their navigation will depend on the space they are invited to traverse. For example, a statue or sculpture in a public garden allows the viewer to navigate the space around the object, controlling their perspective of the work by altering their speed and proximity to it. If the garden becomes the artwork, rather than the statue, the audience have actually entered into the work and are intimately navigating its interior space. Following this example, if the viewer is allowed to touch the sculpture, the space between the viewer and the object has dissolved; however, the viewer's sensory exploration of the object may still be regarded as 'navigation'. They are navigating the spatial surface of the object, exploring its shape and texture. This example highlights how visual perspective is not a necessary precondition of navigation, and as long as there is movement through space, there is navigation. Of course, for the relationship of the viewer to remain purely navigational they must not have an impact upon the work itself. If the work reacts to the viewer's presence in any way, then an interactive relationship between the viewer and the work is established. Navigation offers agency to the audience only in the form of control over movement and direction.

Many performance art and new media installations are based on a model of the museum or gallery 'exhibit', allowing the audience to negotiate their physical relationship to the work and hence construct their visual perspective. Multi-screen video installations such as those originally created by Nam June Paik and more recently by artists such as Gary Hill and Bill Viola do not allow audiences to control that which is being projected, but they do enable the viewer to direct their own path of spatial navigation. In Viola's installation *Stations* (1994), images of bodies suspended in and moving through water are projected onto vertical screens that reflect the image down onto other perpendicular pieces of granite lying beneath each screen. The position of the spectator in the surrounding space will dramatically alter their perception as their focus moves between single screens, and to the screens as a unified work.

Gary Hill (born 1951), an American artist, is one of the pioneers of video art. His works are renowned for their poetic exploration of the self and 'other', such as his immersive work, *Tall Ships* (1992). Another large-scale work, *Viewer*, (1996) features life-size video portraits of around 20 labourers silently gazing out at the other 'viewers', creating a degree zero interactive environment in which spectators choose which portraits to interact with. His work also makes extensive use of his own body, usually performing basic tasks, as content, but the work remains highly conceptual.

This type of physical navigation is also reflected in computer-generated environments. For instance, in computer gaming the user can enter an artificial environment or 'world' through which they are able to direct themselves and make their path. In some cases these environments exist primarily as a display for navigation or as an arena within which user-to-user interaction can occur. Examples of such navigable virtual environments include virtual museums and online galleries as well as some more basic 'chase-based' computer games. These offer a virtual space that allows the user to control their perspective, speed, and navigational path.

A particular instance of navigation of virtual space in a live context is presented in the new media installation, *Eavesdrop* (2004), created by Jeffrey Shaw and David Pledger and discussed in earlier chapters. In this work the spectators enter into a space surrounded by a 360-degree film screen. An individual user stands on a podium and is able to direct the path of the projection, so that they effectively navigate the world presented on the screen for the entire audience. The individual user's navigation constructs the choices for all spectators and in this way it becomes a performance in its own right.

The navigation of virtual environments adds an extra element of viewer activity, for the user must physically manipulate technological tools that facilitate navigation (the podium in *Eavesdrop*; the mouse, keyboard or joystick in computer-based worlds). Other than in the specific case of head-mounted VR displays, there is distance between the

Figure 33   *Eavesdrop* 2004, Jeffrey Shaw and David Pledger

user and the navigable world, and the navigation is mediated through the use of technology. This raises the question of whether clicking a button to open a virtual door or pushing a joystick to 'zoom in' constitutes a physically interactive relationship. Insofar as the programme reacts to the commands of the user, the system manifests a degree of interactivity. Whatever the degree, we can say that this process of audience engagement is primarily navigational.

The action of hyperlinking through cyberspace may also be viewed as a navigational process. The information being accessed already exists in network structures awaiting user access. It is a kind of 'blind navigation' where the user cannot see the consequences of selection prior to making a choice. The links in a hypertext exist independently of the users' actions, and the user may select any number of paths through given information, ignoring some possible avenues and weaving their way relatively blindly through other maze-like paths.

While the basic principle of the hypertext is navigation, there is also an added degree of interaction established as soon as the agent, object or environment responds to the presence of the user. Despite the fact that the object or environment may not have agency of its own with which to directly influence the user, as soon as it reacts to the user's influence, interaction is established, for even a passive reaction on behalf of the environment will reciprocally still affect the user by offering a different image, new information, or an alternative perspective.

Response-based interaction

The term 'response-based interaction' can be used to describe interaction where the audience has agency and engages in a process of action–reaction with a responsive environment, object, or agent. As the 'reactor' does not itself have agency, its reactions are either completely passive, as in the case of a malleable object or environment, or are pre-programmed, such as interactive new media artworks. Unlike hot media such as film, media capable of responsive interaction enable the user to participate fully in the creation of media content and to control the direction and pace of their engagement with the presented information. Marshall explains:

> In new media such as the web, the individual is asked to choose the link and thereby be part of the process of making his media form. This may seem minor, but the changed relationship to media is very significant and has repercussions throughout all cultural industries and into the wider dimensions of contemporary culture. This action of choosing from a menu of choices, the very tactile dimension of clicking on a mouse, shifts our default media consumption from that provided for us to one that is fabricated by us. (2004, p. 25)

New media culture positions the user as an active participant and potentially a co-producer of the mediated experience. However, many examples of 'interactive' contemporary art and performance function via responsive interaction, and this system is not necessarily limited to the domain of new media. An example of response-based interaction is articulated in Ross Gibson's vision of the 'changescape', which describes a model of environmental art. Gibson defines 'changescapes' as

> aesthetic systems that are built purposefully to intensify our experience and to enhance our understanding of the complex dynamics that are at play when our natural, social and psychological domains commingle and alter each other. (Gibson, 2005, p. 200)

A changescape is dynamic and immersive. It is an 'interactive ecology' (Murphie, 2001, p. 203) designed to awaken sensory perception and an awareness of the 'paradoxically unstable "status" of the world' (Gibson,

2005, p. 203). An example used by Gibson to explain this concept is that of the aquarium. Within the aquarium a complex system of natural forces is at work which are influenced and manipulated by the spectator in order to achieve a desired aesthetic.

Gibson describes the artist David Rokeby as one of the 'canniest' practitioners working with 'changescapes'. In Rokeby's work *Silicon Remembers Carbon*, (first presented in 1993–5 and redesigned in 2000) a large video image is projected downwards onto a bed of sand, which forms the floor of the installation. The projection is affected by the reflection of the viewers as they look down on it, with layers of computer-generated imagery merging with the real shadows and reflections to create a 'live virtual shadow'. Rokeby describes the installation as

> some sort of fake reflecting pool, an inversion of Narcissus's experience. Whereas Narcissus's tragedy is that he cannot recognise himself in his reflection, the visitors to the space would find themselves identifying with shadows and distorted reflections that had only circumstantial relation to them. (Rokeby, http://homepage.mac.com)

The viewer's presence triggers reactions in the receptive surface and as the viewer alters the work, they co-create the media content.

Figure 34   *Silicon Remembers Carbon* (1992–5 and 2000), David Rokeby

In this way Rokeby attempts to develop a better understanding of complexity through artistic interaction, with the actions of the participant 'bringing new elements into the componentry' and the artwork 'always becoming something other than it was a moment ago' (Gibson, 2005, p. 204). Rokeby's works are a pertinent example of responsive interaction and create an extremely intimate relationship between the work and the viewer. The work's development is contingent on the physical involvement of the spectator, and the boundary between the viewer and the work is dissolved. Gibson's discussion of these interactive landscapes illustrate that response-based interaction, though not the most complex manifestation of interactivity, can still form a creative system in which the work is constantly evolving.

Australian sculptor Geoffrey Drake-Brockman created an unusual example of a responsive artwork functioning as an 'interactive environment'. *Floribots* (2005) is a play on 'flowerpots' which presents 128 computer-controlled robot origami flowers that cover 35 metres of gallery space and react as a collective organism to the movements of the viewers. Each mechanical flower is able telescopically to 'grow' up to a metre high and fold out from its original bud-state into an open bloom, then shrink and retract into its dormant state. The behaviour of the flowerbed senses and reflects the behaviour and movement of the viewer, flowing from chaotic movement to organised wave-like patterns, with the 'hive mind' of the Floribot controlling the transition between these states. The Floribots function only in response to the actions of the viewer; once the viewer has become familiar with the programmed responses of the Floribot-bed, they are able to choreograph complex movement sequences. It becomes a performance, and as the viewer learns the rules of engagement and their skill level increases, their level of creative interaction becomes more sophisticated.

A different manifestation of response-based interaction can be seen between the performer and the technology in Stelarc's *Exoskeleton*, a six-legged, pneumatically powered walking machine. Stelarc is positioned on a rotating platform with his upper body clad in an 'exoskeleton' that reads his movements. His arms choreograph the movement of his six prosthetic limbs, performing a cyborg dance to accompanying mechanical sounds. Here the human and machine form a 'complex system' of action and response, of conversation through movement. While this example of

Figure 35   *EXOSKELETON,* Cankarjev Dom, Ljubljana 2003. Photographer: Igor Skafar. STELARC

response-based interaction occurs between the performer and technology rather than the audience and the artwork, the process of action and reaction remains.

How interactive is interactive drama?

The field of 'interactive drama' offers another more complicated mode of responsive interaction. The web-based drama, as articulated by Janet Murray's description of the 'cyberdrama', varies in its level of openness and has the possibility of offering 'complex' interaction in the form of human–human (or character to character) interaction. However, Christy Dena states in her article 'Elements of "interactive drama": Behind the Virtual Curtain of "Jupiter Green"' that, '(a)lthough there are works that react to the input of users, none of them have outcomes that are not pre-scripted in some sense' (Dena, 2005). This, of course, restricts interaction to a process of user action–computer reaction, and so it is not 'complex' interaction but response-based.

In the interactive drama *Jupiter Green* discussed by Dena, the audience spy on five characters as they go about their melodramatic everyday lives in an apartment block called 'Jupiter Green'. The user activity is limited to navigation of the fictional environment with occasional hyperlinking to access information enclosed within the space, such as clicking to 'unlock' and enter into a character's personal diary. There are also occasional instances of responsive interaction that occur when, for example, a user can email a character in the drama and receive a reply. Dena describes how this process inadvertently encouraged her to believe that her actions could influence the plot of the drama, and she describes the frustration of realising that 'none of what was said had any influence on the characters and plot' (Dena, 2005). The emailed responses are effectively pre-scripted, providing generic 'answers' to the user's specific questions.

There is certainly the possibility for a narrative to develop between characters and for the users to produce a story collaboratively. However, most current hypertext-based interactive dramas do not produce collaboratively authored stories. Dena refers to Joseph Tabbi, who highlights this difference: 'Hypertext readers might enrich the work by contributing to it new content, but as yet their activity is for the most part limited to making choices about how to *operate* the text-selecting narrative pathways' (Tabbi in Dena, 2005). This description forces us back to the activity of 'navigation' and the issue of whether hypertext navigation can be considered 'interactive'.

> Unsurprisingly, social networking sites such as Facebook and Bebo have become a forum for participatory stories. Bebo commissioned three interactive dramas over six months in 2007 – *Kate Modern*, *Sophia's Diary* and *The Gap Year* –, that included video clips and 'chat' on Youtube and Myspace: 'Each format revolves around original video content but also features a variety of interactive elements. Casting, for example, is conducted among Bebo users with shortlisted participants in each project voted on by the rest of the community. For the two interactive dramas, storylines and characters have been discussed with Bebo users before the first piece of video was shot while audience feedback shapes how plots develop and characters evolve' (Carter, 2007).

Similarly to web-based interactive dramas, live interactive dramas offer viewers the opportunity to navigate through a fictional environment and witness an unfolding narrative. Auslander addresses the 'interactive plays' *Tamara* and *Tony 'n' Tina's Wedding* in which the audience are able to interact with the characters as they dine and dance together (Auslander, 1999, p. 47). However, the interaction is limited by the pre-scripted

Figure 36   *Kate Modern,* Bebo. Produced by LG15 Studios

narrative and, in the words of Barry Wexler, the Californian producer of *Tamara*, '(i)t's like staying at the Hilton, everything is exactly the same no matter where you are' (Wexler in Auslander, 1999, p. 47). Auslander uses these examples to support his view that live performance (as well as cinema or media product) can also be mass-produced. Interactive dramas, whether live or web-based, appear to offer a combination of navigation and responsive interaction. They do not often accommodate 'complex interaction' in the form of conversation, which would require the characters to converse freely with the users, with both groups of participants endowed with the agency to both ask and answer questions beyond a menu of topics.

Complex interaction

Of course, computers do not have the capacity to engage in complex inter-action of the conversational kind, for their actions are all reactions, the result of programmed algorithms. For instance, in the case of Australian cyber artist Stelarc's *Prosthetic Head* (2003), we see these limitations pro-duced in the experience of the work. The animated, automated head of the title is designed with human behaviours such as facial expressions, nods, tilts, turns and changing eye 'contact', and is able to hold a limited conver-sation with a human participant. The head demonstrates a certain agency and the appearance of personality; however, its actions are, of course,

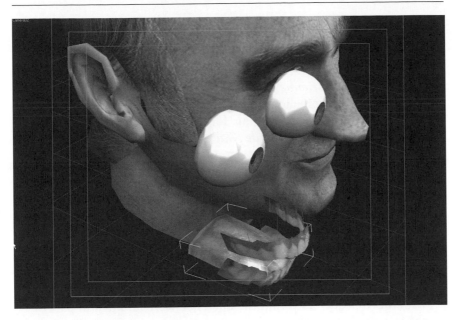

Figure 37 *PROSTHETIC HEAD*, San Francisco, Melbourne 2002, 3D Model: Barrett Fox, STELARC

responsive, the result of embedded algorithms that generate certain behaviours in reaction to the movements and questions of the participant.[1]

Packer and Jordan's definition of 'interactivity' connotes a degree of complexity as 'the ability of the user to manipulate and affect her experience of media directly, and to communicate with others through media' (Packer and Jordan, 2001, p. xxx). This definition suggests two versions of interactivity: user-to-media interaction and user-to-user interaction through media. The former offers audiences the possibility of affective or interpretive engagement, navigation, and responsive interaction. The latter offers the possibility of 'complex interaction' as conversation or collaboration.

Over the last few years, Britain has seen a spate of interactive live performance that demands different levels of interactive participation from the audience. Lyn Gardner, theatre critic for *The Guardian*, writes 'The success of shows from companies such as Punchdrunk, Oily Cart and Dreamthinkspeak (has changed) not just our relationship with spaces and theatres, but also (that with) with the actors. Just as we like to press the red button on our remote control, so we like shows that are interactive' (Gardner, 2007). Referring to the Edinburgh Fringe Festival of 2007, she declares 'touching is all the rage', referring to shows such as *An Audience with Adrienne*, in which the audience are encouraged to share their deepest feelings; *The Smile Off Your Face*, in which the audience are chained to a chair for 20 minutes; and *Six Women Standing in Front of a While Wall at C Soco*, which invites the audience to show physical affection to six performers by touching and hugging them. In the same year, Punchdrunk presented their epic show *Masque of the Red Death*, which transformed the Battersea Arts Centre into an elaborate Victorian scene that referenced the classic tales of Edgar Allan Poe. Here the audience donned a cape and mask and were given free rein of the space, and invited to investigate the various rooms, characters, and scenarios. Often the characters would lead a participant off for a private chat, or guide them into a hidden dungeon. The work climaxed with the 'masque' itself and the audience were an integral part of the festivities. Though participation is only one option for interactivity, the possibility for haptic interaction (based on touch) is an experience that, currently, live theatre alone can provide.

Complex interaction requires the real-time and mutual activity of both agents. Within the relationship, both parties have agency and the ability to assert creative intelligence. Ross Gibson, referencing Paul Cilliers, describes complexity as 'dynamic and relationally intricate' (Cilliers in Gibson, 2005, p. 202). To know it you must experience it, to

> be with its changes through time, to feel its shifts whilst also being attuned to the historically determined tendencies and feedback patterns of stimuli and responses that organise it systematically. (Cilliers in Gibson, 2005, p. 202)

Gibson describes the ecology of the changescape as a 'complex system' in the sense provided by Cilliers, who explains complex systems as having

> to grapple with a changing environment.... To cope with these demands the system must have two capabilities; it must be able to store information concerning the environment for future use; and it must be able to adapt ... when necessary. (Cilliers in Gibson, 2005, p. 202)

In processes of complex interaction, both parties themselves can be recognised as 'complex systems', and the relationship forged between them is 'dynamic and relationally intricate'.

Performances that involve complex interaction occur within a frame that defines the particular circumstances of interaction. This may involve a type of narrative premise, with the interaction occurring between characters, and/or a specifically designed environment. For example, in the famous performance installation, *Two Undiscovered Amerindians* (various locations 1992), Guillermo Gomez-Pena and Coco Fusco performed the characters of primitives from the lost island of Guatinau, the two undiscovered Amerindians of the title, in a cage. The pseudo-ethnographic display offered the potential for complex interaction between viewers and the personae of the Guatinauis. The audience members could choose from a menu of possible interactions with the artists. G\For example, they could ask for an 'authentic dance', a souvenir photo or a story in the character's fictional native language of 'Guatinaui'. However, the possibility for complex interaction was always a tension within the relationship between the audience and the performers. Because the performers had a certain degree of agency over their actions and reactions, they were always an unpredictable force and the work became most exciting when instances of interaction were provoked, for example, in the interactions that took place during the taking of souvenir photos, a scripted activity that nonetheless evolved in real time and was essentially co-authored by both the audience and the performers. This work, while not multimedia in the sense we have given that term, set up a simple interactive system predicated on the uncertain ontology of the Guatinauis which engendered a kind of unconscious collaboration between the artists and the spectators as the spectators were either duped and reacted accordingly (disbelief, outrage) or were not duped and enjoyed the event as ironic spectacle.

Guillermo Gomez-Pena is a Mexican performance artist and founder of the Pocha Nostra performance company. In his multi award-winning performances and books he explores 'border culture' and a 'trans-cultural' identity. As one of his personas he performs as *El Mexterminator*, a 'hyper-Mexican', Spanglesh-speaking, macho, karate trained ethno-cyborg developed using anonymous confessions about Mexicans posted on the project website. In Gomez-Pena's vision, the cyborg has a sense of humour!

Complex interaction is perhaps most commonly found within computer-generated environments that allow for human-to-human interaction via media. Of course, this type of interaction may still be considered 'live' performance as it occurs in real time between real people, but the actual location of interactive connection is within a virtual environment. The theatre and multimedia company, Blast Theory, creates works that require the audience to engage in processes of complex interaction. Works such as *Desert Rain* (1999) and *Can You See Me Now?* (2001) present a virtual world that the audience navigate through the use of computer controls, and in which they communicate with other participants who appear as avatars. The production *Desert Rain*, addressed in Chapter 7, systematically employs all the modes of audience interactivity discussed in this chapter. Participants have to navigate a virtual world to find their target. They must converse with their team members (fellow-users) and with the technical advisors (Blast Theory), and finally they receive a swipe card to access information about their target in a hotel room at the end of the virtual phase of the work. If participants do not succeed in their virtual task and do not locate and rescue their target, then they cannot access any information about them in the hotel room phase of the work. In this sense they must collaborate to experience the work fully.

An unusual example of human-to-human interaction as collaboration occurs in Stelarc's *Fractal Flesh* (1995), in which the participants remotely accessed a website that allowed them to manipulate Stelarc's body, effectively choreographing his movements. *Fractal Flesh* was produced as part of the November 1995 'Telepolis' event, in which the Pompidou Centre in Paris, The Media Lab in Helsinki and the Doors of Perception Conference in Amsterdam were electronically linked through 'a performance website allowing the audience remotely to access, view, and actuate the body via a computer-interfaced muscle-stimulation system based at the main performance site in Luxembourg' (http://www.stelarc.va.com.au). In this piece Stelarc surrenders agency over his body's movements in relation to leg and arm extension but could activate his robotic third hand. Here the onus is placed on the participants to become collaborators in the artwork. Without this aspect of the work Stelarc's body would not have moved, so the performance would not have occurred according to its design. This is, again, a limitation on the degree of interactivity in this piece, since the architecture of the work is not reconfigured in the process of the interaction but, as Stelarc permits remote access to his body, he also distributes the role of 'performer' to the other users in the system. His body becomes the site for the performance rather than the originating entity or authorial figure.

The most complex collaborative interactivity still resides in the quotidian human-to-human give-and-take with its limitless potential for alternative narrative outcomes. Yet sometimes these encounters do not occur and remain purely potential. In this sense the usefulness of multi-media systems may be simply to provide the occasion for these interactions between people, to provide the spaces in which they can become perceptible, as in the changescape or in certain public art contexts where the interactions between members of the public is a key aspect of the work's design. As a way of visualising this process of complex interactivity in urban space we now turn to some recent examples of public art using mediated systems to provide a *mise en scène* for these otherwise invisible person-to-person interactions.

Performative architectures: *Underscan and Body Movies*

Rafael Lozano-Hemmer's public artworks use enormous interactive projections of photographic portraits or video portraits in public spaces. These projections are designed to trap the gaze of passers-by and provoke a disruption of the use of public space by triggering a small, interactive encounter between a pedestrian and the image of someone who lives in the area (the portraits are local people). In this sense his works reveal the usefulness of media in providing occasions for interaction.

Lozano-Hemmer's public artworks use projections in a manner superficially similar to the technique developed by Polish artist Krzysztof Wodiczko but there are some key differences. Wodiczko uses iconic buildings and public monuments as the canvas for his projections to focus attention on the ways in which art and architecture reflect collective memory. Lozano-Hemmer is less invested in collective memory and engages the more immediate sensory data of individuals negotiating public space.

Krzysztof Wodiczko (b. 1943) has created more than 70 large-scale slide-and-video projections since 1980. His images refer to politically controversial topics and have been projected onto facades, or more recently onto the internal walls of significant buildings, in more than 12 different countries worldwide.

His *Underscan* and *Body Movies* are part of the artist's ongoing project in 'relational architecture'. Both works transform public space with enormous interactive projections that reveal themselves over time, not as in Wodiczko, to 'reveal the languages of power and authority operating within the cityscape' (Kaye, 2000, p. 34), but to affirm the power of inter-active media to bring people together in a temporal structure, which de-conceals the playfulness inherent in public space. This work is also political, since it challenges the normative assumptions about the behav-iour of citizens in public space; but it is not directed at explicitly political topics in the way Wodiczko has done.

Body Movies was developed in 2001 for the V2 Cultural Capital of Europe in Rotterdam and uses powerful light (7kW) projectors to throw light onto the facades of public buildings. When passers-by, on the Schouw-burgplein, cross the light beams, their shadows form on the facades to reveal another projection, this time of a portrait of a person taken in the host city itself. These images can be as large as the shadow, so between 'two and twenty-five metres depending on how close or far away they are from the powerful light sources positioned on the ground' (http://www.lozano-hemmer.com). Although the projections are inadvertent, in the sense that the system generates them according to the movement of members of the public in the delineated space, Lozano-Hemmer describes them as 'interactive projections' since they rely on the silhou-ettes of the participants. The system makes use of video surveillance

Figure 38 *Body Movies, Relational Architecture 6* (2006) Rafael Lozano-Hemmer, Museum of Art, Hong Kong, China. Photo: Antimodular Research

tracking devices to monitor the movements of the people in the space and to determine where to throw the images. There are more than 1000 images in the project database.

Lozano-Hemmer claims that '*Body Movies* attempts to misuse technologies of the spectacular so they can evoke a sense of intimacy and complicity instead of provoking distance, euphoria, catharsis, obedience or awe.' These claims are borne out by the evidence of the documentation, which shows crowds of people playing with their shadows and engaging with the portraits. It's partly a question of scale, since the huge size of some of the portraits makes them impossible to ignore and generates a sense of emphatic sensorial engagement. The projections work in the same way as Wodiczko's to (in Nick Kaye's formulation): 'challenge the distinction between the built monument and the projected image' and transform the urban architecture into 'a play of representations' (Kaye, 2000, p. 36) The scale of the projections threatens to disrupt the 'orderly performance' of the city by allowing pedestrians to become aware of their own 'performance *in* and *of* the city (Kaye, p. 2000, p. 40).

A variation on this approach was developed in the work *Under Scan* (2005), in which 'passers-by are detected by a computerized tracking system, which activates video-portraits projected within their shadow' this time not onto the walls of buildings but onto the ground of public spaces such as Trafalgar Square, London, UK in 2008. The work draws upon some 1500 video-portraits of volunteers that were shot throughout the UK by local filmmakers. In these recordings 'people were free to portray themselves in whatever way they desired', so 'a wide range of performances were captured'. The video portraits appear in the shadows of passers-by at random locations and extend the interactivity of *Body Movies* by attempting to create eye contact with the spectator as soon as they are revealed. Some of the documentation reveals an intensity of interaction as viewers focus on the video portraits, but experience of the work suggests that the delay in the appearance of the portraits worked against an effective interactivity. In this sense the simplicity of *Body Movies*, which used ordinary still-life portraits, provoked a more complete sensorial interaction.

In *Under Scan* the system is designed to respond to the viewer's movement so that when someone walks away, the portrait 'reacts' by 'looking away, and eventually disappears if no one activates it' (http://www. lozano-hemmer.com). The smaller scale of the images and the delay in the response time of the video to the locomotion of the viewer limited the interactivity of this work to a fairly basic level of spectatorship in public space and was not as disruptive and energetic as *Body Movies*, where viewers' responses were more embodied and kineticised. This approach to public art, though spectacular, is also very importantly engaged with

Figure 39   *Under Scan, Relational Architecture 11* (2008), Rafael Lozano-Hemmer. Trafalgar Square, London, UK. Photo by: Antimodular Research

the body and its relation to urban space. The sheer complexity of the tracking systems designed to anticipate pedestrian itineraries suggests the importance of this to the work's successful execution.

> Artists such as Lozano-Hemmer, Blast Theory and Builders Association create what Lev Manovich has labelled 'augmented space' (Manovich, 2002). Augmented space is 'physical space overlaid with dynamically changing information' so as to create a new kind of physical space. Manovich derived the term 'augmented space' from the term 'augmented reality', although the two concepts are usually placed in opposition to one another: 'In the case of VR, the user works on a virtual simulation; in the case of AR, she works on actual things in actual space. Because of this, a typical VR system presents a user with a virtual space that has nothing to do with that user's immediate physical space; while, in contrast, a typical AR system adds information that is directly related to the user's immediate physical space' (Manovich, 2002).

In the next case study we see a very different conception of interactivity in public space artwork. Blast Theory's *Can You See Me Now?* is also self reflexively situated in an urban environment, in a way that encourages participants to reflect on their place in this environment; but it more explicitly frames questions of mediated spaces and the 'condition of virtuality' as a core experience of the contemporary world.

Interactivity in Blast Theory's *Can You See Me Now?*

Can You See Me Now? explores the ubiquitous presence of the virtual in our everyday lives as a result of media technologies, self-reflexively presenting the interpenetration of the real and the virtual in society. Participant interaction is integral to the work and evolves from the familiar format of an escape-based computer game.[2] Unlike traditional computer games, this game is played in both real and virtual realms, which enables multiple forms of interaction.

From various locations around the world, participants access an online virtual environment constructed to replicate the actual streets of a selected city. Before accessing the virtual environment, a loose narrative framework is established that requires players to answer the question: 'Is there someone you haven't seen for a long time that you still think of?' At first this questions seems superfluous, but it introduces the concepts of absence and presence as key themes to be explored throughout the work. Blast Theory explains: 'this person – absent in place and time – seems irrelevant to the subsequent game play; only at the point that the player is caught or "seen" by a runner do they hear the name mentioned again as part of the live audio feed' (www.blasttheory.co.uk).

As they navigate the virtual city, they are chased by members of the Blast Theory team, who appear as avatars but are actually using GPS tracking devices to track the participant around the streets of the real city. The online players must avoid the runners; if a runner gets within five metres of an online player, the player is 'seen' and out of the game. When this occurs, the runner takes a digital photo of the real space where the participant was 'seen' and this photo is displayed on the webpage. The online participants have certain tools at their disposal in the virtual world: they can alter the speed at which they can move through the virtual space (with a fixed maximum speed); they can access a city map view; and can see themselves represented in the form of a running avatar as if through the eyes of other participants. Participants are also able to see the avatars of other players and runners, and can choose to exchange typed messages with them. This can evolve into the building of camaraderie between the participants, which can be further explored through the strategies and proxemics employed over time. Online players are also able to hear the continual communication between the runners via their walkie-talkies as a live audio stream.

In most computer games or virtual realities, the participant exists in two dimensions: as a body in the real world, and as an avatar in the computer-generated virtual reality. The doubling of reality in *Can You See Me Now?* places the participant in three different locations simultaneously. They exist as a body in front of the computer, as a constructed identity in the online gaming world, and then are also represented by the locative technology of the runners as a blip, a disembodied entity moving through the streets of the city. With every participant existing in three spatialities, there is potential for interactivity to occur on many levels.

First, agency is exercised on a basic level through spatial navigation. To successfully engage with the work the audience must utilise the tools provided to navigate the computer system and the virtual world, controlling their own speed and path through the work. Here the participant interacts with the medium, determining the specific nature of its mediation and testing the limitations of their agency. This audience experience builds over time as the rules of engagement are gradually learned and participation with the technology becomes more skilled. The technology extends the capabilities of the human participants, and the communication of two or more participants via the technological extensions means that a dynamic two-way flow of information is created that is not predetermined.

Can You See Me Now? presents a navigable virtual world that becomes a platform for participants to communicate with other individuals via the technology. The various relationships established within the work – between all the runners, between the runners and the gamers, and between the gamers themselves – each involve complex interaction. The interaction functions at many levels: the gamers can communicate with each other and with the runners via typed text, the runners are constantly speaking to each other on walkie-talkies, their conversation audible to the gamers; and then there is the spatial relationship between all the players, who appear as avatars on the map of the virtual city. This 'physical' engagement between runners and gamers is a play of proxemics, a performance of chasing, hiding, teasing, testing, eluding, and eventual capture. All parties have agency over their direction and movement and their use of the spoken (or typed) word. The interactivity is essentially human-to-human via media, but for the participants the experience of interactivity often blurs the demarcation of the real and the virtual, of the human and the computer-generated. For the most part, the participants' interaction is limited to their immediate experience of the media interface, and the realms of the real and the virtual, the human and the

Figure 40   *Can You See Me Now?* (2001) © Blast Theory. *Can You See Me Now?* is a collaboration between Blast Theory and The Mixed Reality Lab, University of Nottingham

media, are seemingly compressed into a single realm accessed via the computer, a realm of information.

However, the work is more dimensional than a standard computer game where human-to-human interaction occurs in a virtual environment, for here the space is both real and virtual; it is a hybrid space. The fact that online players are able to hear the continual communication between the runners via a live audio stream creates a sense that they are eavesdropping on the privacy of the runner's strategising. It also serves to emphasise the representative nature of the avatars, highlighting the fact that they relate to a physical referent. Runners discuss the reactions of other people on the streets and are heard crossing traffic and dodging crowds. Players become aware that they are themselves located within the material environment inhabited by the runners; they overhear the mention of a certain landmark or street in the runners' conversation that coincides with the virtual representation they are viewing. It is this affirmation of the reality of the space that adds a fourth dimension to the virtual gaming environment: the players not only exist as a virtual entity but as an informational entity elsewhere in the real world, and actions in either one of these realms translate into consequences in the other (see the discussion in Chapter 9 on the implications of this for the debate on post-humanism).

Access, audience and community

Can You See Me Now? focuses on the impact on our lives brought about by the ubiquity of networked technologies such as mobile phones, internet and GPS devices. In doing this, it challenges accepted understandings of privacy and proximity and reminds us of how these devices enable almost constant social contact. In this work we see technology used to locate and track, to chase, to connect, and to eavesdrop. Involvement in the work also makes prominent the issue of 'access', which Hayles contends is a key concern in determining the impact of the cultural transition into a condition of Virtuality (Hayles, 2000, p. 78). Hayles explains, 'Access has already become a focal point for questions about how information as a commodity is going to be integrated into existing capitalist structures' (Hayles, 2000, p. 78). As interactivity refers at a basic level to the process by which users access information, so an awareness of different modes of interactivity is integral to an understanding of how humans engage with a virtual culture. The interactive capabilities of new media, as highlighted in *Can You See Me Now?* reflect some of the wider concerns regarding the shift into a virtual culture, such as how consumer access should be controlled, how interactivity alters our sense of subjectivity, and even what happens to intellectual property rights and when access to the work of artists is online, unlimited and free.

In the field of multimedia theatre practice, the most prominent impact of interactive access upon traditional conventions is the challenge posed to previously held ideas of 'audience'. Complex interaction potentially dissolves the concept of 'audience' altogether. New media theorist Clay Shirky, in the influential essay 'Communities, Audiences, and Scales' suggests that new media users function as either members of an 'audience' or of a 'community'. The difference between these two modes of engagement in a media environment is that, 'though both are held together in some way by communication, an audience is typified by a one-way relationship between sender and receiver, and by the disconnection of its members from one another – a one-to-many pattern' (Shirky 2002). Alternatively, in a community there is not a one-way flow of information; Shirky explains that, in a community '[p]eople typically send and receive messages, and the members of a community are connected to one another, not just to some central outlet – a many-to-many pattern' (Shirky, 2002). Though Shirky argues for the inherent opposition of audience and community, *Can You See Me Now?* positions its participants as members of both an audience and a community.

The participants are drawn together into a community of users, yet there is still a separation between the 'audience' and the group of 'live performers'. Blast Theory also clearly acts as 'facilitator'; the online

Figure 41 *Can You See Me Now?* (2001) © Blast Theory. *Can You See Me Now?* is a collaboration between Blast Theory and The Mixed Reality Lab, University of Nottingham

participant is led through specific paths of information and images both prior to and immediately after the game; and during the game the runners act as 'hosts' for the networked participants, restricting the number of participants allowed and determining the length of their involvement. However, unlike the format of an audience, there is a two-way flow of information between the groups; the actions of individuals in either group affect the choices of individuals in the other. What is in fact established is two groups that can each be identified as forming a separate community.

These two groups, of runners and online players, function not only as 'communities' but as 'teams' who are required to strategise against one another with the aim of out-manoeuvring their opponents. The scenario of the 'game' appears to be a significant framework for enabling complex interaction. Other Blast Theory works such as *Desert Rain* (1999) (discussed in Chapter 7) and *Uncle Roy All Around You* (2003) facilitate competitive gaming situations that utilise either portable locating technologies or a virtual gaming world. The importance of the video or computer game as social network, and the function of multi-user domains as performative, community-centred social spaces, have been well articulated

(Dixon, Causey). The format of the 'game' may also hold potential as a framework upon which to build interactive performances that do not have to rely on networking technologies. Indeed, theatre practitioners such as Brecht, Grotowski, and particularly Boal, have experimented with game-like scenarios as a means of involving the spectator and creating a sense of community-based interaction. 'Interactive' performance in theatre need not necessarily involve the use of digital media. However, the use of network technology is enabling theatre practitioners to access new communal spaces for performance, to extend the number of participants involved in a work, and establish new formats for involving the spectator in the creative process.

Conclusion

While interactivity is an important concept for determining the efficacy of contemporary performance and the nature of audience experience, it has perhaps not yet manifested its full potential within the realm of multimedia performance. Birringer reminds us that, despite the rapid advance of creative technologies,

> The world has not become a better, more democratic place, participatory design is rare, and interactive art has not necessarily made the "user" a co-author nor allowed the user–player the kind of active role and freedom of expression that is implied in an interactive exchange involving autonomous development. (Birringer, 2006, p. 47)

Certainly, the interactive works discussed in this chapter do not allow the participant complete freedom of expression. The argument in this chapter is basically that interactivity is a matter of degree, and that there are various forms of interactivity operating within the field of contemporary multimedia performance that each offer a different experience.

While interactivity may reach its 'fullest' form only when participants collaborate with equal agency and have complete access to freedom of expression to create a work, there are numerous capacities in which the audience can be involved within the artwork. The role of the spectator is never entirely passive, and audience interpretation will always have a bearing on the significance of an artwork or a performance. Forms of interactivity such as navigation, response-based interactivity (participation), and complex interactivity (conversation and collaboration) each set up a different relationship between the user and the medium. While overuse of the term 'interactivity' had previously rendered it too broad for meaningful application in relation to performance practice, this chapter has attempted to rectify that situation by offering specific terms drawn from media discourse, and presenting a typology of forms of audience engagement to help clarify the various modes of audience activity manifesting in multimedia works.

Further reading

The best way to research online dramas and interactive platforms such as SecondLife is to go online and explore them yourself. However, for some help with understanding the dramatic potential of multi-user online platforms within a historical context see Toni Sant's article 'A Second Life for Online Performance' in the *International Journal of Performance Arts and Digital Media* May 2008, Vol. 4.1. Two key texts linking computer–human interaction and performance are Brenda Laurel's *Computers as Theatre* (1993) and Janet Murray's *Hamlet on the Holodeck: The Future of Narrative in Cyberspace* (1998). Both these books have been influential in the field, and Murray in particular offers an accessible exploration of agency, immersion, gaming, and storytelling in virtual environments. The more recent *Modes of Spectatorship* (2009) edited by Alison Oddey and Christine White also provides thought-provoking analysis of active audiences and interactive spectatorship in both theatre and virtual spaces. For further information on Blast Theory and descriptions of their previous works see their website www.blasttheory.co.uk.

Chapter 9

Digital Aesthetics and Embodied Perception: Towards a Posthuman Performance

The ubiquity of digital technologies in all cultural media reminds us that performance must be considered in relation to 'digital aesthetics', and so the first section of this chapter identifies the characteristics of digital media and the terms in which a digital aesthetic may be articulated. We then examine an important example of digital art in performance and discuss the ways in which this work proposes a posthuman form of experience. The evolution from human to posthuman subjectivity is addressed through a discussion of N. Katherine Hayles's theoretical framework mapping the semiotics of Virtuality. This framework then provides a structural foundation for the concluding arguments around understanding multimedia performance.

Digitalisation

The distinct properties of digital media are addressed by Lev Manovich in his seminal work, *The Language of New Media* (2001). Manovich addresses the significance of the influence of new media and digital technologies upon the field of cinema, and highlights that new media are not 'new' in a revolutionary sense but have developed through the evolution of previous forms of media. Aspects of this discussion are similar to those developed by Bolter and Grusin in their previously discussed book, *Remediation*, where they describe the way in which new media evolves through the remediation of older media. Manovich suggests that new media is defined by the principles of Numerical Representation, Modularity, Automation, Variability, and Transcoding. He discusses the key forms and operations of new media and, while the focus of his work is the development of digital cinema, his 'language', and the principles and forms of new media he identifies, holdis potentially applicable to other media, such as multimedia theatre and performance.

178

The first principle outlined by Manovich, that of numerical representation, is obviously the defining characteristic of the digital. At a fundamental level, the 'digital' consists of numerical code representing, processing, storing, transmitting, or displaying data in the form of numerical digits. The digital is the representation of a varying physical quantity, such as sound waves, as discrete signals interpreted through numbers. The difference between media and 'new media' is that new media have been translated into numerical representation so as to be made accessible to the computer. While new media objects may be computer-generated, they can also be the product of the conversion of an analogue or old media form into digital format. Indeed the move from 'old' media to 'new' media is the move from analogue to digital.

Digitisation has profound consequences for the nature and status of the notion of a 'medium'. As Mark Hansen explains, digitisation transforms media 'from forms of actual inscription of "reality" into variable interfaces for rendering the raw data of reality' (Hansen, 2004, p. 20). Media come to function simply as 'surface differences', and the reality contained in the digital database can easily manifest in any number of accessible interfaces, from a video to an immersive world. Hansen claims that when viewed as such, the

> digital era and the phenomenon of digitisation itself can be understood as demarcating a shift in the correlation of two crucial terms: media and body. Simply put, as media lose their material specificity, the body takes on a more prominent function as a selective processor of information. (Hansen, 2002)

Hansen is assuming a position critical of the vision projected by media theorist Fredrick Kittler, who argues that not only does the digitisation of media erode the notion of 'media' itself, but it eradicates the necessity for human interface. Kittler understands that

> When films, music, phone calls, and texts are able to reach the individual household via optical fibre cables, the previously separate media of television, radio, telephone, and mail will become a single medium, standardised according to transmission frequency and bit format. (Kittler, 1997, p. 31)

Once this occurs, any media can be converted into any other, turning the formerly separate data flows into standardised numerical sequences. Kittler argues that not only does this 'total media link' on a numerical base erase the very idea of medium, but 'With numbers, everything goes. ... Instead of wiring people and technologies, absolute knowledge will run as an endless loop' (Kittler in Hansen, 2002).

Kittler sees information as autonomous, and perceives digitisation as potentially creating a medium able to record and write reality independent of human interference. Hansen claims that Kittler's vision is clearly post-humanist, for

> in the future scenario he depicts – one where optical fibre networks will have become ubiquitous and the digitilisation of information will have encompassed the previously separated and incommensurate media – there will, quite simply, be no need for the human. (Hansen, 2002)

Hansen, as we have demonstrated in previous chapters, argues for the privileged position of the body in the flow of information. The argument made by Hansen, Hayles, Munster, and other informatics and new media philosophers is that information is not autonomous, because it can develop from the transmission of patterns of numerical data into 'informational' form only when it is received by a conscious being. Hansen refers to Raymond Ruyer, who argues that

> transmission itself, insofar as it remains mechanical, is only the transmission of a pattern, or structural order without internal unity. A conscious being, by apprehending this pattern as a whole, makes it take on form ... sound waves on the telephone have been redrawn ... by electrical relays, and if an ear, or rather a conscious 'I' was not, in the end, listening to all the stages of the informational machine, one would only ever discover fragmented functions and never a form properly speaking. (Ruyer in Hansen, 2002)

In this view of the digital situation, information can be meaningful only in relation to the reality it encodes, and only insofar as it relies on embodied perception. Embodied perception focuses on the ways in which we are affected by new media, the processes of bodily engagement that are produced through interaction with the technical processes and products of the digital media. Put simply, without embodied perception (that of both spectators and artists) we don't have art, we have patterns of unrendered code.

Embodied perception is a feature of the poetics of multimedia performance and it inherently explores the materiality of how 'media do things to us' and how in turn 'we do things to media' (Murphie and Potts). The following case study of *Modell 5* by Granular Synthesis looks at a digital work in terms of its performativity and the ways spectators are affected by it. We also suggest that this work manifests a 'posthuman' perspective on subjectivity and embodiment.

Modell 5: Digital performance

Modell 5, an immersive video installation with live audio mixing, is a work which both explores and manifests the concept of the 'posthuman perspective'. It was initially created by art collective Granular Synthesis between 1994 and 1996, with subsequent iterations such as the 45-minute version exhibited in Australia as part of the 2004 Melbourne Festival, in which it occupied its own square gallery inside the Australian Centre for the Moving Image. As audiences were required to attend at given times (two performances per night), the work was presented as a performance rather than a gallery installation. Using the medium of the projection screen, the work does not offer the audience the agency to interact with the work. Rather, it holds the spectator hostage, drowning their senses in a wash of audio-visual effects.

Having received earplugs and health warnings regarding the level of noise and strobe effects, the audience enter the room and are placed before a wall covered by four adjoining projection screens. Accompanied by a very high-volume industrial-techno sound score, which pulses through the floor and walls, video images of performance artist Akemi Takeya's face are manipulated, her features becoming violently distorted as they tremor and convulse.

The pace and noise slowly build and the work creates a visceral and unusually disturbing experience for the audience. The scale of the imagery

Figure 42   *Modell 5* (1994–6), Granular Synthesis. Photo: Bruno Klomfar und Gebhard Sengmueller

and the invasive, frenetic rhythms envelop the senses, immersing the spectator in the immediate space of the work, with the 'entire spatial-acoustic setting devised to disjoint the viewer's perception of time and self, to confront them with their physical limits' (Richard, 2004). The work develops into an extreme sensory symphony composed from the rhythms and repetition of human sounds made inhuman. The rhythms in the soundscape correspond to the patterns of movement in the images, so that sound and image seem to merge as they enter the brain at maximum velocity.

Behind the audience is an enormous mixing/editing desk at which a figure mixes the live sound score. While this figure may be considered a live performer, he is a performer under erasure, merging into the background like a rogue element of the 'behind the scenes' organisation. At no stage does he draw attention to himself; he retains a technical anonymity, with the medium itself functioning as the main performer. Yet the knowledge that this work is being produced in 'real time' makes the audience aware of the work as more than a mere static installation. Indeed, the work is not an 'installation' per se, as it does not exist as an independent structure within a gallery space. The audience members enter into the space as a group, as they would do a live theatre work, and take their places as they await the beginning of the performance.

This work should be considered as 'performative' and as 'new media performance' rather than as installation or visual art not only because of the live mixing of audio elements or the situation of the audience but due to its intensive re-framing and remediating of the singing of Akemi Takeya, which is really the core of the work. Her facial expressions in the act of singing are amplified and broken into constituent microgestures, not fragments from which the whole could be reconstituted, but bits which stutter and stammer and remix the act of singing into a new hybrid event.

Kurt Hentschläger and **Ulf Langheinrich** worked together as Granular Synthesis from 1991 to 2003. Since then they have worked individually, creating internationally recognised media art projects. Hentschlaeger creates immersive environments that explore the sublime and aim to saturate the senses of the audience. His 2005–6 production *Feed* is a two-part 'Performance for Unreal characters, Fog, Stroboscopes and Pulse Light' that engulfs the audience in larger than life projections of multiple moving figures before spatially disorienting the audience using fog, visual effects and a spooky sub-low bass score.

Since 2003, Langheinrich has created large-scale visual and aural installations that, again, encompass the audience physically, emotionally, and sensorially. His 2006 work, *Hemisphere*, creates an artificial space by projecting five high-definition projectors onto a suspended cupola.

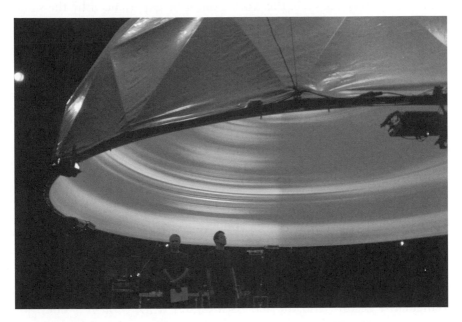

Figure 43   *Hemisphere* (2006), Ulf Langheinrich © Tibor Bozi

Figure 44   *Feed* (2005–6), Kurt Hentschläger © Kurt Hentschläger

Modell 5 revolves around the remix of the *act* and while its form is digital, its presentation is indubitably *live*. Many versions of the same work exist and the bits of information that form the basis of the work are, of course, permanently stored as digital code. But as Birgit Richard explains, '[a]fter being organised in time cells (grains), the data is stored on parallel, autonomous levels. The resultant modular image system allows the data to be continuously re-organised and/or recomposed' (Richard, 2004). As such, the work cannot be experienced by the same audience in 'exact form and context' and while the digital content of the work will never 'disappear', the audience certainly experience the work as being 'transient, intuitive, and experiential'. The work does not aim at conveying meaning, but creates meaning as it acts upon the audience to produce an immediate experience in a very literal version of Phelan's 'maniacally charged present' (Phelan, 1993, p. 148). As such, the medium itself is the key performer, following the digital 'script' but incorporating the variables of improvisation.

Remediation, immediacy and hypermediacy

Birgit Richard suggests that 'Granular Synthesis present us with the character of the technical image, and its special significance for the representation of the human' (Richard, 2004). In *Modell 5*, we do not see the analogue image of a performance by Takeya, but we do recognise her face. This work is not portraiture (the primary aim of which is representational) but digital performance, which affirms the values of the remediated gesture and the act. As a digital work *Modell 5* does not present us with representations of a real or 'live' human body, however tempting this is. What we see is digital information rendered in the image of the performer and allowing this image to act in ways that a human performer would find impossible.

Media theorist Frederick Kittler, in reference to the bodies deployed by early silent films, states: 'Every one of them is the shadow of the body of the one filmed, or in short, his Double' (Kittler, 1997, p. 93). He describes the image of the body in film as 'celluloid ghosts of the actor's bodies' (Kittler, 1997, p. 96). In *Modell 5* the images cannot be considered a 'double' – a representation of a tangible referent, as in filmic media, and yet they remain figurative images which are not entirely computer-generated. This is the crisis of reference that all digital images provoke, a situation which for Geoff Batchen results in the 'diminution of our collective faith in the photograph's indexical relationship to the Real' (Batchen, 1999, p. 227). We can say that these images, which feature live remixing of the video performance of Takeya, constitute a remediation of this video performance. Through its meddling with the structure of the representational image, the ability of the digital medium to augment the simulation of reality, and so create new possibilities for performance, becomes apparent.

Digital artist Jeffrey Shaw explains:

> The digital domain allows Granular Synthesis to denature and deconstruct image and sound components, and bring them into a space of abstraction where they can undergo shared algorithmic procedures. These algorithmic procedures are also conceptual formulations that Granular Synthesis apply to fusions of image and sound elements in order to alchemically renature and thus convert them back into lucid and persuasive fields of meaningful representation. (Shaw, 2004)

This work highlights the impact of digitalisation on representational imagery and explores the ramifications of this in relation to the representation of human bodies.

The medium in this work is not attempting to hide itself, to become immediate, but is foregrounded in the audio-visual field and re-emphasised in the repetition of the image across the four channels. As such, the work is primarily 'hypermediated' in that the digital mediation of the sound and images is overt, and a key visual element is the *acting* of the digital medium upon the representational image. This process is called 'granular synthesis', the name given to a technique derived from the principles of digital sound design in which samples are split into tiny pieces of less than 50 milliseconds' duration. These are called grains, which are then recombined and layered to form clouds of sound in which the different packets of grains are played at different speeds, creating phases. The volume and pitch may also be varied. In *Modell 5* the same process is applied to the somewhat larger grains of single video frames (www. granularsynthesis.info).

Scott Gibbons uses a similar method of grain recombination to piercing effect in his work with Romeo Castelluci's Societas Raffaello Sanzio. Gibbons is a composer of electronic and electro-acoustic 'micromusic' and has created music and 'sonic events' for a number of the company's theatre productions, including *Genesi: From the Museum of Sleep* (1999) and *Tragedia Endogonodia* (2002–4).[1]

The distinct nature of the mediation is prominent; however, the audience experience of the work is live. Granular Synthesis plunge their viewers into an intense experience of sound, image, vibration, and an awareness of other bodies in the room. Richard explains that in *Modell 5*

> Physical reactions are unavoidable, and make their performances and installations a 'dreadful' experience wholly in keeping with Burke's notion of 'negative delight'. This disconnection from the everyday is like being taken hostage in a vibrating color-space(ship). (Richard, 2004)

The work invades our senses, assaulting and penetrating them. The pulverisingly phat base-driven techno soundtrack feels as if it is doing permanent damage to our hearing even through the ear plugs provided while the video component of Takaya is shown in extreme close up. These effects are hypnotic, and the atmosphere changes from an initially oppressive feeling to the experience of immersion. Jeffrey Shaw suggests: 'The often seemingly aggressive audiovisual installations shake the viewer out of the stupor of habitual consumption and, in the best traditions of the avant-garde, bring about an unusual, even shocking, level of experiential intensity' (Shaw, 2004). Yet the odour of sweaty bodies squashed into a small, hot room and the pounding base rhythms punctuated by Takeya's synthesised screams affirms the liveness of the event even as it accompanies the inhuman four-channel projection.

Performing posthuman perspective

Although the digital performer's disembodied head exists as a simulation, as a manipulated configuration of information particles with no reference to the real, the work still plays on the significance of the dispersion of human presence as it explores the remediation of the live performer in digital media. It may be apparent to the audience that it is not a 'real' face, merely a projection, but the work simulates a vision of human embodiment within the space of technology, and in this way facilitates the perception of posthuman embodiment.

At an immediate level, the work functions to produce the 'hyperreal'. The hyperreal is created when the mediated, virtual, or simulated are perceived as the real: 'simulation of the real produces the hyperreal' (Stevenson, 2002, p. 166). The images presented in *Modell 5* are recognisably human features, though they are based on digital information which produces this hyperreal effect. Takeya's face gradually transforms and mutates, and an image of an exotically beautiful woman becomes an entirely alien thing. The confusion of reality and virtuality creates a haze of hyperreality in which the 'mediatedness' of the images is accentuated.

CREW, a Belgium-based company under the artistic direction of Eric Joris, create highly immersive, interactive events that explore posthuman embodiment and push the boundaries of performance. Their 2008 work *W (Double U)* is an experience for two participants using 'head swap' technology designed by EDM (Expertise Centre for Digital Media at Hasselt University) and CREW. Each participant is given a 'helmet' that enables her to see exactly what the other participant is seeing, and is invited to navigate a public space. Using videogoggles, a camera, and a 'head tracking system', one user is able to send the other the live feed from her camera. The company describe the experience as taking place at several levels: 'a sense of 'double space', that is, public versus personal space, the clash between physical and virtual space; and, last but not least, the schizophrenic relationship with your immersive counterpart' (www.crewonline.org).

In other work by Granular Synthesis – such as *We Want God Now* (1995), in which the torso of male dancer Michael Ashcroft is filmed dancing within a 'coffin-like' square box – the creators sampled ten seconds from the original seven minutes of film and resynthesised those moments into a 60-minute work. While the form of the work is digital and the distinct nature of this form is emphasised, the content of the work is indubitably the human body. Here we encounter the total deconstruction and reconstruction of the live performer, and while the figure is clearly no longer live, the efficacy of the work relies on the fact that it retains a degree of familiarity as an expressive body. *We Want*

Figure 45   *'W' (Double U)* (2008), CREW

God Now not only stages the remediation of the video performance, but it reconstructs the rhythmic movement we associate with live dance. Instead of the dance being controlled by bodily impulses, where the human body is the site of expression and the medium of communication, in this form of dance the body is almost immobile, it is trapped and forced into movement. It becomes a contorted puppet, a 'bastard mixture of the performer and the artists' (Richard, 2004). The body itself is presented as material to be restructured, manipulated, accelerated.

The work presents an exploration of the place of the body in the 'posthuman' age. Hayles explains, 'the posthuman view thinks of the body as the original prosthesis we all learn to manipulate, so that extending or replacing the body with other prostheses becomes a continuation of a process that began before we were born' (Hayles, 1999, p. 3). In the work of Granular Synthesis, the body is presented as material to be sampled and remixed. The manipulation of this expressionless body functions to dehumanise the image and makes visible the posthuman perspective, which 'privileges informational pattern over material instantiation, so that embodiment in a biological substrate is seen as an accident of history rather than an inevitability of life' (Hayles, 1999, p. 2). Here the body becomes neither absent nor present, for it is reconstituted into a boundless form that exists outside the realm of physicality.

Multimedia performance such as *Modell 5* positions the spectator's body in relation to informational pattern to confront the perceived boundaries between these domains; the spectator's experience of the virtual via the technical problematises the parameters of their own sense of 'presence'. At the same time, multimedia performance often also places the audience in a proximal relation to both the presence of the live performer and the slightly different presence (active and potentially even intelligent, but not actually living) of the virtual performer. By presenting these two entities alongside one another, performance forces a comparison of the different ways in which participants connect with the material and the virtual. While most multimedia performance does not really merge man with machine, as a genre it problematises perceptions of the separateness of bodies and media. In this sense it is a matter of rematerialisation, as Munster argues (see Chapter 5) in her study of digital systems and corporeal experiences. This notion of affectual re-emergence as a function of a dialogue with information is a product of posthuman thinking.

The posthuman

The idea of a 'posthuman' is illustrated in detail by N. Katherine Hayles, whose work, along with the 'cyborg' social feminism of

Donna J. Harraway, envisions the emergent relationship between the human and the machine as creating a hybrid subjectivity that is continuously moving between the material realm of bodily agency and the informational realm of digitality. As Brian Lennon elucidates, 'cyborg or posthuman neither dystopically rejects the automaton, nor transcendentally dissolves itself in it, but instead moves continually between nature and culture, organic and synthetic, individual and collective' (Lennon, 2000, p. 66). This kind of formulation represents the context for the performer in multimedia performance, the constant moving between registers of perception and between material and informational modes of being in the world, between image and flesh. But before we seek to apply these ideas in performance culture we need to ask where this kind of thinking is coming from and what the posthuman is.

Hayles's influential book, *How We Became Posthuman: Virtual Bodies in Cybernetics, Literature, and Informatics* (1999), explores the complexity of the human-machine interface and argues for an 'embodied virtuality'. Hayles looks into the history of cybernetics to demystify the emergence of inhabited virtuality as the new condition for social existence and outlines the nature of this cultural shift. Hayles's 'posthuman point of view' is characterised by four key assumptions that precondition its formation. First, informational pattern is privileged over material presence, so that biological embodiment is not viewed as a fixed and immutable origin or destiny of life but rather as an 'accident of history', as contingent and subject to creative mutation (Hayles, 1999, p. 2). Secondly, consciousness, widely understood as the locus of human identity, is viewed as an 'evolutional upstart trying to claim that it is the whole show when in actuality it is only a minor sideshow' (Hayles, 1999, p. 3). Thirdly, the body is viewed as a manipulable prosthesis, so that extending or altering the body with other prostheses is essentially just the continuation of an ongoing process that begins before birth. Fourthly, the posthuman view constructs the human being so that it can be 'seamlessly articulated' with intelligent technology.

The Brazilian performance artist Eduardo Kac explores the intersection of the digital and the biological in his 'transgenic art', a field of art that explores post-organic life and evolution. In 1999 Kac produced *Genesis*, a work that included an 'artists gene', and *GFP Bunny* in 2000, a project in two parts: the creation of a green fluorescent rabbit (GFP stands for 'green fluorescent protein), and the public dialogue generated by the rabbit. 'Alba' the bunny was born in 2000. She is an albino rabbit created with EGFP, a mutation of the fluorescent gene found in the jellyfish, *Aequorea victoria*. In relation to the project Kaz states:

> As a transgenic artist, I am not interested in the creation of genetic objects, but on the invention of transgenic social subjects. In other words, what is important is the completely integrated process of creating the bunny, bringing her to society at large, and providing her with a loving, caring, and nurturing environment in which she can grow safe and healthy. This integrated process is important because it places genetic engineering in a social context in which the relationship between the private and the public spheres are negotiated. (http://www.ekac.org/gfpbunny.htm)

The posthuman subject rejects the 'natural' self, having become a composite, 'an amalgam, a collection of heterogeneous components, a material-informational entity whose boundaries undergo continuous construction and reconstruction' (Hayles, 1999, p. 3). As fantastical as this may sound, this kind of posthuman subject negotiates and is interpolated within informational space as an ongoing feature of its social existence. When we check our bank balance online and navigate the portals of the online business environment, we live this hybrid experience. We are, for the purposes of the transaction and the entire online world, a username and a password in combination. At our terminals we are grounded in a different and sensorial world but this world in its social manifestations is also informationally coded and lived. This informational existence is a cybernetic state in which our virtual and real experiences combine in a continuously constructed hybrid subjectivity. Hayles further elucidates her vision in terms of this subjectivity:

> If my nightmare is a culture inhabited by posthumans who regard their bodies as fashion accessories rather than the ground of being, my dream is a version of the posthuman that embraces the possibilities of information technologies without being seduced by fantasies of unlimited power and disembodied immortality, that recognizes and celebrates finitude as a condition of human being, and that understands human life is embedded in a material world of great complexity, one on which we depend for our continued survival. (Hayles, 1999, p. 5)

Hayles argues strenuously against the apocalyptic vision of a 'postbiological' future in which the mind exists separately from the dematerialised body, which has been substituted by information. She warns us, '[a]s we rush to explore the new vistas that cyberspace has made available for colonization, let us remember the fragility of a material world that cannot be replaced' (Hayles, 1999, p. 49). These 'ecstatic pronouncements and delirious dreams' of a disembodied existence

> should be taken as evidence not that the body has disappeared but that a certain kind of subjectivity has emerged', a subjectivity constituted by the interplay of the materiality of informatics with the immateriality of information. (Hayles, 1999, p. 193)

This embodied subjectivity is not necessarily a 'body', or even an 'identity', but a configuration 'enmeshed within the specifics of place, time, physiology, and culture' (Hayles, 1999, p. 196). The inherent physicality of the body is never fully dematerialised, never completely absorbed into information architectures, and likewise, digitalised data is not totally removed from its material context and, as we have seen with Hansen and Munster, depends on embodied agents for its meaningfulness and usefulness.

> Other recent developments include Sally Jane Norman's research into the advent of BANs (body area networks). These use the body as a 'natural conductive resource' to facilitate the use of electronic devices embedded in the body itself such as heart pacemakers powered by the body and not by batteries (Norman, 2006, p. 121).

As we have already pointed out, it is the continuous tension between materiality and information that is the defining dialectic in what Hayles labels the 'condition of virtuality'. She defines virtuality as 'the cultural perception that material objects are interpenetrated by information patterns' – a basic proposition for the study of multimedia performance (Hayles, 2000, p. 69). For Hayles, the virtual condition means that the balance in the relation of information and materiality is uneven, with information being viewed as subordinating the material. This is the most prominent characteristic of Virtuality as an emerging cultural paradigm. Her example is new molecular biology, which understands human physicality to be 'encoded' as information in genes: 'The content is provided by the genetic pattern; the body's materiality articulates a pre-existing semantic structure. Control resides in the pattern, which is regarded as bringing the material object into being' (Hayles, 2000, p. 70).

Information consists of bits of data that have been sequenced to create recognisable forms. It relies on the organisation of otherwise random units and, as such, information may be characterised by the interrelation of pattern and randomness. Materiality implies physical presence, the existence of matter, and may be characterised by the interrelation of presence and absence. So, in the virtual condition, Hayles asserts that the dialectic of pattern–randomness, the basis of information, is beginning to develop prominence over the dialectic of presence–absence. While the dialectic of pattern–randomness may also have prominence over the dialectic of presence–absence, Hayles explains that it would be a mistake to view the dialectic of presence–absence as no longer having relevance, for it 'connects materiality and signification in ways not possible within the pattern/randomness dialectic' (Hayles, 1999, p. 247). Both dialectics are central in the formation of the posthuman point of view.

As we have seen, the 'posthuman being' exists simultaneously as both body (material entity) and digital information. As such, the posthuman perspective does not view information and materiality as discrete concepts. There are a number of problems with the notion of information and materiality as being inherently demarcated and mutually independent: for media theorists such as Hansen and Munster information provides new access for the material in the world and re-sensitises human perception by amplifying and reordering sensory perception in the world; for both of them the material body is the site of meaning-making, it is where information becomes significant. Hayles summarises these concerns as follows: 'the efficacy of information depends on a highly articulated material base (Hayles, 2000, p. 72). Information is reliant on material properties, and so too is materiality dependent on informational pattern.

Semiotics of virtuality

Presence	Absence
Pattern	Randomness

To summarise the argument so far: for Hayles the interplay of presence and absence produces the synthetic term *materiality*, whereas the dialectic of pattern and randomness forms the basis of *information*. The 'posthuman point of view' perceives the boundary between information and materiality as fluid and ever dissolving, and it is the merging of these two realms that, for Hayles, defines our current posthuman condition. The other terms also interact and result in different products: the effect of the injection of randomness into the material world produces *mutation*: 'mutation testifies to the mark that randomness leaves upon presence' (Hayles, 2000, p. 72). Finally, following Baudrillard's understanding of the precession of simulacra, the interplay between absence and pattern is labelled *hyperreality*, which exists when there is informational pattern with no original, a signified without signifier. These four terms – information, materiality, mutation, and hyperreality – are the four central concepts Hayles attributes to the posthuman.

The purpose of going into this detail here is to explore how these perspectives are exhibited in contemporary multimedia performance and to ask how the relationship of presence and absence (materiality) to pattern and randomness (information) is encoded in performance works. In theatrical performance, the dialectic of presence–absence is a traditional binary opposition which regulates the notion of representation in stage drama (actor–character etc.) but it continues to have relevance as the quality of 'liveness' that is often seen as defining theatrical performance as the derivative of material presence. The dialectic of pattern–randomness is less familiar and best fits the new multimedia environments in which performance now occurs. This binary can be used to structure our understanding of the modes, means, and complex processes of aesthetic presentation in multimedia performance.

While information theory may use a specific definition of 'pattern' in relation to data management, with computers using patterns to manipulate and organise data, pattern and randomness are concepts with many profound resonances. They are also terms with strong roots in avant-garde theatrical performance, with notions of chance and repetition a feature of Fluxus and the works of John Cage, among others. Pattern is experiential and is closely related to the concept of rhythm. It can accumulate diachronically (across time periods) and can also spread synchronically across a depth of media, layering a present moment (granular synthesis). Pattern can move across many media simultaneously, regardless of their materiality or digitality, creating narrative and compositional forms. At the end of his article on digital poetics Brian Lennon suggests that

> the informational concepts of noise, pattern, and recombination may (through no intention of their originators) provide new ways to read and to write about the poetries of the past, as well as informing those of the continuous or unacknowledged present. (Lennon, 2000, p. 85)

The terms 'pattern' and 'randomness', and related terminologies, may also provide new ways to experience and understand the poetics of multimedia performance.

Posthuman time: *Modell 5*

If we return to our discussion of *Modell 5*, we can see a number of these concepts in action. In this piece, pattern emerges largely as a result of the way in which sound and image are combined to create something like an extended music video, but the randomness of the edits disrupts this reading. The patterning of the image is undone as the video material is reworked using non-linear editing and motion-control videotape systems to create the effect of a stammering or stuttering image in which the face can be seen in the briefest fragments of time, almost in between durations. The facial gestures, produced according to a pattern of movements, are re-ordered at a micro temporal level so that even the blink of an eye is disrupted and a scream is fragmented into component intensities. This is a form of mutation of the video as document in which the natural movements of a face are randomised to create a mutant machinic performance.

But what of the live aspect? Apart from the 'cyborg choir' (the four heads on screens), the live component of the performance consists in the mixing of images onto the four screens and the sound into the speakers and controlling the levels of sub-bass. The presence at the missing desk of one of the Granular Synthesis group is hardly the stuff of conventional performance aesthetics, but it is nonetheless linked to the notion of presence. In Hayles's terms we can say that *Modell 5* produces a mutation of the notion of presence. In the work, presence is reinforced by the power of the sound, but serially subverted by the temporal disintegration and restructuring of the audio and visual data. It is a performance based on the digital recomposition of presence; micro-durations, smaller than the experiential present, are endlessly repeated and phased in and out. In this sense it is a properly posthuman performance since the perception of time that the piece affords, and the fracturing of gesture that the audio-visual signals present, become available to the viewer from the point of view of the machine. The human perception of time, gesture and affect is challenged here.

The time signature of *Modell 5* is not a readily identifiable rhythm but at different moments the piece emphasises differential speeds and affords a glimpse of machine time as micro-durational and multilayered. It is profoundly posthuman in this sense; it opens the experience of machine time to the perception of the embodied spectator. In this way *Modell 5* differs from a number of other significant video performance works in recent times in that it does not deprivilege the technical frame in the way Mark Hansen suggests of Bill Viola's video performance work, *Quintet of the Astonished*. For Hansen, Viola's work provides new perspectives on time for its audience, arguing even more broadly that it brings 'the properly imperceptible, microphysical machinic inscription of matter (time) into the sphere of human experience' (Hansen, 2006, p. 266). In Viola's video work in the *The Passions* series, time slows down, so that the moment of an expression of emotion, the time of affect, can be visually experienced by the viewer as well as experientially known.

The significance of this is that the 'now' can then be perceived as well as 'felt'. Hansen's examples (he also discusses Gordon's *24 Hour Psycho*) are both somewhat restrained in that the artists refrained from hacking the original performance and instead allowed the space of the now to dilate, placing technology at the service of human perception but not challenging that perception, which remains unchanged.

In *Modell 5*, on the other hand, the time signature is not a user-friendly anthropomorphised rhythm but emphasises differential speeds and affords a glimpse of machine time. After all, if we can accept a model of time as cybernetically enhanced, then surely we can expect digital artists to reconfigure the performance of the perceptual apparatus of the spectator so that a spectator can witness the action from the point of view of the machine? This new 'now' feels more constricted and compressed than Viola's. This time is intelligible rather than experiential, but it is also not normally perceptible without the intervention of the digital.

In this work a more self-consciously cybernetic performativity is evident in which the body's movement in time is not fluid and extended but is itself intensive and granular. In this kind of remixed performance, actions are no longer returned to their constituent gestures, as in Brecht, but into micro-gestures which bear no direct relation to the originating action, creating a strongly hypermedial effect. Like Bill Viola's *Passions* works and Douglas Gordon's *24 Hour Psycho*, Granular Synthesis are also using the mediated image to 'contaminate the perceptual present', but it is not with 'the material infrastructure of the enlarged now' (Hansen, 2006, p. 259). Instead, they produce a less sympathetic and more critical take on human affect. The now is not extended and enlarged, as in Gordon and Viola, but fragmented into grains and pulses of information. In *Modell 5* we glimpse the edges of our perception of the temporal. What remains is something posthuman, as the song of Akemi Takeya becomes a shriek. In presenting this perspective, these artists certainly 'contaminate the now' with 'elements that are properly inhuman' and this now, much more than Gordon or Viola, suggests a new chronotope structured around a different assemblage of machine time and the virtual body.

Stelarc's *Movatar* and other posthuman moments

Another kind of posthuman performance can be found in Stelarc's performance of Movatar in August 2000 at the Casula Power House art centre in Sydney. This was performed as part of the *Posthuman Bodies* exhibition curated by Kathy Cleland, a writer on and theorist of digital culture. In this work Stelarc used a device called a 'motion prosthesis' that looked like a metal backpack with hydraulic muscle actuators, making his arms move in accordance with the movements of an avatar on a screen above him in the performance space. In this work it is the avatar that initiates the movement and not the human subject, but the two are connected and can both influence the choreography as the piece develops. The system is designed as a Servo-mechanism, a term from cybernetics which means a machine for staging feedback loops, in this case from the avatar to the body and back. Stelarc likens the Motion Prosthesis to the 'muscles of the avatar' in the physical world.

This kind of literally cybernetic event constructs a posthuman body through the randomising of motivation and motion. There is no intention to move expressed in Stelarc's arm motions, only the embodied response to the avatar's 'intentions'. Its code randomises certain movements and the artist's body responds. It is a kind of posthuman puppet show, with the artist as a prosthesis for the avatar. Like all Stelarc's performances, it also makes visible a rite of passage, namely the passage of Western culture into a posthuman relation to technology. The work enables the perception that a properly cybernetic way of living and being in the world is already open to us.

> There are a number of individuals who exemplify this 'cybernetic way of living', including the Toronto-based film director, Rob Spence, who lost an eye and replaced it with a tiny video camera hidden in a false eye. Computer programmer Jerry Jalava's finger is a detachable USB drive, while Kevin Warwick from the University of Reading has implanted a radio chip in his arm, and has connected his central nervous system to robot arms.

All his performances embody, in the enhanced symbolic behaviour characteristic of performance art, the myriad connectivities already operating between organic human and non-organic machinic entities. In this respect Stelarc has consistently challenged the way our culture has imagined the body, whether it is seen as a sacred object, a fetish of the natural, an organic unity. Stelarc has been making challenging and technically sophisticated performance actions since the late 1970s. As such he is one of the key figures in a generation of major artists who have used the body as the work of art itself (Marina Abramovic, Vito Acconci, Mike Parr etc.) and manipulated it as an artefact rather than as a biological given (and therefore a kind of destiny). Stelarc is more concerned with the cybernetic body than with subjectivity, and more involved with

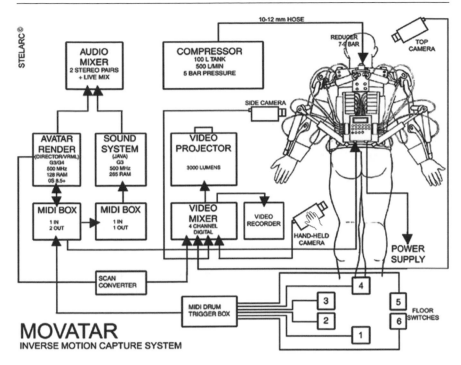

Figure 46   *Movatar, STELARC*

pluralizing and problematising the ways we speak of bodies and imagine them. He is also concerned with how we get them to do things and
how they might do them differently. These are properly performative
considerations, but in the context of an event such as Movatar, in which
a human agent is not at the origin of the motivation for the action, it
becomes more properly a posthuman question.

Stelarc provokes in his audiences the anxiety of the cyborg in arguing that 'we've always been hooked up to technologies and have always
been prosthetic bodies, augmented and extended' (Stelarc interview). He
knows that when he says this part of his audience imagines that he is
describing an unfeeling, dehumanised droid self. Both the figure of the
zombie and that of the cyborg can seem disturbing insofar as they displace our sense of the humanistic self, separate from others and from the
world, present to itself, in charge of its intentions and agency and located
within its own affective field. But Stelarc is not referring to a concept of
subjectivity in his work, rather to a model of the body as 'an evolutionary
architecture for operation and awareness in the world', in other words,
'an engineering entity, always modifiable, and never defined essentially'
(Galison in Scheer, 2002, p. 88).

Stelarc: ' the internet is not so much a case of a lack of physicality at all, but an alternate kind of operational system which connects physical bodies and machines with physical bodies in other places.'

...

'cybernetic corporeality is an extended and extruded embodiment that connects a multiplicity of remote bodies, spatially separated, but electronically connected.'

...

'technology does not only replace what is missing from the body, but rather it constructs unexpected operational architectures. The body is not about lack, but rather about excess. It always has been. (Even the biological body alone performs with redundancy.) We are all prosthetic bodies with additional circuitry that allows us to perform beyond the boundaries of our skins and beyond the local space we inhabit. Operating in electronic space and electronic architectures, the body has spatially extended, telematically scaled loops of interaction.'

(Stelarc in Scheer, 2005)

In an interview with Gabriella Giannachi, Stelarc argues that technology 'allows us to extrude and extend, extrude our awareness and extend our physical operations and the Internet becomes the medium through which the body can do this' (Stelarc in Giannachi, 2004, p. 61). So in virtual contexts the Internet not only extends the 'body' of the participant into virtual reality, but also extends their 'presence' in the real world. Stelarc suggests that the posthuman realm

> may not simply be in the realm of the body or the machine but the realm of intelligent and operational images on the Internet. Perhaps connected to a host body, these viral images may be able to express a physical effect and so the idea of a virtual and actual interface. (Stelarc in Giannachi, 2004, p. 62)

In his performances Stelarc brings this vision of posthuman possibility into existence, exploring the juncture of the virtual and the material beyond the current everyday cybernetics of online work and social life and continually connected mobile telephony by using online images, such as the Movatar, that produce physical effects in the world.

The Australian Dance Theatre's *Devolution* integrates human dancers and robotic apparatus, exploring in an overtly visual manner the relationship between body and machine. The dancers share the stage with mobile contraptions of all shapes and sizes, and both flesh and machine are integral to the choreography. The company says of the work: 'Filled with symbolism and ritualised process *Devolution* highlighted that for all of our technology we are still primitive, of the flesh and live as instinctive biological beings' (www.adt.org.au). The dancers and the robots move as animals, the humans are primal and the robots organic, and together they perform as a cyborg chorus reminiscent of a hive of insects or an underwater ecosystem.

Figure 47   *Devolution,* a work by Garry Stewart and Louis-Philippe Demers. Performed by Australian Dance Theatre. Photographer: Chris Herzfeld

Figure 48 *Devolution*, a work by Garry Stewart and Louis-Philippe Demers. Performed by Australian Dance Theatre. Photographer: Chris Herzfeld

From presence to pattern: Posthuman perspectives in *Can You See Me Now?*

This process is also evident in Blast theory's works, such as *Can You See Me Now?*, discussed in the previous chapter. As the participant in this work exists as an informational entity that has a physical location in the material world, we can say that the participant is constructed by it as posthuman in the sense of Hayles's 'material-informational entity, whose boundaries undergo continuous construction and reconstruction' (Hayles, 1999, p. 3). Within the parameters of the game, the participant's actions in the virtual world have very real physical effects on the presence of others, and as users invest themselves within the technology, they become enmeshed in a system that enables them to move beyond the limitations of the interface and to impact upon material reality in new ways. The subjectivity experienced by the user is no longer a discrete 'body', but a composite configuration.

The distribution of embodiment in *Can You See Me Now?* illuminates how the conceptual dialectic of 'presence' and 'absence' associated with the physical is inadequate to describe the posthuman interactivity of information and materiality. The doubling of the physical reality in *Can*

Figure 49   *Can You See Me Now?* (2001) © Blast Theory. *Can You See Me Now?* is a collaboration between Blast Theory and The Mixed Reality Lab, University of Nottingham

You See Me Now? simultaneously locates the existence of the participant in three spaces: in the physical body before the computer interface; within the online virtual reality as a constructed identity (an extension of the self in which the physical is absent); and they are also represented via the locative technology of the runners as an informational entity moving through the city streets. Each participant exists as a virtual representation, that is, as physically absent, in both the real and the virtual dimension.

In the virtual world we may consider the physical self as being absent, and in the real world we recognise the physical self as being present; however, when the virtual self is no longer limited to the virtual world but becomes a functioning double, spatially located in material reality, the participant simultaneously exists in the real world as both a physical body and an informational pattern. Here the physical cannot be regarded as absent, but rather as 'other', for the user's pattern exists alongside their physical body in the real world, illustrating how materiality can be 'interpenetrated by information patterns' (Hayles). In *Can You See Me Now?*, the participant exists in a hybrid space as both 'material' and 'informational'. Peggy Phelan argues that in performance the body is metonymic of presence (1993, p. 150); however, in *Can You See Me Now?* the concept of presence becomes disassociated from the material body and becomes distributed. When this occurs, the distinction of presence and absence is no longer the key operational principle in the work.

Can You See Me Now? and *Modell 5* illustrate how the perceived multiplication of performative presence across different media spaces results in a convergence of the material and the informational. When the boundary of the physical 'self' becomes viewed as permeable and exists as an 'informational–material entity', information and materiality can no longer be perceived as discrete arenas. These works play with combinations of pattern and presence, exploring the slippages between them and exploiting our confusion between the two, confronting us with our tendency to attribute presence to pattern. We are shown the transition from presence to pattern, the process whereby the representational image of the body loses connection to the physical referent when it enters into the virtual realm, where image becomes pattern to be re-patterned and mutated by randomness. To reflect upon the nature of embodiment in these works, we must, as Hayles suggests, think beyond the opposition that previously associated presence with truth and absence with simulation. For when the body is perceived as capable of being 'seamlessly articulated with intelligent technology', it exists between absence and presence, reconstituted as an expandable form that exists outside the perceived limits of materiality.

Conclusion

The theorists we have discussed in this chapter argue that virtuality is a condition now inhabited by societies all over the developed and developing world. They say that it engenders a 'posthuman perspective' which is inevitable for the technology-saturated subjects of these societies. In our view, Hayles' succinct explanation of 'Virtuality' as defined by a number of clear overlapping components (materiality and information) and sublated characteristics (pattern and randomness) is a valuable contribution not only to media theory and cybernetics, but to performance studies as well. Hayles's schematic of the semiotics of virtuality offers enormous potential as a framework for understanding the influence of digital information technologies and the posthuman perspective on performance.

Not all contemporary performance work in the information age makes such extensive use of the notion of the virtual or the posthuman perspective it provides but even in the reception and critique of more traditional forms of theatre an analytical framework that can be informed by the dialectic of pattern and randomness as well as the familiar discourse of presence and absence would enhance our understanding of this work. It would also enable an analysis to emerge that would avoid reinforcing the distinction of the 'live' and the 'mediated', and focus instead on the patterns and rhythms created in performance across media. It is one of the key aims of this book.

Further reading

Donna Haraway's 'A Cyborg Manifesto: Science, Technology, and Socialist-Feminism in the Late Twentieth Century' in *Simians, Cyborgs, and Women* (1991) is a seminal text in this area, and her ideas are further extended in the writings of N. Katherine Hayles discussed here. Rosi Braidotti's *Metamorphoses: Towards a Materialist Theory of Becoming* (2002) and *Transpositions: On Nomadic Ethics* (2006), provide provocative philosophy that analyses the binary distinctions of categories such as the self and other, human and non-human, and promotes diversity above cultural relativism. For an innovative study of 'cyborg theatre' see Jennifer Parker-Starbuck's *Cyborg Theatre: Corporeal/Technological Intersections in Multimedia Performance* (2011). Parker-Starbuck uses the term cyborg metaphorically to re-imagine posthuman subjectivity. To further understand 'digitalisation' see Lev Manovic's *The Language of New Media* (2001) and *Software Takes Command* (2010), and for more information on Stelarc visit his website http://stelarc.org which presents an overview of his artistic aims, works and publications.

Conclusion: Posthuman Corporealities and Augmented Spaces

As theatre and performance continue to engage a digital aesthetic, characteristics from the world of media art such as intermediality, immersion, and interactivity become more relevant to the understanding and experience of performance. Theatrical forms become more open, they develop more complex interactive features and are therefore more susceptible to mutability and reformation. Their structures take shape out of the negotiation between the participant and the configuration of elements within the work. It falls to the spectator to enter into a conversation with the work and in doing so complete it, forming a continually evolving complex system. In this sense multimedia performance embraces an aesthetic that offers constant process in its product, an unfinished aesthetic, with the threads of meaning permanently left dangling to be woven into multiple forms. While the spectator moves centre stage, the performer in multimedia work must adapt to the convergence of media and live performance, must balance their own embodiment and the increasingly virtual spaces it inhabits.

As performance increasingly assimilates multimedia technologies and artists progressively explore intermedial, even telematic performance spaces, the position of the performer as defining the essence of theatre as a medium, or the ontology of performance in theatre, is changing. Tori Haring-Smith posits that the current attention to media spectacle is distracting theatre 'from its essential task of bringing a live human actor together with a live human spectator to explore issues of common concern' (Haring-Smith, 2002, p. 100). The live performer has previously been viewed as defining theatre, their physicality the ultimate means of expression. The corporeality of the actor has been the foundational site of meaning in performance, and the body the essential medium of communication within the hypermedium of theatre.

However, as this body is being remediated, relocated and reframed, the corporeal dimension in multimedia theatre is being transferred from the body of the performer to the body of the spectator. The distinction between a material performer, a mediated performer, and a digitally constituted virtual performer is becoming less vital, as the perception of these media as separate and ontologically discrete channels is waning. Rather,

204

with multimedia theatre embracing an 'aesthetic of unfinish' (Lunenfeld), and demanding the sensual engagement of the audience, the performance occurs not only at the site of its transmission, but also at the site of its reception. This reception is an embodied reception that approaches the condition of posthuman embodiment: part actual/part virtual, part material/part information due to the positioning of the spectator's body between these domains. This experience of the virtual, for the spectator as for the performer, problematises the parameters of their own sense of 'presence'. By presenting these two entities alongside one another multimedia theatre-makers force a comparison of the different ways in which participants connect with the material and the virtual. Not merging man with machine, but problematising perceptions regarding the body and enabling the experience of new forms of embodiment and subjectivity.

With performance embracing a multimedial aesthetic, performance analysis too must reflect a multimedial, paradigmatic focus. A 'reading' of performance through the Hayles dialectic of pattern and randomness, as opposed to presence and absence, provides one avenue leading away from humanist limitations and acknowledges the post-humanism of contemporary multimedial performance. A post-humanist perspective recognises the body itself as 'unfinished', as open to the world, with its boundaries altered by technologies, objects, and other animals. A post-humanist reading of performance does not focus on one element of the performance such as the body of the performer, but views performance as a multimedial system that is accessed by the body of the audience member, a body that is open to the work and affected by the work.

Virtuality and/augmented reality

Most of the multimedia performance practices discussed in this book do not attempt to relocate the performance experience entirely into the virtual as in Second Life or computer-gaming environments. The artists we have focused on do not construct an alternative space or time that requires the suspension of disbelief for participants to engage fully with the work. In works such as *Wages of Spin, 40 Part Motet* and *Modell 5*, the artists discussed in this book work instead to overlay patterns onto the actual environment inhabited by the participant. Virtual reality requires the participant to experience only a strong sense of 'immediacy', while multimedia performance is functioning to create both immediacy and 'hypermediacy'.

Even in cinematic new media performance such as *Eavesdrop*, the participant does not become transported into another world, but is continuously panning across the surface of a virtual world from a distance, and the nature of the audience interaction functions to emphasise the single dimensionality of the screen. While users can 'zoom' in to the view the 'interior landscapes' of the presented characters, this serves to highlight the opacity of the medium and the nature of the work as hypermedial, as able to link separate media elements to one another. The user navigates the imagery, piecing together the various components as they restructure the composition. In Blast Theory's *Can You See Me Now?*, which involves the participant navigating a virtual space accessed online, the constructed space is not a fully realised virtual reality requiring the suspension of disbelief, but exactly corresponds to a real city. The participants in this piece are effectively tracing a map of an actual physical space. It is the connection between the virtual map and the real space it represents that produces the multimedial effect of *Can You See Me Now?*

Similarly, while 'immersion' is a key characteristic of contemporary multimedia theatre, this quality does not tend to manifest in multimedia theatre as immersion in a virtual world. 'Immersion in a virtual world' may imply either the cognitive transposition of the self into a purely fictional space constructed upon the architecture of language or the transposition of the self into a computer-generated space built on the architecture of digital code. Immersion in a virtual reality involves an imagined sense of changing one's actual physical location into a different location, about exchanging real space for virtual space. Immersive multimedia works are embracing an aesthetic of Virtual Reality in the sense that they are extending and augmenting the experience of actual reality, of 'being' in an immediate present with enhanced visual scope. For example, the work of companies that bring media into the theatrical frame – such as Lightwork, Version 1.0, The Builders Association, and The Toneelgroep – utilise media as dramaturgical tools, emphasising themes and narrative elements. Here onstage media can function both within a diegetic world and simultaneously as a hypermedial element distancing the audience from this world.

Multimedia performance-makers have embraced an aesthetic of virtual reality insofar as it reflects a rejection of the rhetorics of presence that have limited the theoretical discussion of theatre practice to an archive of dramatic forms. The move from presence to pattern in multimedia theatre is responding to the convergence of materiality and information in the 'Virtual' aesthetic. This move from presence to pattern in theatre practice is literally enacted in the move into virtual spaces. However, multimedia theatre-makers also display a marked resistance to the virtual as an experience of disembodiment, and explore the perception 'that materiality is being interpenetrated by informational pattern' (Hayles), not rejecting materiality but manifesting the fundamental principle of the condition of Virtuality: that information and material are not perceived as discrete entities. Multimedia performance-makers are playing with the in-between, exploiting the slippages, creating spaces in which the material and the digital converge.

Hayles explains that 'the technologies of virtual reality, with their potential for full-bodied mediation ... foreground pattern and randomness and make presence and absence seem irrelevant' (Hayles, 1999, p. 26). This kind of argument would seem to suggest that theatre and performance as it has been understood until now have been replaced entirely, but this is not what we note in our research. Presence and absence are not yet irrelevant in multimedia theatre, and performance is not reducing itself to technologies of virtual reality. The 'aesthetic of virtual reality' we see in recent multimedia performance is about creating spaces in which both material presence and informational patterns are placed in proxemic relations to one another, creating what Lev Manovich has labelled 'augmented space' (Manovich, 2002). Augmented space is 'physical space overlaid with dynamically changing information' so as to create a new kind of physical space. Manovich derived the term 'augmented space' from the term 'augmented reality', although the two concepts are usually placed in opposition to each other:

> In the case of VR, the user works on a virtual simulation, in the case of AR, she works on actual things in actual space. Because of this, a typical VR system presents a user with a virtual space that has nothing to do with that user's immediate physical space; while, in contrast, a typical AR system adds information that is directly related to the user's immediate physical space. (Manovich, 2002)

Instead of transporting the participant into an alternate virtual space, most of the examples of performance discussed in this book project patterns of information, imagery and sound into material space to create a layered environment. Alternatively, digital technologies are used within the selected works to intervene mechanically in physical reality, as in Stelarc's cyborg performances. All these works utilise digital media to create augmented spaces that reflect, and comment upon, the manifestation of a cultural condition of Virtuality in which informational patterns interpenetrate materiality. In The Builder's Association's *Supervision*, the script addresses how communication technologies augment reality, and we see the creation of an augmented space on stage in the intermedial *mise en scène*. Blast Theory's *Desert Rain* projects a map of a warzone onto a wall of water, and *Can You See Me Now?* uses locative devices to manipulate the movements of performers within real space. The works of Bill Viola and Janet Cardiff overlay the immediate space of the participant with sound and images that stimulate sensory immersion and create the sense that actual space has been embellished. And in Version 1.0's *Wages of Spin*, the live projection of the onstage performers on the background screen affects the perception and perspective of the immediate space.

Multimedia performance is a space for acting out attitudes and reactions to an emergent cultural condition of Virtuality. The examples of practice addressed in this book, both through the content and in the demands of the form, foreground the ways in which digital technologies are affecting everyday modes and means of communication and reshaping traditional forms of representation. One of the defining characteristics of multimedia is that it functions as 'hypermedia', making the viewer aware of the workings of the opaque medium as it 'remediates' other media. As multimedia performance functions within an aesthetic of multimedia, manifesting the qualities of intermediality, immersion, and interactivity, it too functions as hypermedia, drawing attention to its specific form of mediation and revealing the circumstances of its construction. By remediating digital technologies, multimedia performance enables participants to experience the augmentation of embodied, lived reality through technological intervention.

Notes

Chapter 2   The Evolution of Multimedia Performance

1. Cage also took his cues from Duchamp, whom Michael Rush attributes with making 'explorations into different media and artistic forms seem very natural, almost expected' (Rush, 1999, pp. 21–2).
2. It is interesting to look at the emphasis on the process of painting and the performance of art in the Untitled Event, in relation to Michael Fried's controversial position in his essay *Art and Objecthood* (1967). Fried criticises Minimal Art for being what he describes as 'inherently theatrical', and suggests that the future of art lies in its ability to 'defeat theatre'. He views theatre – the 'negation of art' (Fried 1998, p. 153) – as involving the beholder (a subject) experiencing a work (an object) in time, over a duration. Art, he suggests, must defeat both this objecthood and temporality.

Chapter 3   The Theatre of Images Revisited

1. For further discussion of the televisual in the work of the Wooster Group, read Phaedra Bell's article 'Fixing the TV: Televisual Geography in the Wooster Group's *Brace Up*', and Phillip Auslander's exploration of their work in his book *Presence and Resistance: Postmodernism and Cultural Politics in Contemporary American Performance*.
2. Under John Howard's leadership, the government maintained power partly through a skilful manipulation of popular perceptions about race and ethnicity in immigration. See also Scheer (2008).

Chapter 4   Liveness and Re-Mediation

1. In *Body Pressure* (1974) 'Nauman constructed a false wall nearly identical in size to an existing wall behind it. A pink poster with black typeface invited visitors to perform their own action by pressing against the wall' (http://pastexhibitions.guggenheim.org/abramovic/).
2. In *Seedbed* (1972) Acconci positioned himself beneath a false floor upon which the audience walked while he masturbated and spoke through a microphone in an attempt to establish 'an intimate connection'.
3. In *Action Pants: Genital Panic* (1969), Valie Export proposed walking through an art cinema wearing pants with the crotch removed, substituting her very real female body for the virtual imagery the spectators were expecting.

4. In *The Conditioning* (1973) Gina Pane lay for around half an hour on a metal bed heated by a number of lit candles below.
5. In *How to Explain Pictures to a Dead Hare* (1965) Joseph Beuys, in full shamanic mode, dripping with honey and with gold leaf on his head, cradled a dead hare, showed it some of his pictures on the wall, and whispered to it.
6. In *Lips of Thomas* (1975) 'Abramovic ate a kilogram of honey and drank a litre of red wine out of a glass. She broke the glass with her hand, incised a star in her stomach with a razor blade, then whipped herself until she "no longer felt pain". She lay down on a cross made of ice, while a space heater suspended above caused her to bleed profusely' (http://pastexhibitions. guggenheim.org/abramovic).

Chapter 5   Framing Media Theory for Performance Studies

1. The terms 'information age' and 'global village' have been widely used since first coined by McLuhan in *Understanding Media: The Extensions of Man* (1964).
2. The argument "Dance + Virtual = Virtual" was originally made by Philip Auslander in his book *Liveness: Performance in a Mediatized Culture*. This notion is explored in further detail in Chapter 6.

Chapter 6   Dance + Virtual = Multimedia Performance

1. When I attended the performance, I was struck by the odd effect of shaking Hellen Sky's hand and seeing the gigantic avatar moving its own arm in an identical fashion on the wall facing us across the street. This was not a disembodied experience at all but, on the contrary, the exoskeleton provided a strangely enhanced, amplified sensation of movement (Edward Scheer).
2. The fact that both Tim Etchells of Forced Entertainment and Liz Lecompte of the Wooster Group have both, separately, made the same remark about their own work also suggests that it is not an incidental comment, and perhaps even an important paradigm for making multimedia performance.

Chapter 8   Forms of Interactivity in Performative Spaces

1. This scenario brings us back to Turing's Chinese Room hypothetical, which poses the questions, 'Is the appearance of intelligence and the existence of intelligence one and the same?' 'And if the participant believes in the agency and complexity of the agent, does it effectively *have* agency and complexity?'

2. Rosie Klich participated online in the Cambridge, England version of the work in April 2005 and in person at the *May You Live in Interesting Times* Media Festival in Cardiff, Wales in October 2005.

Chapter 9   Digital Aesthetics and Embodied Perception: Towards a Posthuman Performance

1. We are indebted to Dr. Helena Grehan for this connection between Castellucci, Gibbons and the use of granular synthesis as a sampling technique.

Bibliography

E. Aarseth (1997) Cybertext (Baltimore and London: Johns Hopkins University Press).

B. Anderson (1983) Imagined Communities (London: Verso).

A. Artaud, (1938, 1994) *The Theatre and its Double*, trans. Mary C. Richard, (New York: Grove Press).

P. Auslander (2008) *Liveness: Performance in a Mediatized Culture* (New York: Routledge).

P. Auslander (2006) 'The Performativity of Performance Documentation', *PAJ: A Journal of Performance and Art* 84, 28, 3, 1–10.

P. Auslander (2005) 'After Liveness: An E-Interview', *Performance Paradigm: A Journal of Performance and Contemporary Culture*, 1, March 2005.

P. Auslander (2003) 'Good Old Rock and Roll: Performing the 1950s in the 1970s', *Journal of Popular Music Studies*, 15, 2, 166–94.

P. Auslander (1999) *Liveness: Performance in a Mediatized Culture* (London and New York: Routledge).

P. Auslander (1992) *Presence and Resistance: Postmodernism and Cultural Politics in Contemporary American Performance* (Ann Arbour: University of Michigan Press).

R. Barthes (1977) 'Introduction to the Structural Analysis of Narratives', *Image Music Text*, trans. S. Heath (New York: Hill & Wang).

G. Batchen (1999) 'Post-Photography: After but not yet Beyond' in B. French (ed.) *PhotoFiles: An Australian Photography Reader* (Power and ACP: Sydney), 227–34.

J. Baudrillard (1988) *Selected Writings*, Introduction by Mark Poster (Stanford, CA: Stanford University Press).

J. Baudrillard (1994) *Simulacra and Simulation* (Ann Arbour: University of Michigan Press).

C. Baugh (2005) *Theatre, Performance and Technology: The Development of Scenography in the Twentieth Century* (New York: Palgrave Macmillan).

S. Bay-Cheng, C. Kattenbelt, A. Lavender and R. Nelson (eds) (2010) *Mapping Intermediality in Performance* (Amsterdam: Amsterdam University Press).

W. Benjamin (1969) '"Epic Theater"' and '"The Work of Art in the Age of Mechanical Reproduction"' in *Illuminations*, trans. Harry Zohn (New York: Schocken).

P. Bell (2005) 'Fixing the TV: Televisual Geography in the Wooster Group's Brace Up', *Modern Drama*, 48, 3, 565–84.

G. Berghaus (2005) *Avante-Garde Performance: Live Events and Electronic Technologies* (New York: Palgrave Macmillan).

J. Birringer (2008) *Performance, Technology and Science* (New York: PAJ Publications).

J. Birringer (2006) 'Saira Virous: Game Choreography in Multiplayer Online Performance Spaces' in Broadhurst and Machon (eds) *Performance and*

Technology: Practices of Virtual Embodiment and Activity (New York: Palgrave Macmillan).

J. Birringer (2002) 'Dance and Media Technologies', *PAJ*, 70, 84–94.

J. Birringer (1999) 'Contemporary Performance/Technology', *Theatre Journal*, 51, 4, 361–81.

J. Birringer (1998) *Media and Performance: Along the Border* (London: John Hopkins University Press).

J. Birringer (1993) *Theatre, Theory, Postmodernism* (Bloomington: Indiana University Press).

Bjork Family Tree and Greatest Hits, http://unit.bjork.com/specials/gh/SUB-01/index.htm, accessed May 2010.

Blast Theory Website, *Desert Rain*, www.blastthoery.co.uk/bt/work_desertrain.html, accessed November 2005.

Blast Theory Website, *Can You See Me Now*, www.blasttheory.co.uk/bt/work_cysmn.html, accessed November 2008.

R. Blossom (1966) 'On Filmstage', *The Tulane Drama Review*, 11, 1, 68–73.

P. M. Boenisch (2006) 'Mediation Unfinished: Choreographing Intermediality in Contemporary Dance Performance' in F. Chapple and C. Kattenbelt (eds) *Intermediality in Theatre and Performance* (Amsterdam and New York: Rodopi Press).

P. M. Boenisch (2003) 'coMEDIA electrONica: Performing Intermediality in Contemporary Theatre', *Theatre Research International*, 28, 1, 34–45.

J. Bolter and R. Grusin (2000) *Remediation: Understanding New Media* (Cambridge, MA: The MIT Press).

J. Bolter, B. MacIntyre, M. Gandy, and P. Schweizer (2006) 'New Media and the Permanent Crisis of Aura', *Convergence*, Vol. 12, No. 21–39.

R. Braidotti (2006) *Transpositions: On Nomadic Ethics* (Cambridge, UK: Polity Press).

R. Braidotti (2002) *Metamorphoses: Towards a Materialist Theory of Becoming* (Cambridge, UK: Polity Press).

E. Brannigan (2010) *Dancefilm: Choreography and the Moving Image* (New York: Oxford University Press).

T. Brejzek (2006) 'Physicality and Virtuality: Memory, Space and the Actor on the Mediated Stage', in A. Oddie and C. White (eds) *The Potential Of Spaces: The Theory and Practice of Scenography and Performance* (Bristol: Intellect Books).

S. Broadhurst and J. Machon (eds) (2006) Performance and Technology: Practices of Virtual Embodiment and Interactivity (Basingstoke, England and New York: Palgrave Macmillan).

S. Broadhurst (1999) *Liminal Acts: A Critical Overview of Contemporary Performance and Theory* (London and New York: Cassell).

F. Brody (2000) 'The Medium is the Memory' in P. Lunenfeld (ed.) *The Digital Dialectic* (Cambridge, MA and London: The MIT Press).

J. Burton (2006) Marina Abramovic, *Artforum*, http://www.artforum.com/archive, accessed January 2006.

P. Cabanne (1971) *Dialogues with Marcel Duchamp*, trans. Ron Padgett (London: Thames and Hudson).

M. Carter (2007) 'Online Drama Proves a Lucrative Hit', *The Guardian*, 12 November, www.guardian.co.uk/media/2007/nov/12/mondaymediasection. technology, accessed April 2010.

M. Causey (2009) *Theatre and Performance in Digital Culture: From Simulation to Embeddedness* (London and New York: Routledge).

M. Causey (2002) 'A Theatre of Monsters: Live Performance in the Age of Digital Media' in M. M. Delgado and C. Svich (eds) *Theatre in Crisis?: Performance Manifestos for a New Century* (Manchester: Manchester University Press).

M. Causey (1999) 'The Screen Test of the Double: The Uncanny Performance in the Space of Technology', *Theatre Journal*, 51, 4, 383–94.

M. Causey (1998) 'Postorganic Performance: The Appearance of Theatre in Virtual Spaces' in M. Ryan (ed.) *Cyberspatial Textuality* (Bloomington: Indiana University Press).

T. N. Cesare (2005) 'Reperforming the Score', *NY Arts Magazine*, http://www.nyartsmagazine.com, accessed July/August 2005, 10.

A. Chandler and N. Neumark (2005) *At a Distance: Precursors to Art and Activism on the Internet* (Cambridge, MA and London: The MIT Press).

F. Chapple and C. Kattenbelt (eds) (2006) *Intermediality in Theatre and Performance* (Amsterdam and New York: Rodopi Press).

Company in Space, Company Website, www.companyinspace.com, accessed April 2010.

N. Couldry (2003) *Media Rituals: A Critical Approach* (London and New York: Routledge).

C. Cunningham, *Bjork: All is Full of Love*, www.director-file.com/ cunningham/ bjork.html, accessed May 2010.

M. Cunningham (1999) *Public Release of Merce Cunningham's Loops Choreography*, http://www.merce.org/dev/documents/1.31.08Loops.pdf, accessed April 2010.

Gina Czarnecki's *Nascent*, Forma: Arts and Media Producers, http://www.forma.org.uk/artists/represented/gina-czarnecki/works-nascent, accessed April 2010.

G. Dasgupta and B. Marranca (eds) (1999) *Conversations on Art and Performance* (Baltimore: The Johns Hopkins University Press).

J. Davidson (2006) *Alex Ross: The Rest is Noise*, http://www.therestisnoise.com/2006/01/spem_in_moma_re.html, accessed November 2006.

S. Delahunta (2005) 'Isadora "almost out of beta": Tracing the Development of a New Software Tool for Performing Artists', *International Journal of Performance Arts and Digital Media*, 1, 1.

S. DeLahunta (2000) *Choreographing in Bits and Bytes: Motion Capture, Animation and Software for Making Dance*, http://www.daimi.au.dk/~sdela/bolzano/, accessed April 2010.

G. Deleuze (1989) *Cinema 2: The Time-Image* (London: The Athlone Press).

C. Dena (2005) 'Elements of "interactive drama": Behind the Virtual Curtain of Jupiter Green', *Performance Paradigm: A Journal of Performance and Contemporary Culture*, 1, www.performanceparadigm.net/issue1.shtml, accessed July 2006.

E. Diamond (1997) *Unmaking Mimesis: Essays on Feminism and the Theatre* (London and New York: Routledge).

A. Dills (2002) 'The Ghost in the Machine: Merce Cunningham and Bill T. Jones', *PAJ*, 24, 1, 94–104.

S. Dixon (2007) *Digital Performance: A History of New Media in Theatre, Dance, Performance Art, and Installation* (Cambridge, MA: MIT Press).

S. Dixon (1998) 'Autonomy and Automatism: Devising Multi-Media Theatre with Multiple Protagonists', Studies in Theatre Production, 18, 60–79.

R. Drain (1995) *Twentieth-Century Theatre: A Sourcebook* (London and New York: Routledge).

T. Druckrey (ed.) (1996) Electronic Culture: Technology and Visual Representation (New York: Aperture).

U. Eco (1989) *The Open Work*, trans. A. Cancogni (Cambridge, MA: Harvard University Press).

A. Enigma (2010) *Underground Culture of Balls*, http://balls.houseofenigma.com/, accessed May 2010.

M. Featherstone and R. Burrows (1995) Cyberspace, Cyberbodies, Cyberpunk (London: Sage).

R. Fensham (2000) 'Mediating the Body: Dance and Technology' in P. Tait (ed.) *Body Show/s: Australian Viewings of Live Performance* (Amsterdam: Rodopi) 229–43.

M. Fenske (2004) 'The Aesthetics of the Unfinished: Ethics and Performance', Text and Performance Quarterly, 24, 1, 1–19.

J. Feral (1982) 'Performance and Theatricality: The Subject Demystified', *Modern Drama*, 25, 1.

E. Fischer-Lichte (1997) 'Performance art and Ritual: Bodies in Performance', *Theatre Research International*, 22, 1, 22–37.

S. Freud (1953) 'The Uncanny' in James Strachey (ed. and trans.) *The Standard Edition of the Complete Psychological Works of Sigmund Freud: Vol. XVII* (London: Hogarth).

M. Fried (1968) 'Art and Objecthood', Artforum (June 1967), rpt. Minimal Art Gregory Battcock (ed.), New York: E. P. Dutton.

L. Gardner (2007) 'Interactive Theatre is all the Rage', *Guardian Theatre Blog*, www.guardian.co.uk/stage/theatreblog/2007/aug/15/interactivetheatreisalltherage, accessed May 2010.

G. Giannachi (2004) *Virtual Theatres: An Introduction* (London and New York: Routledge).

R. Gibson (2005) 'Changescapes' in S. Attiwill, G. Lee, and J. Franz (eds) *IDEA Journal* 2005, http://www.idea-edu.com/alt_content/pdf/2005/Professor_Ross_Gibson.pdf, accesssed August 2006.

G. Giesekam (2007) *Staging the Screen* (Basingstoke and New York: Palgrave MacMillan).

S. Glickman (2006) 'Review – Chunkymove's Glow', *The Herald Sun*, 5 September, 2006.

Granular Synthesis, *Modell 5*, www.granularsynthesis.info/start/nsl?goto=modell%205, accessed January 2007.

O. Grau (ed.) (2007) *Media Art Histories* (Cambridge, MA and London: The MIT Press).

O. Grau (2003) *Virtual Art: From Illusion to Immersion* (Cambridge, MA and London: The MIT Press).

O. Grau (2002) Interview – conducted in German on the Deutschlandfunk Program on Deutschland Radio, http://www.switch.sjsu.edu, accessed June 2003.

E. Grauerholz and B. A. Pescosolido (1989) 'Gender Representations in Children's Literature: 1900–1984', *Gender and Society*, 3,1, 113–25.

S. Hall (1997) *Representation: Cultural Representations and Signifying Practices* (London: Sage/The Open University).

M. Hansen (2006) *New Philosophy for New Media* (Cambridge, MA and London: The MIT Press).

M. Hansen (2002) 'Cinema Beyond Cybernetics, or How to Frame the Digital Image', *Configurations*, 10, 1, 51–90.

D. Haraway (1991) 'A Cyborg Manifesto: Science, Technology, and Socialist-Feminism in the Late Twentieth Century' in *Simians, Cyborgs and Women: The Reinvention of Nature* (New York: Routledge) 149–81.

D. F. Harrell (2005) *Shades of Computational Evocation and Meaning: The Griot System and Improvisational Poetry Generation*, (http://cseweb.ucsd.edu/users/fharrell/pps/Harrell-DAC2005.pdf, accessed May 2010.

G. Hawkins (2005) 'Taste' in T. Bennett, L. Grossberg, and M. Morris (eds) *New Keywords* (London: Blackwell Publishing).

T. Haring-Smith (2002) 'On the Death of Theatre: A Call to Action' in M. Delgado and C. Svich (eds) *Theatre in Crisis?: Performance Manifestos for a New Century* (Manchester: Manchester University Press).

N. K. Hayles (2000) 'The Condition of Virtuality' in P. Lunenfeld (ed.) *The Digital Dialectic: New Essays on New Media* (Cambridge, MA and London: The MIT Press).

N. K. Hayles (1999) *How We Became Posthuman: Virtual Bodies in Cybernetics, Literature, and Informatics* (Chicago: University of Chicago Press).

M. Heim (2000) 'The Cyberspace Dialectic' in P. Lunenfeld (ed.) *The Digital Dialectic: New Essays on New Media* (London and Massachusetts: The MIT Press).

R. Higgins (2001) 'Intermedia' in R. Packer and K. Jordan (eds) *Multimedia: From Wagner To Virtual Reality* (New York: W. W. Norton and Company).

T. J. Hines (1991) *Collaborative Form: Studies in the Relations of the Arts* (Ohio: The Kent State University Press).

S. Holden (1982) 'Cultural Collisions on "Route 1 and 9"', *New York Times*, 2 January, 1982.

K. Hudson (2005) *Unpopular Art: Local Stories and Spatial Narratives*, http://www.canadianshakespeares.ca/anthology/unpopular_art.pdf, accessed May 2010.

E. Huhtamo, 'Silicon remembers Ideology, or David Rokeby's meta-interactive art' David Rokeby Homepage, http://homepage.mac.com/davidrokeby/src.html, accessed June 2006.

M. Huxley and N. Witts (1996) *The Twentieth-Century Performance Reader* (London and New York: Routledge).

A. Jones (2011) 'The Artist is Present: Artistic Re-enactments and the Impossibility of Presence', *TDR*, 55, 1, Spring 2011.

P. Kaiser (1999), *Steps*. Catalog essay for Ghostcatching, Cooper Union (out of print) http://www.openendedgroup.com/index.php/publications/older-essays/steps/, accessed May 2008.

P. Kaiser, *BIPED* essay, http://www.openendedgroup.com/index.php/artworks/biped/essay/, accessed May 2008.

A. Kaprow (2001) 'Untitled Guidelines for Happenings' in R. Packer and K. Jordan (eds) *Multimedia: From Wagner to Virtual Reality* (London and New York: W. W. Norton and Company).

N. Kaye (2000) *Site-Specific Art: Performance, Place and Documentation* (London and New York: Routledge).

S. Kern (2003) *The Culture of Time and Space, 1880–1918* (Cambridge, MA and London: Harvard University Press).

F. Kittler (1997) *Literature, Media and Information Systems* (Amsterdam: Overseas Publishers Association).

R. Klich (2005) 'On Eavesdrop and New Media' Interview David Pledger, *Performance Paradigm: Journal of Performance and Contemporary Culture*, 1, http://www.performanceparadigm.net/issue1.shtml, accessed July 2006.

R. Klich (2005) Interview with Marianne Weems, conducted at The Walker Arts Centre, Minneapolis, Minnesota, 16 October 2005.

G. Landow and P. Delaney (2001) 'Hypertext, Hypermedia and Literary Studies: The State of the Art' in R. Packer and K. Jordan (eds) *Multimedia: From Wagner to Virtual Reality* (London and New York: W. W. Norton and Company).

A. Lavender (2006) 'Mise en scene, Hypermediacy and the Sensorium' in F. Chapple and C. Kattenbelt (eds) *Intermediality in Theatre and Performance* (Amsterdam and New York: Rodopi Press).

A. Lavender (2002) 'The Moment of Realised Actuality' in M. Delgado and C. Svich (eds) *Theatre in Crisis?: Performance Manifestos for a New Century* (Manchester: Manchester University Press).

N. Leach (ed.) (1997) *Rethinking Architecture: A Reader in Cultural Theory* (London and New York: Routledge).

H. Lehmann (2006) *Postdramatic Theatre*, trans Karen Jurs-Munby (London: Routledge).

B. Lennon (2000) 'Screening a Digital Visual Poetics', *Configurations*, 8, 1, 63–85.

T. Lenoir (2006) 'Haptic Vision: Computation, Media and Embodiment in Mark Hansen's New Phenomenology' in M. Hansen *New Philosophy for New Media* (Cambridge, MA and London: The MIT Press).

P. Levy (1995) Welcome to Virtuality, *Ars Electronica Festival Homepage*, http://www.aec.at/en/archives/festival_archive/festival_catalogs/festival_artikel.asp?iProjectID=8616, accessed May 2006.

R. Lozano-Hemmer, Artist's Homepage, http://www.lozano-hemmer.com/english/projects/bodymovies.htm, accessed May 2010.

J. F. Lyotard (1984) 'The Postmodern Condition: A Report on Knowledge', trans. G. Bennington and B. Massumi, Theory and History of Literature 10 (Minneapolis: University of Minnesota Press).

F. MacCarthy (2006) "The Fiery Stimulator", *The Guardian*, http://www.guardian.co.uk/artanddesign/2006/mar/18/art.modernism, 18 March 2006.

M. Maclean (1988) *Narrative as Performance: The Baudelairean Experiment*, London: Routledge.

L. Maholy-Nagy (2001) 'Theatre, Circus, Variety' in R. Packer and K. Jordan (eds) *Multimedia: From Wagner to Virtual Reality* (London and New York: W. W. Norton and Company).

L. Manovich (2002, updated 2005) *The Poetics of Augmented Space*, http://www.manovich.com/DOCS/Augmented_2005.doc, accessed November 2006.

L. Manovich (2001) *The Language of New Media* (Cambridge, MA and London: The MIT Press).

L. Manovich (2000) 'What is Digital Cinema?' in P. Lunenfeld (ed.) *The Digital Dialectic: New Essays on New Media* (Cambridge, MA and London: The MIT Press).

F. T. Marinetti, B. Corra, E. Settimelli, A. Ginna, G. Balla, and R. Chiti (2001) 'The Futurist Cinema' in R. Packer and K. Jordan (eds) *Multimedia: From Wagner To Virtual Reality* (New York: W. W. Norton and Company).

F. T. Marinetti, E. Settimeli and B. Corra (1998) 'The Futurist Synthetic Theatre' in G. W. Brandt (ed.) *Modern Theories of Drama: A Selection of Writings on Drama and Theatre* 1850–1990 (Oxford: Clarendon Press).

B. Marranca (1996) The Theatre of Images (Baltimore and London: The Johns Hopkins University Press).

P. Marshall (2004) *New Media Cultures,* (London: Arnold Publishers).

M. McLuhan (1994) *Understanding Media: The Extensions of Man* (Cambridge, MA: The MIT Press).

M. McLuhan and Q. Fiore (1967) *The Medium is the Massage: An Inventory of Effects* (New York: Bantam Books).

M. McLuhan (1962) *The Gutenberg Galaxy: The Making of Topographic Man* (Toronto: The University of Toronto Press).

A. Monks (2005) '"Genuine Negroes and Real Bloodhounds": Cross-Dressing, Eugene O'Neill, the Wooster Group, and The Emperor Jones', *Modern Drama*, 48, 3, 540–64.

A. Munster (2006) *Materialising New Media: Embodiment in Informational Aesthetics* (Dartmouth: UPNE).

A. Murphie (2001) 'Vibrations in the Air: Performance and Interactive Technics', *Performance Paradigm: A Journal of Performance and Contemporary Culture*, 1, www.performanceparadigm.net/issue1.shtml, accessed July 2006.

J. Murray (2000) Hamlet on the Holodeck: The Future of Narrative in Cyberspace (Cambridge, MA: The MIT Press).

S. J. Norman (2006) 'Instant Conductors', *International Journal of Performance Art and Digital Media*, 2, 2, 109–21.

Not Yet It's Difficult, Company website, www.notyet.com.au, accessed August, 2006.

G. Obarzanek (2010) *Glow*, Dance Week Festival, http://dwf.danceweekfestival.com/93/glow/ accessed April 2010.

A. Oddey and C. White (eds) (2009) *Modes of Spectatorship* (Bristol and Chicago: Intellect Books).

The OpenEnded Group, company website, http://www.openendedgroup.com/, accessed April 2010.

R. Packer and K. Jordan (eds) (2001) *Multimedia: From Wagner To Virtual Reality* (New York: W. W. Norton and Company).

J. Parker-Starbuck (2011) *Cyborg Theatre: Corporeal/Technological Intersections in Multimedia Performance* (Basingstoke and New York: Palgrave Macmillan).

J. Parker-Starbuck (2006) 'Becoming-Animate: On the Performed Limits of Human', *Theatre Journal*, 58, 4, 649–66.

J. Parker-Starbuck (2005) 'Shifting Strengths: The Cyborg Theater of Cathy Weis' in C. Sandahl and P. Auslander (eds) *Bodies in Commotion: Disability and Performance* (Michigan: University of Michigan Press) 95–108.

R. Petterd (2002) *Liquid Sensations: Evoking Sensory Experiences with Interactive Video Installation Art*, www.artschool.utas.edu.au/petterd/htdocs/central.htm, accessed October 2006.

P. Phelan (1993) *Unmarked: The Politics of Performance* (London and New York: Routledge).

F. Popper (2007) *From Technological to Virtual Art* (Cambridge, MA: The MIT Press).

G. Quasha and C. Stein (2002) 'Performance Itself', *Performance Research*, 7, 2, 75–89.

R. Remshardt (2008) 'Beyond Performance Studies: Mediated Performance and the Posthuman', *Culture, Language and Representation*, Vol. 6, pp. 47–64.

B. Richard (2004) 'Immersion in the Resonance Chamber, and Blinding: On the Craving of Images in the Work of Granular Synthesis', essay accompanying the DVD *Granular Synthesis: Immersive Works*, produced by ZKM Centre for Art and Media, Karlsruhe.

David Ross (1973) 'Nam June Paik's Videotapes' in John Hanhardt (ed.) *Nam June Paik* (NY: Whitney Museum of American Art).

M. Rush (1999) *New Media in Late 20th Century Art* (Singapore: Thames and Hudson).

M. L. Ryan (1999) 'Cyberage Narratology: Computers, Metaphor, and Narrative' in D. Herman (ed.) (1999) *Narratologies: New Perspectives on Narrative Analysis* (Columbus: Ohio State University Press).

M. L. Ryan (2001) *Narrative as Virtual Reality: Immersion and Interactivity in Literature and Electronic Media* (Baltimore: Johns Hopkins University Press).

T. Sant (2008) 'A Second Life for Online Performance', *International Journal of Performance Arts and Digital Media*, 4, 1.

E. Scheer (2006) 'Read the Pictures. Mike Parr and Performance Documentation as Remediation', *Brought to Light II: Contemporary Australian Art 1966–2006* (Brisbane: Queensland Art Gallery Publications), 88–97.

E. Scheer (2005) 'Performing Indifference: An Interview with Stelarc', *Performance Paradigm: Journal of Performance and Contemporary Culture*, 1, www.performanceparadigm.net/.

E. Scheer (2002) 'What Does an Avatar Want? Stelarc's E-Motions' in J. Zylinska (ed.) *The Cyborg Experiments: The Extenstions of the Body in the Media Age*, (London and New York: Continuum), 81–101.

J. Shaw (2004) *Eavesdrop, iCinema Centre for Interactive Cinema Research*, http://www.icinema.unsw.edu.au/projects/prj_eavesdrop.html, accessed July 2006.

J. Shaw (2004) *Preface to the DVD Granular Synthesis: Immersive Works*, produced by ZKM Centre for Art and Media, Karlsruhe.

D. Shewey (1983) 'The Devil in Liz Lecompte', *The Village Voice*, 13 December 1983.

C. Shirky (2002) 'Communities, Audiences, and Scale', *Clay Shirky's Writings About the Internet: Networks, Economics, and Culture*, www.shirky.com/writings/community_scale.html, accessed November 2006.

R. Shuker (1994) *Understanding Popular Music* (London: Routledge).

M. Singer (1972) *When a Great Tradition Modernises* (New York: Praeger Publishers).

Z. Soboslay (2005) 'On Moving and being Moved', *RealTime*, 69, www.realtimearts.net/rt69/soboslay.html, accessed August 2006.

The Southbank Show (1987) [TV Programme] ITV, 22 February 1987, 22.30.

Stelarc (1999) *Stelarc*, http://www.stelarc.va.com.au/fractal/index.html, accessed May 2010.

S. Springgay (2002) 'Thinking Through Bodies: Bodied Encounters and the Process of Meaning Making in an E-mail Generated Art Project', *Studies in Art Education*, 47, 1, 34–50.

N. Stevenson (2002) *Understanding Media Cultures: Social Theory and Mass Communication* (London and Thousand Oaks, CA: Sage).

T. Sutton (2005) 'Immersive Contemplation in Video Art Environments', *Contemporary Aesthetics*, www.contemporaryaesthetics.org/newvolume/pages/article.php?articleID=288, accessed July 2006.

P. Tait (2002) *Magicians for the Age of Electronic Artistry. Performance Review: The Lighthouse*, http://www.companyinspace.com/lightroom/downloads/infopack.pdf, accessed April 2010.

Tate online (2000), Tate Modern Gallery-Past exhibitions-level 5-*Nude/Action/Body*, www.tate.org.uk/modern/exhibitions/nudeactionbody/, accessed August 2006.

R. Taylor and I. Christie (1994) *The Film Factory: Russian and Soviet Cinema in Documents 1896–1939* (Oxon and New York: Routledge).

C. Thompson and K. Weslien (2006) 'PURE RAW Performance, Pedagogy, and (Re)presentation: Marina Abramovic', *PAJ: A Journal of Performance and Art*, 82, 29–50.

Time, *Top 10 of Everything*, 2007, http://www.time.com/time/specials/2007/top10/article/0,30583,1686204_1686303_1690904,00.html, accessed May 2010.

M. Trimmingham (2010) *The Theatre of the Bauhaus: The Modern and Postmodern Stage of Oskar Schlemmer* (London: Routledge).

C. Vernallis (2004) *Experiencing Music Video: Aesthetics and Cultural Context* (New York: Columbia University Press).

Version 1.0, *Version 1.0 Website*, www.versiononepointzero.org, accessed August 2006.

B. Viola (2003) *Tate Magazine*, 6, 3 June 2003, http://www.tate.org.uk/magazine/issue6/fiveangels.htm, accessed 19 April 2010.

P. Virillio (2004) 'The Third Interval' in S. Graham (ed.) *The Cybercities Reader* (London and New York: Routledge).

M. Wagner (2006) 'Of Other Bodies: The Intermedial Gaze in Theatre' in F. Chapple and C. Kattenbelt (eds) *Intermediality in Theatre and Performance* (Amsterdam and New York: Rodopi Press).

R. Wagner (2001) 'Outlines of the Artwork of the Future' in R. Packer and K. Jordan (eds) *Multimedia: From Wagner To Virtual Reality* (New York: W. W. Norton and Company).

R. Wagner (1998) 'The Work of Art of the Future' in G. W. Brandt (ed.) *Modern Theories of Drama: A Selection of Writings on Drama and Theatre 1850–1990* (Oxford: Clarendon Press).

L. Ward (2005) *Bill Viola*, www.nga.gov.au/viola/, accessed August 2006.

M. Warschauer (2003) 'Demystifying the Digital Divide', *Scientific American*, 289, 2, –7.

B. Wiens (2006) 'Hamlet and the Virtual Stage: Herbert Fritsch's project Hamlet-X' in F. Chapple and C. Kattenbelt (eds) *Intermediality in Theatre and Performance* (Amsterdam and New York: Rodopi Press).

Judy Tzu-Chun Wu (2000) 'Exclusion: Orientalism and American Identity', Review of 'New York Before Chinatown: Orientalism and the Shaping of American Culture 1776–1882' by John Kuo Wei Tchen, *American Quarterly*, 52, 4, 742–9.

W. B. Yeats (1998) 'The Theatre' in G. W. Brandt (ed.) *Modern Theories of Drama: A Selection of Writings on Drama and Theatre 1850–1990* (Oxford: Clarendon Press).

J. Zinoman (2005) 'The Wooster Group: An Oral History', *Time Out New York*, 487, 27 January–2 February 2005.

S. Zizek (2001) *Welcome to the Desert of the Real* (New York: The Wooster Press).

J. Zylinska (2002) *The Cyborg Experiments: The Extensions of the Body in the Media Age (Technologies: Studies in Culture and Theory)* (London and New York: Continuum).

Index

Page numbers followed by "*f*" and "*n*" indicate figure and note respectively.